GUIDE
TO PRODUCING
A FASHION SHOW

SECOND EDITION

Judith C. Everett
Northern Arizona University

Kristen K. Swanson
Northern Arizona University

Original Photography
Christopher C. Everett

Fairchild Publications, Inc.
New York

Executive Editor: Olga T. Kontzias

Assistant Acquisitions Editor: Carolyn Purcell

Editor: Sylvia Weber

Associate Production Editor: Elizabeth Marotta

Art Director: Adam B. Bohannon

Director of Production: Priscilla Taguer

Editorial Assistant: Suzette Lam

Copy Editor: Jennifer Plum/Words & Numbers

Interior Design: Ron Reeves

Cover Design: Adam B. Bohannon

Fourth Printing 2007
Copyright © 2004

Fairchild Publications, Inc.

Library of Congress Catalog Card Number: 2002108016

ISBN: 1-56367-253-7

GST R 133004424

Printed in the United States of America

CONTENTS

PREFACE

The fashion show should be an entertaining and rewarding experience for show producers, participants, and the audience. It is an exciting and theatrical presentation of apparel and accessories on live models conducted by many different market levels—from haute couture designers presenting their latest innovations, to the ultimate consumer extravaganza held by community groups and retail stores. The purposes of the second edition of Guide to Producing a Fashion Show are to lead individuals through the process of planning and presenting a fashion show, and to outline the steps necessary for organizing a successful event.

Public interest in supermodels and celebrities, as well as other media coverage, contribute to the popularity of the fashion show in the 21st century. This second edition has changes that reflect the changing nature of fashion shows as a business practice and as an entertainment vehicle. We have incorporated many real-world examples into every chapter, including featured readings on the topic, which provide perspective for the reader from experts in the fashion industry. Additional changes include the use of Web sites to direct readers where they may view fashion shows online. Fashion show media coverage on television and in print has also grown since the first edition, and we have included discussions about these two important fashion media sources.

We begin this edition with a discussion on the background and development of the various types of fashion shows. Fashion shows began over two centuries ago as displays of fashion on dolls. Yet, in the 21st century they have emerged into a multi-million dollar business for supermodels and celebrities alike. This framework includes the primary purpose of producing a show—to sell merchandise. This first part of the book also traces the history of the fashion show through a review of designers, special events, and associations that influenced its advancement. This chapter concludes with a discussion of the business of fashion shows and their relevance today.

In the second chapter we continue the discussion on background, detailing the various types of shows. European fashion shows have set the pace for innovation and theatrical presentations. The unique styles of the French, Italian, British, and American retailers and designers—couture and ready-to-wear—are thoroughly reported in this chapter along with emerging countries, such as Brazil, Denmark, Spain, and others. Los Angeles is also discussed as a new fashion center.

The next section of the book outlines the steps in planning the fashion show, beginning with the first stages of planning—establishing the audience, type of show, site, theme, and budget. The message—presented through publicity and advertising—is fully discussed. Preparation of press materials and advertising for newspapers, magazines, television, and radio, as well as electronic presentations, is investigated. We have provided examples of press releases and photographs, as well as step-by-step instructions on how to write a press release, which we know will assist fashion show planners with this activity. E-mail has become an important communication tool since the writing of the first edition and a discussion of its use is also part of this chapter.

The merchandise selection process involves pulling, fitting, and preparing merchandise. The workroom and runway chapter highlights these important tasks. Grouping merchandise in a creative and interesting lineup that fits the theme is also part off this activity and is fully examined. The role of the models, who display the merchandise on the catwalk, is an important feature of how the show looks. Therefore, selecting and training models is critical to the overall success of any show. We have considered advantages and the difference between using professional or amateur models in a fashion show and the responsibilities of all the models during the fitting, rehearsal, and show. A change from the first edition, we have incorporated choreography into this chapter. Choreography sets the dramatic opening, pace, and finale for the models.

Music has taken center stage in fashion-show production. Show planners and the audience know that music can enhance or detract from the ambiance of a show more than almost any other theatrical element. Using music is one of the major focuses of this chapter. In a change from the first edition, we consider commentary to be another element of the sound check and discuss it with music in this chapter. Determining whether or not to use a commentator and commentary must be considered. If commentary is used, techniques and examples of how to write good and aid bad commentary are provided.

This chapter is followed by a discussion of the framework, which consists of the theatrical stage and runway design that can enhance the image or theme established in the early stages of planning. Distinct patterns for runways, seating arrangements, and the appropriate use of lighting and props are featured.

All of the advance preparation pays off on the day of the show. Rehearsal is complete and participants are excited to see everything pulled together, finally having the opportunity to introduce the show to the target audience. The thrill of all activities coming together results in a truly rewarding experience for the fashion show organizers, models, designers, technical staff, and audience. We also discuss the often-neglected portion of producing a fashion show—striking the stage and returning merchandise to the designers, manufacturers, or retailers. Another responsibility at this point is addressed—sending thank you notes and paying promptly for services.

The last chapter in the second edition of *Guide to Producing a Fashion Show* outlines the final step in fashion-show production—the evaluation process. This much-overlooked step in fashion-show production is really the first step in the production of the next show. Each time a fashion show is presented, the participants learn how to make the next show even better.

Producing a fashion show is a hands-on learning experience. One last feature of this second edition is the use, by example, of *Rock the Runway*, a student-produced fashion show from Northern Arizona University. This was truly a hands-on learning experience for students who produced one of the best shows ever produced at NAU. The students were enthusiastic and proud of their achievements in producing the show. Meanwhile, the university recognized the show as an outstanding educational project by giving the Service Learning Award to students who produced *Rock the Runway*.

It is our hope that the techniques discussed throughout this book will provide a foundation for fashion show planners to organize this enormous project and that the behind-the-scenes photographs support and enhance this information. This in-depth study of fashion-show production will serve as a valuable tool for fashion professionals, instructors, and students of design, merchandising and modeling, and civic or community leaders, giving them a view of all the aspects of the dramatic and exciting event. We enjoyed updating this edition and hope you will find the new information entertaining and helpful as *you produce a fashion show.*

2004

Judy Everett

Kris Swanson

ACKNOWLEDGMENTS

The authors wish to thank the many business associates, students, personal friends, and family who helped to make working on this project a pleasurable and rewarding experience. We appreciate all of the support from those individuals who were eager to answer questions, give counsel, review chapters, and provide entrance backstage to many of their fashion shows.

A special thanks to the following people: Sonya de Roeck, Fashion Coordinator for Printemps (Paris); Wendy Cholfin, Cholfin & Taylor Productions, Inc., Phoenix, Arizona; Kim Dawson, Kim Dawson Agency, Dallas Apparel Mart; Judy Edwards, Robert Black Agency, Tempe, Arizona; Karie Farrally, Special Events Director, Broadway Southwest; Bernie Goldstein, President, Dillard's Southwest Division; Lynette Harrison, W, Fairchild Productions; Milena Jovonic, Relations Clientele Internationale, Galeries Lafayette (Paris); Tony Keiser, Designer for Grey Elk Studio, Flagstaff, Arizona; Sally Leibig, Director, Flagstaff Winterfest, Arizona; Bob Mackie, Designer; Lee Merkle-Kemper, Special Events Director, Dillard's Southwest Division; Albert Nipon, Chief Executive Officer, Albert Nipon; Luciana Polacco, Director of Marketing, Laura Biagiotti, Milan; Beatrice Riordan, Flagstaff Symphony Guild, Flagstaff, Arizona.

We have gained much by working with all of our students. We especially wish to thank the student directors for *Rock the Runway*: Stephanie Gill, merchandise coordinator; Stephanie Hudson, stage manager; Erin Kalafut, promotion coordinator; and Jessica McClain, model coordinator. Thanks to Sara Frain, model coordinator for *Wear to Go*, who provided model composites for the second edition. These students served as inspiration and research assistants for the first edition. Thank you to Angel Gibson, Lynne Gilmore, Betsy Heimerl, Natalie Martin, and Ronnie Silverman.

Additional thanks need to go to the reviewers—Diane Ellis, Marsha Stein, Sharon E. Tabaca, Janice Threw—whose suggestions were extremely beneficial. Elizabeth Marotta and Beth Applebome, editors at Fairchild Publications, for their work on the second edition. Olga Kontzias, editor at Fairchild Publications, for keeping us on track—without her guidance and enthusiasm, this project would not have been completed.

Our mothers, Norma Culbertson and Bonnie Swanson, gave us a great foundation and appreciation of clothing. Thank you for your inspiration and encouragement.

Our husbands, Christopher Everett and James Power, thank you for putting up with the endless hours of fashion show talk and competing to use the computer. Chris served as our photographer and James contributed computer support.

GUIDE TO PRODUCING A FASHION SHOW

THE FASHION DOLLS, SUPERMODELS, AND CELEBRITIES

1

What do George Clooney (Fig. 1.1), Hilary Swank, Mary J. Blige, Gwyneth Paltrow, Paul McCartney, Steven Tyler, Sting, and Dustin Hoffman have in common? Each of them have attended a runway fashion show as part of the nonstop action that takes place at the semi-annual fashion presentations held in New York, London, Paris, or Milan. Star treatment for these events generally includes gift items from the designer's current line and a spot in the plush VIP lounge with champagne and hors d'oeuvres where celebrities relax before facing the mad rush of unending flashbulbs (Parr, 2001).

This whirlwind of activities, profiled in Box 1.1, brings fashion to the consumer via theatrical presentations staged by designers, supermodels, and celebrities from movies, stage, television, and politics. Fashion shows began as a simple method of presenting new clothes to clients. Today, fashion shows are elaborate productions, regularly featured on television broadcasts from Metro Channel or Fashion TV. Metro Channel's coverage of New York Fashion Week is round-the-clock for viewers in the New York region (Braunstein, 2001). Consumers in the Middle East do not have to wait until they see fashion magazine and newspaper articles written by the fashion press about the latest trends in Europe. Fashion savvy consumers from all over the world can watch some of the international fashion presentations live via the Internet.

This chapter, The Fashion Dolls, Supermodels, and Celebrities, introduces the reader to the key reasons why fashion shows are produced. Next, we look at the historical development of the fashion show and acquaint the reader with some of the significant people who were involved in the evolution from simple presentation on fashion dolls to electronic multimedia productions. Public interest in supermodels and celebrities, as well as other media coverage, contribute to the popularity of the fashion show in the 21st century. Thus, we profile some of the designers, rock stars, models, and actors who influence the fashion launches in the 21st century.

Figure 1.1 Brad Pitt, Jennifer Aniston, and George Clooney are among the celebrities who attract attention from photographers by sitting in the front rows of fashion shows such as this Giorgio Armani production in Milan. *Courtesy, Fairchild Publications, Inc.*

With huge expenses and high levels of stress for the designers, models, fashion media, and show producers, fashion critics have questioned whether fashion shows are still necessary. We end this chapter with a look at the future direction of fashion show production.

Fashion shows sell merchandise

Every creative element of theatrical and modern entertainment media is used in a **fashion show** to present the latest colors, fabrics, and fashion trends in apparel and accessories to an audience using live models. Certainly an advantage of seeing merchandise in an exciting live presentation is that the audience can become involved. They are not seeing a "representation" of a garment in a photograph or in an illustration from an advertisement, nor are they viewing a garment on a hanger. A model on the runway is wearing all the elements of apparel and accessories. The audience can react to the total look of an outfit and visualize how they might look wearing the newest and latest developments from the fashion world. The models in Figure 1.2 are exhibiting a joie de vivre on a Paris runway.

After designers or manufacturers create garments, accessories, or beauty products, promotion and merchandising contribute to the ultimate goal of selling these products. Fashion shows are produced with one primary purpose—to sell merchandise to consumers at all marketing levels from people working in the industry (designers, manufacturers, retailers) to fashion-conscious shoppers. The fashion show helps to make an authoritative visual statement about fashion, making it one of the most exciting and dramatic forms of promotion.

Figure 1.2 Fashion shows are a type of promotion that involves presenting merchandise on live models to potential customers. *Courtesy, Fairchild Publications, Inc.*

Promotion is a comprehensive term used to describe all of the communication activities initiated by the seller to inform, persuade, and remind the consumer about products, services, and/or ideas offered for sale (Swanson & Everett, 2000). It is a necessary function for the creators and distributors of fashion items. Promotion activities include: advertising, direct marketing, personal selling, publicity and public relations, sales promotion, special events, and visual merchandising, in addition to fashion shows.

The three major market levels for promotion activities are national, trade, and retail, as illustrated in Figure 1.3. **National promotion** involves primary and secondary resources directing promotion activities toward the ultimate consumer. **Primary resources** are the producers of raw materials. These primary producers typically include textile fiber and fabric firms. **Secondary resources** in the apparel industry generally are the clothing and accessory manufacturers. National promotion is used to pre-sell the consumer. It is not uncommon for a primary or secondary manufacturer to cooperatively produce a fashion show with a retailer to attract the consumer. Several firms participate and financially support cooperative, or co-op, promotion in the presentation of a show.

Trade promotion activities promote products from one business to another. This type of promotion activity takes a product from a primary resource to a secondary resource, a textile mill to a clothing manufacturer. It may also promote products from a secondary producer to a retailer.

Retail promotion typically involves stores promoting their products to consumers. Retailers, the main distributors of fashion items, focus their sales promotion efforts on their target consumers. Retail organizations are considered **tertiary resources.**

Figure 1.3 Market levels of national, trade, and retail promotion activities.

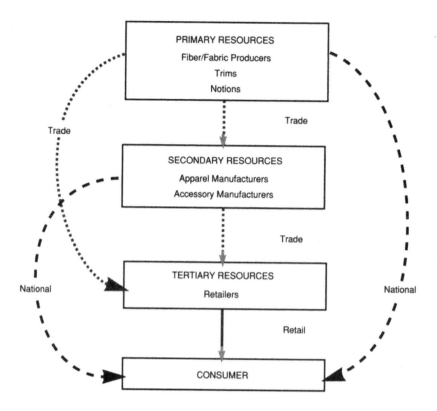

Additional reasons for producing fashion shows

Fashion-related organizations stage fashion shows for many reasons other than to sell merchandise. The most current fashion information on the latest trends in apparel, silhouettes, fabrics, color, or fashion services is transmitted to customers through this entertaining format. Fashion organizations want to attract new customers, build traffic, and encourage current customers to return. Retailers can use fashion shows to solidify the store's position as a fashion authority and leader in the community and promote goodwill with local, regional, or national patrons. A new product or line of merchandise may be introduced to customers through a fashion show.

In order to enhance a store's image as a fashion leader and increase sales for designer merchandise, the designer of the line may be invited to the store for a personal appearance. For example Randolf Duke was the featured guest at an in-store trunk show held at Neiman Marcus in Beverly Hills. The show was produced as a cooperative venture by the designer/manufacturer and the retail store. The trunk show sold more than $150,000 worth of merchandise in six hours, benefiting both the store and designer (Young, 2000).

When a manufacturing company introduces a secondary line targeting a specific type of customer such as Lauren by Ralph Lauren, consumer or trade-oriented fashion shows are used to acquaint customers with the new product.

In addition to introducing new products, retail stores want to inform their customers about the depth, range, and variety of merchandise carried. This will enable the retailer to

continued on page 6

Box 1.1
Opening the Tent To Woo More Fans

You do not have to be on air-kissing terms with Diane Von Furstenberg to have gotten it straight from her lips that James Bond was a primary influence on the collection she unveils tonight. Nor did you need to have lunch with Anna Sui to learn that Ms. Sui has spent the last several weeks poring over a stack of snowboarding magazines, seeking inspiration for her fall show, which takes place on Wednesday.

On the eve of Fashion Week, which opened Friday, both designers made the public privy to their fashion influences by way of Style.com, a Web site run by *Vogue* and *W* magazines. There was a time when such snippets, like tickets to the shows, were served up parsimoniously, dispensed like stock tips strictly to insiders.

No longer. This year, editors, retailers, designers and other impresarios of the runways are broadcasting their insider briefings on the Web, in stores and in other public spaces, sometimes well in advance of the shows, as part of a stepped-up effort to market Fashion Week directly to consumers, those who will ultimately buy the clothes.

Some are wooing shoppers with hot-off-the-runway videotape, others with hair and makeup tips from celebrity hair stylists working behind the scenes, still others with coveted tickets to the shows.

Most are betting the public will take the bait. "Every six months when the tents go up in Bryant Park, there is a mob, with people asking, 'How do I get in? How can I be a part of this?'" said Ed Burstell, vice president and general manager of Henri Bendel, which hopes to dish up at least some thrills with its first Mercedes-Benz Fashion Week boutique on the main floor.

Shoppers, lured inside the store by continuous runway video displayed in its Fifth Avenue windows, will enter a tent much like those in Bryant Park, to hear designers like Stephen Burrows, Matthew Williamson, Patricia Field and Ms. Von Furstenberg, some of whom will preview key looks from their fall collections.

"Our motive ultimately is to draw more shoppers to the store," Mr. Burstell said. He predicted that the boutique would create a spike in store traffic at Bendel's. "You can't beat the advertising of a Fifth Avenue window," he added.

American Express, too, has thrown its weight behind the effort to sell Fashion Week, putting together a package of "high-end runway shows, backstage tours, receptions, V.I.P. gift bags and meet-and-greets with designers, models, fashion stylists and editors." The offer, sent to American Express Platinum cardholders in a newsletter in December, promises behind-the-scenes peeks at Fashion Week.

Forty tickets for the package, sponsored by American Express and Seventh on Sixth, which produces Fashion Week, went on sale the same month for $2,300 each. All were sold. "The event is a good promotion," said Fern Mallis, the executive director of Seventh on Sixth. "Platinum cardholders spend money and buy a lot of fashion."

continued on page 6

Box 1.1 continued from previous page

Ralph Lauren is marketing a piece of the frenzy under the tents on Style.com, which offers an Internet link to Polo.com, his company's Web site, the day after the show on Thursday. Polo will run an online sweepstakes, offering the winner a pair of tickets to Mr. Lauren's show. His Web site will also display fresh film from the runways and will offer visitors the chance to play fashion editor by voting online for their favorite outfit. The campaign, which is also a form of consumer research, has already met with some success. Last fall, when the site was introduced, Polo reported that 70,000 people registered and voted in the three-week period following its introduction.

Not to be outdone, the preview page operated by Style.com, which made its debut last fall, will offer consumers insider tips on new designers and models and on the season's most sought-after events, like Jeremy Scott's after-show party on Friday night and Project Alabama's fashion show and party the same night at Bowlmor Lanes in Greenwich Village.

It also provides preshow tidbits, some of which may have visitors scratching their heads. Consider this sound bite from Narciso Rodriguez, who tells his audience that among his current fashion influences are Giovanni Boldini, the 19th-century society portrait painter, and "the abstract idea of separation."

A surfeit of fashion arcana has hardly put off visitors. Some 500,000 people logged on to the preview page last fall. The company predicts that this season the page will attract at least 700,000 visitors, most of them ordinary shoppers. "We are starting to nibble at the heels of very well-established fashion magazines," said Jamie Pallot, the editor in chief of Style.com. "A lot of new advertisers are coming on board."

The success of the site attests to a "tremendous appetite by ordinary people to know what's going to be in stores as far in advance as next August," said Janet Ozzard, the executive editor for Style.com. "They want a sense of being at the shows."

Source: La Ferla, R. (2003, February 9). Opening the Tent to Woo More Fans. *The New York Times*, Sec. 9. p. 11. Reprinted with permission. © 2003 *The New York Times Co.*

continued from page 4

focus on the different brands carried, features of their private label merchandise, or special merchandise offerings.

Various organizations may wish to show current fashions for a business program, luncheon, or annual meeting. Fundraising activities for such charitable groups as the American Heart Association, Muscular Dystrophy Association, Planned Parenthood, art museums, or symphony guilds may include holding an entertaining fashion show. In order to promote goodwill within a community a retail store or group of stores may support charitable groups by lending clothing and accessories. In addition, a portion or all of the revenues from the ticket sales may be contributed to such charitable groups.

Macy's West launched *Passport*, a fashion show and charity event to raise money and awareness for AIDS and HIV research. *Passport* is held each year and has grown to become a multi-theatrical fashion event with participation by celebrities, models, and musical artists.

Passport 00 featured hosts Elizabeth Taylor, Earvin "Magic" Johnson, and Cindy Crawford at the various fashion shows and musical performances held in San Francisco and Los Angeles ("Yahoo Shopping Presents," 2000). Since the first event staged in 1988, *Passport* has raised more than $13 million to benefit HIV/AIDS research, prevention, treatment, care, and education ("Obituary," 2001).

Fashion shows are also produced to provide training to at least two groups—fashion students and industry personnel. Nearly every fashion school or department produces an annual fashion show. This is the opportunity for students in apparel design to show their creations. Modeling students have an opportunity for practical application of their presentation skills. Merchandising students learn the behind-the-scenes responsibilities for organization, selection of merchandise and models, promotion, presentation, and evaluation of the show.

Students and faculty at the Shannon Rogers and Jerry Silverman School of Fashion Design and Merchandising at Kent State University produce an annual fashion show called *Portfolio*. The show, which features creations made by the fashion design majors, provides an opportunity to learn fashion show production in addition to recognizing outstanding students and alumni. *Portfolio* also raises money for scholarships.

At schools such as Northern Arizona University, which has a merchandising program without a fashion design program, students learn the techniques of fashion show production by staging a theme show, such as *Rock the Runway*, fusing fashion and music trends with merchandise borrowed from local retailers. All aspects of fashion show production, from planning to evaluation are learned by hands-on application.

Store personnel benefit from in-store training shows. During this type of show, the fashion office presents specific themes of merchandise that will be presented to customers during the next season. The training show helps to raise the staff's awareness of these specific trends and to provide selling features to help market this merchandise. In-store training shows help improve the attitude and morale of employees. They also help increase their knowledge about products and upcoming events, greatly enhancing the personnel's loyalty and the store's identification as a fashion leader.

Now that we have learned why fashion shows are produced, we turn our attention to the historical development of fashion shows. At first, fashion trend information was shared with clients by sending them fashion dolls. Next in the evolution of fashion promotion, an in-store model demonstrated the clothes. Then a runway was added, and this humble presentation evolved into the multi-media events we know as fashion shows today.

Fashion show history

The fashion show has been used by ready-to-wear manufacturers from the start of the mass production industry as a promotion event. However, the true inventor of the modern runway fashion show—using live models—is unknown. One of the first methods used by dressmakers to transmit fashion information to reach potential consumers, the women of the royal courts, was to send fashion dolls.

Fashion dolls

Fashion dolls were miniature scale figurines wearing replicas of the latest clothing. The dolls were also known as puppets, dummies, little ladies, or fashion babies. The earliest record of the fashion doll was in 1391 when the wife of Charles VI of France sent a full-size figure wearing the innovative French court fashions of the time to Queen Anne, wife of Richard II, King of England (Corinth, 1970). Although this was more like the modern day mannequin, it was called a fashion doll. Queen Anne was able to wear the garment immediately instead of having it reproduced from a miniature scale garment as was the common practice later.

Rose Bertin was the first dressmaker to be recognized by name. This French fashion creator was the dressmaker to Marie Antoinette, wife of Louis XVI. Dressmakers of the time would make up garments from a pattern, with fabric and trimming selected by the client. Despite her work for the queen, Rose Bertin achieved international fame with fashion dolls that she sent to all the capitals of Europe to solicit orders. As a result of this international fame, Mademoiselle Bertin was given the nickname, Minister of Fashion.

Shipping dolls wearing the latest fashion trends from one royal court to another was a common practice in the European monarchy, reaching its peak during the reigns of Louis XIV, Louis XV, and Louis XVI, from the 1640s to 1790s. Even during the 17th to 19th centuries it was recognized that fashion was best shown on a body, even if it was on a lifeless mannequin. One of the fashion dolls is illustrated in Figure 1.4.

Thêatre de la Mode was a fashion doll presentation unique to the 20th century, which took place at the end of World War II. Paris designers in a liberated France wanted to let the world know that they were ready to resume fashion leadership despite limited resources. Unable to launch a full scale fashion exhibition, designers, artists, and musicians collaborated to present Thêatre de la Mode, allowing the world to see the French spring-summer collection of 1946, the first to be designed for export since the war. Petits mannequins, or fashion dolls, were revived for this exhibition. Although the presentation did not use live models, it did present fashion on the human form in the style of a spectacular fashion show.

This project was coordinated through the Chambre Syndicale de la Haute Couture Parisienne. It brought together designers who otherwise would have concealed their work from competitors (Train, 1991).

An exhibit of 228 petits mannequins featured the latest work of the French designers. The mannequins were presented in 12 theatrical sets to provide the proper environment for morning, afternoon or evening attire (Fig. 1.5). Participating couture houses agreed to create from one to five outfits for display.

The 27.5 inch wire figurines were built from sketches developed by Eliane Bonabel. Plaster heads constructed by sculptor Joan Rebull were added to the figures so they could have real coiffures and hats.

The art director for the project was Christian (Bebé) Bérard, a Parisian artist. He called upon his friends in the arts, theater, and literary world to participate. Balenciaga, Hermés, Balmain, Lanvin, Molyneux, Schiaparelli, Worth, and Ricci were among the fashion designers who were involved.

The show was originally produced to raise money to help war victims. The exhibition traveled to England, Spain, Denmark, Sweden, and Austria. The following year the show was sent

Figure 1.4 This fashion doll is shown in Russian Court Dress of the early 19th century. *Courtesy, Warwick Doll Museum. Copyright © Walter Scott, Bradford, England.*

Figure 1.5 Susan Train prepares a fashion doll for presentation in Thêàtre de la Mode. The doll is dressed in a day suit by O'Rossen complete with suede gloves by Hermés. *Courtesy, Jean Luca Hure.*

to New York and San Francisco with updated fashions. With limited resources, the show's sponsors could not afford to return the mannequins and clothing to Paris. The display was forgotten and it was assumed that the doll collection was lost until it was discovered at the Maryhill Museum of Art in Goldendale, Washington, in 1983. The garments and accessories were returned to Paris for restoration in 1987. An exhibit featuring 171 dolls opened at the Musée des Arts de la Mode in Paris in 1990. The exhibit moved to the Costume Institute of The Metropolitan Museum of Art, New York, later that year. The exhibit is permanently located at the Maryhill Museum of Art.

Barbie is perhaps the most famous fashion doll of the 20th century. Mattel Toy Company introduced her in 1959 ("What a doll," 1998). Barbie was more than a simple toy for girls and boys in the last half of the century; she was a fashion symbol. The doll was sold with exchangeable fashions of the time period, in addition to fantasy dresses. She became a fashion model, wearing her Bob Mackie, Ralph Lauren, Donna Karan, and Anne Klein inspired clothing. Many youngsters dreamed of becoming fashion designers as they created their original Barbie clothing.

Influential designers

The modern runway fashion show has its roots in the French Couture that began in the 19th century. Costume historians agree that Charles Frederick Worth, the English-born fashion innovator, was the first couturier in France, opening his Paris fashion house in 1858. Among Worth's revolutionary ideas was designing clothing for an individual woman, customizing the style, fabric, and trimmings to the wearer. Made-to-order garments were created for his clients from samples in the salon. For his contributions in making the couture world what it is today, Worth was given the nickname, "Father of Haute Couture."

Worth had worked with fabrics and clothes in London before leaving for Paris in 1845. One of his first jobs in France was with Gagelin and Opigez, a retailer that sold fabrics, trimmings, coats, and shawls. It was the responsibility of the demoiselle de magasin (shop-girl) to show customers how the shawls looked on a living form (Diehl, 1976). Marie Vernet, an original demoiselle de magasin who later became Madame Worth, was perhaps the first fashion model when she showed shawls and the latest Worth creations to clients.

The House of Worth called the women who wore garments for clients **mannequins** (Corinth, 1970). Showing clothing on mannequins allowed clients to see how garments would look on a living and moving person. Up to this point, the term *mannequin* had referred to a stationary doll or dummy used as a display fixture. As Worth became more successful, he hired more young women to model at his maison or fashion house. These mannequins continued to show his collections to his customers.

Before the end of the century several other designers opened Maisons de Haute Couture in the manner of Charles Frederick Worth. These designers copied the promotion innovations of Worth and featured their designs on live models. By the 1920s French designers Paul Poiret, Madame Paquin, and Jean Patou also made significant contributions to the development of the fashion show.

Paul Poiret, known for liberating women from the corset, opened his couture house in 1904. This designer had a knack for promotion, and among his contributions were his innovative and controversial window displays. Poiret also toured, making personal appearances to show his fashions at chic resorts. Poiret even traveled to Russia with nine mannequins. He was one of the first couturiers to parade his mannequins at the races (Diehl, 1976). Such appearances had a positive impact on his sales and image.

The House of Paquin was known for parading models at the racetrack, but Paquin also staged events at the opera. Paquin was the first designer to introduce the finale for her events. It is said that in one show 20 mannequins were dressed in white evening gowns as a tableau (Diehl, 1976). This created a positive and lasting impression at the end of the show. Finales—exciting conclusions—have become universal and important to contemporary fashion shows.

Fashion shows were also being regularly held at retail stores in the United States, Paris, and London during the early decades of the 20th century. Fashionable customers enjoyed the entertainment and education provided by these events. Figure 1.6 shows models from a Washington D.C., clothing shop after they had presented merchandise to the customers of the store.

It was common practice for couture houses to show their latest collections on a predetermined opening day. These dates were established by the Chambre Syndicale so that openings of the important designers would not conflict, enabling clients and the press to view several shows. After this premiere the show would be repeated twice each day for a month, with smaller shows for private clients. The ordinary dress rehearsal, which took place the evening before the premiere, was held with the sales personnel and workers as the audience, giving the employees their only chance to see their labors.

Jean Patou, primarily known for his contributions to sportswear and as a rival of Chanel, was associated with two important contributions to the fashion show—the press show and the use of American models in Paris. The press had been coming to report on the fashion collections since 1910. In 1921 Patou scheduled a special preview showing, the repetition generale, a full dress rehearsal for the influential representatives of the press, notable buyers, and exceptional clients on the evening before his regular opening (Etherington-Smith, 1983). With the assistance of Elsa Maxwell, a popular party planner of the era and perhaps the first press agent, Patou converted the ordinary dress rehearsal into an extraordinary way to introduce the fashion season. The salon was festively decorated with flowers and spotlights. Guests were seated at tables with name cards and were treated to champagne, deluxe cigarettes and cigars, and sample bottles of Patou perfumes. The couturier Patou, his **premier/premiere**, head of the workroom, and his **directrice/directeur**, head of the salon, approved each model before she was allowed to show the garment to the audience. Since some fashion styles were rejected at this program, the audience observed the designer as he made his final eliminations from his collection. Patou's events led the way for the twice annual press shows held by the Paris couture throughout the 20th century.

An American client complained that she had a hard time visualizing herself in the Patou clothing as it was shown on the French mannequins, whose figures were round compared to American figures. Patou traveled to America in 1924. With the assistance of Edna Woolman Chase, then editor of *Vogue* magazine, Elsie de Wolfe, decorator and international socialite, Edward Steichen, photographer, and Condé Nast, publisher of *Vogue*, Patou selected six American models—Lillian Farley, Josephine Armstrong, Dorothy Raynor, Caroline Putnam, Edwina Prue, and Rosalind Stair—to return with him to Paris. Although Patou had originally planned on hiring three models, he doubled the number due to the favorable impression they created. The young women "of refined manner" gave prestige to the profession of modeling. They were paid $40 per week and given the opportunity to purchase ensembles from Patou for as little as $25 (Etherington-Smith, 1983). The use of American models changed the ideal

Figure 1.6 Models pose during a 1921 fashion show for the Wells Shop of Washington, D.C. This early specialty store featured corsets, brassieres, hats, and bonnets. *Reproduced from the Collections of the Library of Congress.*

of international physical beauty to the thinner and more athletic shapes that these American women possessed.

Paquin's contribution to the fashion show was the finale, but it was Patou who influenced the dramatic opening. For his spring 1925 presentation, he had French and American models make their first entrance in a single file parade wearing the toile—the simple robe worn between fittings in the dressing room. He demonstrated that the physical form was the same regardless of nationality and served as the inspiration for his designs. The audience was entertained and were preconditioned to like the collection (Etherington-Smith, 1983).

Fashion shows remained as fashion parades through the 1930s, 1940s, and 1950s (Fig. 1.7). The quality of these fashion productions improved as did the technology in this time period. Many of these shows rivaled Broadway musicals with stage sets, lighting, music, and fabulous mannequins.

Christian Dior was acknowledged for changing the format of the fashion parade with his legendary collection in 1947. According to then *Vogue* fashion editor, Bettina Ballard, in her memoirs, "We were given a polished theatrical performance such as we had never seen in a couture house before. We were witness to a revolution in fashion and to a revolution in showing fashion as well" (Quick, 1997, p. 70). Dior asked his models to project the image and lifestyle of the women who wore his clothes, not simply show the cut and cloth. Dior's models, who entered the salon with an electrical tension, stepping fast, walking with provocative swinging movements, and whirling in the room packed with clients and fashion press, might seem tame compared to the energetic fashion shows of the 1960s (Fig. 1.8).

The creativity and energy of the swinging 1960s led to major changes in fashion and the way it was presented. British designer Mary Quant was at the forefront of these changes. Certain models were known for their work in the photographic media while other models

Figure 1.7 Private clients and influential members of the press were always anxious to view the latest Chanel collections. The audience views Chanel's fashion show in 1959. *Courtesy, Marc Riboud/Magnum Photos.*

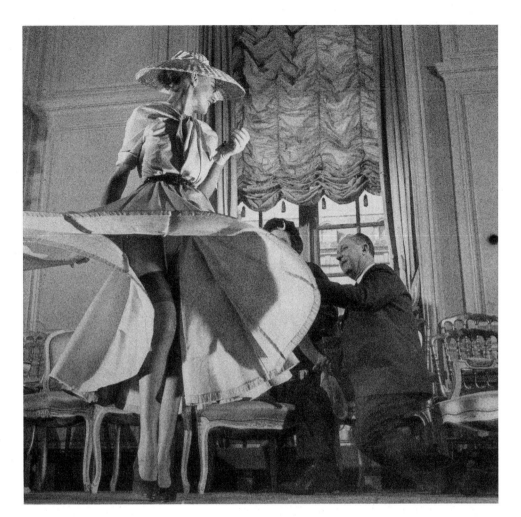

Figure 1.8 Dior encouraged his models to capture an energetic and youthful appearance at his fashion shows after World War II ended. *Courtesy, © Bettmann/Corbis.*

worked the runway shows. However, Quant felt that photographic models rather than runway models knew how to move around in clothes, so she selected nine of them to dance down the stairs and runway at her shop, Knightsbridge Bazaar. Since this era models have worked each field interchangeably.

Quant's staging, use of innovative props, and dancing led to more active fashion shows. Contemporary jazz music was taped for an uninterrupted pace. The show consisted of 40 garments and was shown in 14 minutes. One outfit featured a model wearing a Norfolk jacket and knickers, carrying a shotgun and a dead pheasant for a hunting scene. Models wearing party dresses carried oversized champagne glasses. Absolutely no commentary was spoken (Quant, 1966). This period marked the elimination of commentary from press and trade shows. Music, dance, and choreography set the mood for these fashion shows.

By the 1970s, French Haute Couture started to look sadly outdated. Ready-to-wear clothing was quickly becoming popular, overshadowing the expensive made-to-measure couture. Japanese designer Kenzo introduced his extremely successful Jungle Jap label with a fashion show spectacle (Quick, 1997). Kenzo extended the traditional catwalk into a stage performance, attracting an audience almost four times the size of a traditional salon show. Instead of presenting a neat parade, he asked his models to improvise. The girls went wild—clowning, dancing cancan, doing the rumba, somersaulting, waving sparklers, showering each other

Figure 1.9 Kenzo presented bright and colorful images onto the Paris runway during the 1970s. *Courtesy, Fairchild Publications, Inc.*

Figure 1.10 Claude Montana's 1984 fashion show featured models that walked the runway wearing bright colors and strong shapes. *Courtesy, Fairchild Publications, Inc.*

with confetti, and baring their breasts. The conservative Parisian and worldwide fashion audience had never seen anything like it before. A dress from Kenzo's 1976 collection is shown in Figure 1.9.

After Kenzo, the rules changed. There were no runway rules.

The fashion show as a carnival with punk fashion influenced by street wear was the atmosphere created by British designer Vivienne Westwood in the 1980s (Quick, 1997). Westwood fused the rebellious styles of the street with tribal and historical costume, attracting a fanatical cult following. Each year the models adopted a different guise, and with that guise the models adopted a different set of poses and gestures.

It was during the same decade that John Galliano presented his first show. In 1984, Galliano's graduation collection from Central Saint Martins, entitled "Les Incroyables," foretold of how different his approach would be. His models looked like women resurrected from the French Revolution, as they drifted down the runway barefoot, eyes whitened with pale mascara, in tattered clothes sprinkled with dust and cobwebs (Quick, 1997). Each season a different set of characters emerged from Galliano.

The 1980s were a decade of excess, and everything, including fashion shows, got bigger. Fashion became a global force, with designers licensing their names to perfume, accessories, cosmetics, and even chocolate and wine. The consumer became aware of the biannual fashion events through television coverage, turning the collection presentations into major media events. Satellite and television stations worldwide, broadcast the collections, showing celebrities and fashion editors in front-row seats. There were 1,875 journalists and 150 photographers in attendance at the Paris shows in 1986, nearly 4 times greater than the number who attended in 1976 (Quick, 1997). The European fashion shows were no longer the private reserve of the high fashion clients and fashion journalists. Now everyone knew about these exciting presentations.

French designers Thierry Mugler and Claude Montana produced fashion shows of monumental proportions. Dazzling light shows and epic soundtracks sparked their shows. Mugler's shows became so popular that he attracted 4,000 paying guests to a grand spectacular in 1984 (Quick, 1997). Montana sent his battalions of models onto a runway in clouds created by dry ice. Montana's strong silhouette, with "football" shoulders, from his 1984 collection is illustrated in Figure 1.10. Fashion shows became increasingly fantastic and ostentatious, as designers were attempting to woo the cameras for publicity. International models on the runway seemed to guarantee camera appeal and media coverage.

Reality hit the fashion scene in the 1990s. Real fashion, consisting of minimal and urban clothes similar to those found at the Gap, was shown on the runway. There was a trend to use normal looking girls as models. At his 1996 runway show, American designer Marc Jacobs pinned up the following sign in the dressing room:

Boys and Girls
Please walk at a natural pace-not slow, not fast
Please no hands on hips
No "turns"

No modeling!

Thank you-you are all beautiful and we love you (Quick, 1997).

Minimalist designers like Zoran were able to buck the traditional fashion system, gaining success during the end of the 20th century without advertising, courting celebrities, or putting on fashion shows. His styles changed very little in his more than 20 years in business; his line consisted of a collection of minimally cut garments without zippers or buttons in four or five solid colors. Zoran used expensive fabrics, like cashmere and Tasmanian wool, to construct separates that cost $3,000 for a 2- or 3-piece ensemble (Horyn, 1999). Even with those high prices and styles that compared to an upscale Gap, Zoran attracted a loyal following of customers.

Fashion shows at the start of the 21st century became media spectacles again, departing from the minimalist approach taken by many designers in the 1990s. Dutch design team Viktor & Rolf (Viktor Horsting and Rolf Snoeren) shocked their Paris audience with an all black collection worn by white models painted black (Fig. 1.11). Attempting to delve into the nature of shadow and light, the team did not anticipate the mixed reaction to their show. The girls were said to look beautiful and intriguing, but however unintentional, the connection to blackface and racially sensitive minstrel shows could not be missed (Foley, 2001a).

Figure 1.11 Viktor & Rolf created quite a controversy when they painted their models' faces black for their Fall 2001 fashion show. *Courtesy, Fairchild Publications, Inc.*

Internet fashion shows

Fashion show audience participation was expanded to anyone with a computer modem via the Internet by the turn of the 21st century. Victoria's Secret invited the 1999 Superbowl audience to watch its live fashion show to be broadcast on the Internet during the week following the sporting event (Swanson & Everett, 2000). Millions of people turned on their computers to watch, causing the system to overload. Since then, innovators such as Saks Fifth Avenue and Ralph Lauren have expanded the use of virtual fashion shows. Saks Fifth Avenue projected the Spring 2001 New York fashion shows onto the façade of its flagship store on Fifth Avenue. An advertisement in the *New York Times* invited consumers to get a ringside seat to see the shows. Ralph Lauren launched a Web site (http://runway.polo.com) to allow customers to look at his fashion shows, hair and makeup trends, and behind the scenes activities, and to buy merchandise. The 21st century will offer many new ways to get involved in fashion events.

Models and supermodels

As we previously indicated, Marie Vernet was probably the first fashion model, as her husband Charles Fredrick Worth's muse. However, she was accepted into society as Worth's wife, not as a model. Fashion models during the first part of the 20th century were viewed as figures of scorn and scandal (Quick, 1997). It was not until after World War I that the status of fashion modeling improved and was considered an appropriate career for young women.

High society women, millionaire wives, and the popular actresses from stage and screen became the fashion models, or **mannequins du monde**, as they were known, in the 1930s.

Dressed by couturiers, pressured to appear on the pages of *Vogue* and *Harper's Bazaar*, and complimented in society columns, these women were offered free clothing in exchange for their loyalty and promotion of the designer's clothes (Quick, 1997). Society women were year-round walking advertisements for fashion, resulting in an improved image for fashion models. The professional model was quickly in demand.

The fashion model in the 1950s became the public image of fashion, and girls flocked to New York, London, and Paris to enter this glamorous world. Names of the popular models of the era, including Suzy Parker, were known due to various magazine articles, "how-to" books, and autobiographies. Models found work as house or fit models for specific designers, runway models for retail stores such as Harvey Nichols in London and Neiman Marcus in Dallas, or as photographic models.

London was the place to be in the 1960s. Jean Shrimpton and Twiggy became international fashion icons. Models were the center of media attention and the symbol of the pop generation. Rock stars dated and sometimes married the popular models of the era. George Harrison of the Beatles married top model Patti Boyd, which contributed to the growing interdependence of music and fashion.

Starting with Lauren Hutton (Fig. 1.12), who became the face of Revlon cosmetics for a record $400,000 in 1973, American models dominated the fashion scene in the 1970s. Cover Girl signed Cheryl Tiegs for a staggering $1.5 million, while Fabergé paid Margaux Hemingway $3 million to an exclusive contract (Quick, 1997). This media exposure led these models to acting roles in addition to their lucrative modeling careers.

Figure 1.12 Lauren Hutton became the face of the 1970s when her modeling salary skyrocketed after she was offered an exclusive deal from Revlon. *Courtesy, Fairchild Publications, Inc.*

Fashion in the 1970s also had an appetite for the exotic. Ethnic beauties broke into the business. Somalian born Iman, the beautiful daughter of a diplomat, went on to become one of the highest paid models ever. It was reported that she earned $100,000 for doing a Munich runway show, compared to the $1,500 paid other models at the time (Quick, 1997). Pat Cleveland was the first black runway model, and Beverly Johnson became the first black model on the cover of American *Vogue*.

Nearly 100 years after the first models were picked from among the seamstresses working for Charles Frederick Worth and paid wages on a par with a floor sweeper, the celebrity supermodels emerged. Supermodels Naomi Campbell, Cindy Crawford, Linda Evangelista, Elle MacPherson, Claudia Schiffer, and Christy Turlington became the fashion idols of their time. Their popularity and salaries exceeded rock stars and Hollywood celebrities. Linda Evangelista gained a reputation for being arrogant when she remarked, "We have this expression, Christy and I: We don't wake up for less than $10,000 a day" (Quick, 1997, p. 149).

These supermodels not only continued their fashion careers, they made transitions into related careers. Cindy Crawford acted in several movies, made television commercials, and served as a spokesperson for a number of products, including Revlon and Pepsi. Christy Turlington retained advertising contracts with Calvin Klein and Maybelline for editorial modeling, while launching Nuala, a yoga wear company in partnership with Puma, and Sundari, a natural skincare line with friends (Foley, 2001b).

Model agencies

John Robert Powers was credited with starting the first model agency in 1923. According to Michael Gross (1995), Powers and his wife, Alice Hathaway Burton, were out of work actors who were asked to find models to pose for commercial photographers. Realizing that photographers needed models for a rapidly growing advertising industry and knowing many unemployed actors and actresses, they created a business to bring the two together. Powers had pictures taken of his models, put together a catalog containing their descriptions and measurements, and sent the catalogs to anyone in New York, photographers, department stores, advertisers, or artists, who might be prospective clients. While the first model book contained only 40 models, this project spurred an entire industry of modeling schools and agencies.

In Europe, model agencies evolved from charm schools. In 1928, Sylvia Gollidge, a former department store model from Blackpool, opened Lucie Clayton, a charm school in London (Quick, 1997). Gollidge charged the girls, or their parents, fees to become more socially proficient. The charm school owner and teacher promised to turn any young girl into a lady through her classes in deportment, basic elocution, and social manners. Such charm schools opened throughout Europe and America, expanding the girls' education into modeling techniques such as posing, applying makeup, and dressing quickly.

Eileen Ford, set up a model-booking agency in 1946 (Gross, 1995). As a former model, Ford and her partner, husband Jerry, recognized the special needs of models and their career development. She provided training and professional advice to her models. With her hands-on management style, Ford turned modeling into a more respectable career, and she turned her model agency into a powerful player in the fashion industry. The Ford Agency grew to become one of the largest international agencies, with several offices in the United States, Europe, Canada, and South America. The Ford Agency set the standards in an industry that has become highly lucrative.

Celebrities and fashion shows

Hollywood and the entertainment industry have maintained a symbiotic relationship with fashion since movies were mass distributed. Hair and makeup trends were the primary fashion influence coming from Hollywood in the 1920s and 1930s. Americans watching these movies learned styles from the popular actresses, starting with Clara Bow and later were influenced by such beautiful women as Joan Crawford, Jean Harlow, Marilyn Monroe, Lauren Bacall, and Mia Farrow.

Actresses and entertainers learned about the power of clothing from the preeminent Hollywood costume designers, including Edith Head, Adrian, and Bob Mackie. During the era when movie studios dominated the scene, actresses would be dressed for various events by the studios' costume and makeup departments. The biggest Hollywood and fashion event held each year was the Academy Awards Ceremony, which in addition to recognizing the outstanding costume design for a movie, prominently portrayed the glamorous stars as fashion leaders when they presented and received awards. Leaving nothing to chance, the Hollywood studios dressed the actors and actresses for the Oscar ceremony throughout its early years.

Later in the 20th century, international fashion designers started interacting with Hollywood stars more frequently. Italian fashion designer Giorgio Armani had always been a fan of Hollywood and the movies, creating Oscar night clothing for Diane Keaton (1978) and designing film images for Richard Gere in *American Gigolo* (1980). With sales of $90 million the year after that movie was released, Armani and his competitors saw the significance of courting Hollywood stars (Fox, 2000). Armani went on to dress such stars as Jodie Foster, Mira Sorvino, and Michelle Pfeiffer for their Oscar appearances. Today, Oscar nominated actresses and presenters have unlimited choices of dresses and jewelry to wear on such occasions.

Fashionable actresses realized by attending the designers' fashion shows, they might end up on the cover of *Women's Wear Daily*, *W*, or *InStyle* magazines, a publicity win for both the actress and designer. Front row seats at fashion shows, once reserved for significant fashion editors and private clients, are now shared with celebrities, such as Melanie Griffith, Penelope Cruz, Uma Thurman, and Sarah Jessica Parker.

With Paul McCartney's daughter Stella gaining an international reputation as a fashion designer, with such models as Christy Turlington becoming clothing manufacturers, and with fashion designers presenting dramatic and theatrical fashion shows, the inter-relationship between the fields of entertainment and fashion are forever dependent upon each other. Exciting fashion design, electrifying music, and fantastic staging are all components of the fashion show in the 21st century.

Fashion show associations

As the American ready-to-wear industry was taking shape in the early years of the 20th century, American manufacturers used live models to present the latest collections at the major regional trade marts. The most important trade shows were held in Chicago and New York.

The Merchandise Buyers Exposition and Fashion Show at the New Grand Central Palace held in 1912 in New York staged two live fashion parades daily (Diehl, 1976). While a local orchestra played the popular songs of the day, live models walked across a stage carrying cards with simply the manufacturer's name indicated. No evidence of commentary was reported at this time.

In 1914, the Chicago Garment Manufacturers Association presented an elaborate fashion show to the 5,000 people attending this market. One hundred mannequins showed 250 garments in nine scenes. The rehearsal was filmed and distributed to local theaters across the United States. This show used a stage and a large platform or runway to bring the clothing closer to the audience. This was perhaps the first use of a fashion show "runway" (Corinth, 1970).

Edna Woolman Chase, editor of *Vogue* magazine, combined several elements, including trade shows, society leaders, and a charitable benefit for a wartime cause into the first major fashion show for the public. On November 4, 1914, the Fashion Fête was produced featuring American designs at the time that Paris was threatened by World War I. The show was held as a benefit for widows and orphans of the allied countries (Fig. 1.13).

With the assistance and patronage of the society women of the day, *Vogue* presented fashions at a gala event held at the Ritz-Carlton hotel. Clothing from Henri Bendel, a fashion leader of the time, was selected by a committee of seven society women as well as Mrs. Chase and Helen Koues also from *Vogue*. The evening started with dinner; it was followed by a fashion show and later dancing. The show was repeated for two days in the afternoons and evenings.

Vogue advertised for models for the Fashion Fête. At this time no formal schools existed for models, and dressmaker models, although an integral part of French couture, were employed by only a few New York dressmakers. The applicants were rehearsed by *Vogue* and instructed how to walk, pivot, and show the garments. The following year, partly because of the influence of the first Fête, mannequins as models started to become an important factor to the American fashion scene (Chase, 1954). The use of the fashion show to raise money for philanthropic organizations has been common throughout the 20th century.

By the 1920s fashion shows were an accepted form of introducing new lines of apparel to the fashion press, retailers, and consumers. Fashion shows were no longer a novelty, they were professionally staged events that people looked forward to.

One group that helped to set high standards for professionalism in the production of fashion shows was the Fashion Group International, which was founded in 1928 by 17 women fashion executives (Corinth, 1970). One of the purposes of the group then, as it is now, is to provide a central source of information on fashion trends. Fashion shows for members and guests were presented almost from the beginning of the organization. The first Fashion Futures event was held on September 11, 1935 (1970). It was described as the first unpropaganda, un-commercialized, and un-subsidized fashion show ever presented.

By 2001 The Fashion Group International, Inc. had more than 5,500 members in 40 regional groups (Fashion Group International, 2000). Members can be found in the United

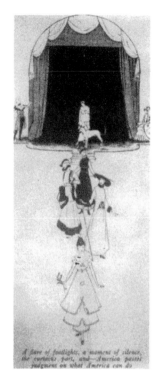

Figure 1.13 In 1914 Edna Woolman Chase, editor of *Vogue*, decided to feature American designers in the Fashion Fête. *Copyright © 1914 by The Vogue Company. Courtesy of* Vogue *Magazine, The Condé Nast Publications Inc.*

States, Canada, England, France, Mexico, Korea, Japan, South Africa, and South America. Membership is made up of women and men with executive status, representing the fields of fashion, cosmetics, and the home.

Various volunteer committees provide unique programs. The most important international programs are the multi-media presentations of seasonal fashion trends from New York, Paris, London, and Milan. The visual programs and print Trend Reports are available to all members in regional groups.

Regional groups take on fashion leadership in the various markets. For example the Fashion Group International of Dallas, Inc. sponsors an annual "Career Day" for students of fashion merchandising and design. The day concludes with a fashion show featuring apparel and accessories created by fashion design students. The show is professionally produced by the Kim Dawson Agency—the fashion show production and modeling agency affiliated with the Dallas Apparel Mart. The show serves as a design competition with trips to Paris and scholarships as the awards.

Fashion show's finale

According to Teri Agins (1999), four megatrends sent fashion retailing in a new direction at the end of the 20th century.

- *Women let go of fashion.* Baby-boomer women entered careers and were moving up in the workplace. As executives, these self-confident women became secure enough to ignore the foolish fashion frippery that no longer connected to their way of life.
- *People stopped dressing up.* Most Americans wore jeans, loose knit tops, and athletic style shoes, which even became acceptable as office apparel.
- *People's values changed with regard to fashion.* Target gained a reputation for providing fashionable clothing at discount prices. Soon, customers questioned why they should pay high prices for designer originals, when they found similar clothing at such stores as Gap, Ann Taylor, The Limited, Banana Republic, and J. Crew.
- *Top designers stopped gambling on fashion.* The financial managers from Chanel, Isaac Mizrahi's parent company, closed his fashion business in 1998 when they realized Mizrahi had shown zero in the profit column. Mizrahi (Fig. 1.14) mistakenly believed that enough fashion followers were willing to believe in his taste level.

With these dramatic changes taking place in the fashion world, some critics questioned the future role of fashion shows.

Despite the expense, stress, and overall craziness associated with fashion show production, these events continue to attract media attention and large audiences. Media coverage and consumer accessibility to international fashion productions through the Internet, continue to make these events popular. A panel discussion held by Fashion Group International members in Arizona concluded that fashion shows will continue to be a viable method of intro-

Figure 1.14 Isaac Mizrahi, shown here with Cindy Crawford, rose to fame in the 1990s with the release of the fashion themed movie, *Unzipped. Courtesy, Fairchild Publications, Inc.*

ducing new and creative fashion lines to retailer buyers, celebrities, journalists, and fashion clients for a long time into the future.

This chapter introduced the fashion show as a special event to exhibit clothing and accessories on live models to a potential audience. The primary purpose of a fashion show is to sell merchandise. A number of secondary objectives, including training employees or students and establishing fashion leadership, were identified. We also presented a historical perspective on fashion show production and evaluated the role of the fashion show.

Key fashion show terms

directrice / directeur	national promotion	retail promotion
fashion dolls	premier / premiere	secondary resources
fashion show	primary resources	trade promotion

mannequins   promotion   tertiary resources
mannequins du monde

References

Agins, T. (1999). *The end of fashion: The mass marketing of the clothing business*. New York: William Morrow.

Braunstein, P. (2001, April). Chic excess: There is no such thing as fashion media overload. *Women's Wear Daily: The Magazine*, 86-88.

Chase, E. W., & Chase, I. (1954) *Always in Vogue*. New York: Doubleday.

Corinth, K. (1970). *Fashion showmanship*. New York: Wiley.

Diehl, M. E. (1976) *How to produce a fashion show*. New York: Fairchild.

Etherington-Smith, M. (1976). *Patou*. New York: St. Martin's.

Fashion Group International. (2002). *Membership directory*. New York: Author.

Foley, B. (2001a, April). Great expectations with their endless possibilities for intrigue, the collections are a thrill seekers paradise. *Women's Wear Daily: The Magazine*, 45-48.

Foley, B. (2001b, June). Princess Bride: Christy Turlington revels in her new life as an entrepreneur and wedding planner. *W*. Retrieved June 22, 2001 from http://www.style.com/w/ feat story/09/19/01/full page.html

Fox, P. (2000). *Star style at the Academy Awards*. Santa Monica, CA: Angel City Press.

Gross, M. (1995). *Model the ugly business of beautiful women*. New York: Morrow.

Horyn, C. (1999, April 20). Zoran, the master of deluxe minimalism, still provokes. *New York Times*. Retrieved April 20, 1999 from http://www.nytimes.com

Obituary. (2001, June 4). *Women's Wear Daily*, 13.

Parr, K. (2001, May). Fashion report: At clothes range. *In Style*, 222-30.

Quant, M. (1965). *Quant by Quant*. London: Cassell.

Quick, H. (1997). *Catwalking: A history of the fashion model*. Edison, NJ: Wellfleet Press.

Swanson, K.K., and Everett, J. C. (2000). *Promotion in the merchandising environment*. New York: Fairchild.

Train, S. (Ed.) (1991). *Théâtre de la Mode*. New York: Rizzoli.

What a doll. (1998, September). *Women's Wear Daily Century*, 98

Yahoo Shopping, (2000). *Macy's fashion and compassion: Passport 2000*. Retrieved June 21, 2001 from http://www.yahoo.com/promotions/macyspassport.

Young, K. (2000, July 5). Trunk show hits. *Women's Wear Daily*, 15.

THE BACKGROUND

After watching how beauty writers studied and predicted trends from cosmetics looks coming down the fashion runway, Sephora, a leading retail beauty chain in Europe and the United States decided to do something about it by offering the first-ever beauty formal runway show (Naughton, 2001). The show, held at the Bryant Park tents (Fig. 2.1) in February 2001, featured cosmetics visions of 15 Sephora vendors, including Stila, Lorac, Christian Dior, Givenchy, and Urban Decay. Necessary planning included handling more than 70 models. Each cosmetic vendor was allowed to show four looks. Unlike a conventional apparel fashion show, the makeup could not be stripped off of a model's face and replaced rapidly. Therefore, each look had to be presented on a different model.

Similar to apparel and accessory fashion shows, Sephora used a fashion show to showcase trend forecasts. According to Betsy Olum, Senior Vice President of marketing for Sephora and Sephora.com, "So many times, beauty is an afterthought . . . we wanted to give these brands the chance to help define makeup looks for the next season" (Naughton, 2001, p. 6). Additionally, Sephora used the show to benefit its brick-and-mortar business by tying the show into in-store, online, and catalog marketing.

As illustrated in Chapter 1, fashion shows are full of entertainment and excitement. But before the readers of this text plunge into the details of producing a fashion show, some background information is necessary to understand the different types of fashion shows and how they are used as promotion tools. This chapter, The Background, will provide needed background information.

This chapter begins with a discussion of fashion show categories, production shows, formal runway shows, informal fashion shows, and multimedia production shows. Next, we will turn our attention to specialized fashion presentations including haute couture shows, ready-to-wear shows, trade shows, and press shows. Many of these fashion presentations are

Figure 2.1 Sephora leads the way showing new trends in cosmetics during Fashion Week. *Courtesy, Fairchild Publications, Inc. Photographer: George Chinsee.*

worldwide media events presented to an international audience of buyers and journalists. The chapter concludes with a description of different types of retail and consumer shows.

Fashion show categories

As the opening example illustrates, fashion shows are staged to sell a variety of products at various market levels in the distribution channel. Shows take on diverse forms based on the desired outcome of the individual, business, or group sponsoring the event. Some shows can be very small informal activities with limited preparation and casual execution, while other spectacular events take months to prepare and involve a large staff to execute a flawless performance.

Fashion shows are defined by four different production styles (Fig. 2.2). These include:

- Production shows
- Formal runway shows
- Informal shows
- Multimedia production shows

Production shows

The most elaborate fashion show is the **production show**, also called a dramatized or spectacular show because of the dramatic or theatrical elements used in the performance. The purpose of a production show is to create impact, and to that end fashion trends are emphasized using special entertainment, backdrops or scenery, lighting effects, live or exclusively produced music, and dancing or unique choreography.

Type	Style	Merchandise
Production	Dramatized Spectacular	Couture Evening Bridal Ready-to-Wear
Formal Runway	Fashion Parade	Seasonal Trends Specialty Markets Ready-to-Wear
Informal	Tea-Room Trunk Show Mannequin Modeling	All Types of Merchandise
Multimedia Production	Video CD-ROM Internet	All Types of Merchandise

Figure 2.2 Fashion Show Categories

Production shows require a great deal of organization and advance planning. Production shows may be as short as one-hour presentations during an afternoon or evening with mood setting preshow entertainment and post event music, dancing, and frivolity. In addition to the entertainment, hors d'oeuvres and cocktails, lunch, or dinner may be served. As few as 15 or as many as 50 models, including guest celebrity models, may walk the runway to emphasize current trends. More elaborate production shows may last over multiple days focusing selected events at different target audiences. Often the event is keyed to a special event such as a fundraiser for a charity.

The Macy's *Passport* fashion benefit show featured in Chapter 1 is an example of this dramatic show type. *Passport* has grown to a six-event, multiple night celebration held both in San Francisco and Los Angeles. Federated (Macy's parent company) has termed the concept of the event "retail is theatre." The event includes a no-expenses spared fashion show, hot MTV veejays, and muscled hunk models in underwear. Actress Sharon Stone and MAC spokesperson and rap artist L'il Kim among many other celebrities have lent their support to this event to raise money to battle HIV and AIDs (Young & Saeks, 2000).

Formal runway shows

The **formal runway show** is a conventional presentation of fashion similar to a parade in which merchandise is presented in consecutive order (Fig. 2.3). The length of the show is generally 30 minutes to 1 hour and features a series of models who walk or dance on a runway in a sequential manner. Models may walk down the runway alone, in pairs, or in groups. The main characteristic of this show type is the use of a runway and models coming out one after another. This type of show requires advance planning and organization for a professional appearance and involves all of the following fashion show elements:

- Theme (merchandise and scene development)
- Special location (auditorium, hotel, restaurant, or sales floor)
- Staging and lighting

Figure 2.3 Models parade by fashion press, retail buyers, and celebrities in a formal runway show. *Courtesy, Fairchild Publications, Inc.*

- Models
- Music (live or sound system)
- Optional Commentary

A formal runway show may be directed to retailers or consumers. Manufacturers and designers use the runway show as a primary promotion tool to show retail buyers and the fashion press the most recently produced lines. In turn, retailers use the formal runway show to entice consumers to buy the latest trends by displaying new colors, fabrics, and silhouettes on the runway.

A formal runway show was used to present top London designers to an Asian audience in the first full-fledged, all-British runway show in Hong Kong (Daswani, 2000a). The British Consul General in Hong Kong, and the British Department of Trade and Industry in London jointly organized the event. Nine top London designers were flown to Hong Kong for the event held at the luxurious ballroom of the Grand Hyatt Hotel for an audience of 500 retailers, merchandisers, and consumers. Merchandisers were specifically on hand from top Asian retail outlets including Seibu, Lane Crawford, and Joyce, representing stores in Hong Kong, Taipei, Singapore, and China. And, as is common in America, celebrities from local film and music industries pumped up the glamour surrounding the runway fashion show.

Informal fashion shows

A more casual presentation of garments and accessories on models is an **informal fashion show**. In this type of fashion show no theatrical elements such as music, lighting, or runway are used. While there are no special staging requirements for informal fashion shows, props may be used to enhance the image of the garments being featured. Selling is achieved by the model who walks through the store sales floor, manufacturer's showroom, or restaurant often carrying a sign, business card, or handout with information about the merchandise, department, or store where the merchandise is located. This type of fashion show requires very little preparation compared to the production and formal runway shows.

Restaurants might choose to feature fashions from a local retail store on a regular basis. This type of informal fashion show is referred to as **tea-room modeling**. The store selects three to five models, perhaps store employees. These models are fitted into outfits prior to the show. During the show the models walk from table to table showing what they are wearing, careful to interact only with interested patrons.

Informal modeling in a store (Fig. 2.4) may take place in a specific department or throughout the entire store. Usually an assistant fashion coordinator will handle scheduling models and select garments in cooperation with the buyer or department manager. The fashion coordinator will also work with accessories personnel to achieve a total look and project the desired fashion statement.

Informal modeling is not restricted to apparel. Using the movie *Breakfast at Tiffany's* as a theme, the luxury retailer Tiffany's hired models dressed in vintage clothing to walk around the retail show room displaying necklaces, bracelets, and earrings which might have been worn by Audrey Hepburn.

During market weeks, held to present new seasonal items to the trade, manufacturers may hire models to wear the new line and walk around the showroom. Retail buyers may not be able to see a formal fashion show, but they may wish to see how certain garments from the line look on the human form. Models show these garments in an informal manner, putting on sample garments as desired by retail buyers and showroom personnel.

Trunk show   A specific type of informal fashion show that features garments from one manufacturer or designer at a retail store is a **trunk show**. The complete line from the manufacturer or designer is shipped to a store in "trunks" or sales representative's cases. Manufacturers or designers send a company representative to interact with the customers during the in-store event. Models walk through the retail store, emphasizing the garments.

Figure 2.4 Informal modeling gives audiences a chance to see models stroll around showrooms, restaurants, or other intimate settings. *Courtesy, Fairchild Publications, Inc.*

Figure 2.5 Models display merchandise in an informal manner at a John Galliano trunk show at Saks Fifth Avenue flagship store. *Courtesy, Fairchild Publications, Inc.*

Tom Ford used a two-day trunk show at the Yves Saint Laurent Manhattan store to sell his second ready-to-wear line for the YSL collection. The store reported sales in excess of $1 million in 48 hours for the fall collection (Wilson, 2001). John Galliano hosted a trunk show at Saks Fifth Avenue's flagship store and yielded orders of $200,000 in two days (Socha, 2000). Figure 2.5 shows models wearing Galliano designs and posing in an informal manner within the retail environment.

Trunk shows are not strictly an American promotion tool. New York-based designer Douglas Hannant held the first ever trunk show in Hong Kong, and within a few hours sold every item in his Fall 2000 collection, over $120,000 worth of merchandise (Daswani, 2000b). Hannant, who sells at Neiman Marcus and Saks Fifth Avenue in the United States, hosted the trunk show at Lane Crawford, an upscale retailer with four stores in Hong Kong and a fifth store in Shanghai. Hannant used the trunk show strategy to pre-sell the line, with the intent to create a series of events that guarantees sales. Additionally, spending time with clients allows designers or representatives to incorporate clients' needs into future lines.

There are several advantages for the manufacturer and the retailer in conducting trunk shows. Retailers rarely buy entire collections from a particular manufacturer for their stores. Normally, retail stores edit from the manufacturer's offerings, buying only the colors and styles they feel will sell to their customers. With a trunk show, customers are able to see complete collections from the producer. They are able to order any styles, sizes, or colors they like in the line. Retailers benefit by selling merchandise without taking the risk of carrying the merchandise in the permanent stock. Another advantage for the manufacturer as well as the retailer is being able to evaluate consumer reaction to the line, learning customers' preferences and best sellers. Box 2.1 highlights the popularity of trunk shows.

Mannequin modeling Some retail stores, shopping centers, and fashion exhibits at fairs have utilized this simple form of the fashion show. **Mannequin modeling** involves live models in a store window or on a display platform. These live models strike poses like the stationary display props they have been named after. This type of informal modeling requires a lot of discipline and composure by the models who pose in stiff positions. Inevitably, customers try to make these models laugh and move.

Multimedia production shows

Throughout history the fashion industry has always had a fascination with the latest technology. The fashion industry has aggressively adopted video technology and the Internet in presenting fashion at both the wholesale and retail levels. One of the first uses of **video production** was at the designer/manufacturer level. Nearly every designer and manufacturer would videotape their runway shows. These tapes would be used to train the national sales force or given to retailers to show in their stores where customers could stop and view these presentations. The videotape would become a silent salesperson. The consumer was able to view how the designer/manufacturer envisioned the total look of the merchandise. Models are often selected based on their video appeal.

Now there are several types of video productions used. These include the point-of-purchase, instructional, and documentary videos. The **point-of-purchase video** is placed on the

continued on page 30

Box 2.1
Trunk-Show Chic

BIRMINGHAM, Ala.—In December, when most mall shoppers were picking over marked-down cashmere and leather leftovers, Village Sportswear was taking orders for nearly a half million dollars worth of spring fashions for a single clothing label—and all at regular price.

Such a feat is something of an anomaly in today's cutthroat retail environment, where only an estimated 30% of clothing is sold at full price. For Village Sportswear, the secret to its recent sales success is the "trunk show," a decades-old, highly personalized sales tactic that is making a steady comeback with retailers across the country.

Trunk shows are typically two-day affairs where designers send representatives to stores to present their clothes in an intimate setting and then take customized orders from customers. For shoppers who love fashion and want the luxury of reviewing and trying on a designer's entire collection in an uncrowded setting, but don't mind waiting a couple of months for the goods to arrive, trunk shows are a good bet. Philip Kowalcyk, a retail analyst at apparel-industry consultants Kurt Salmon Associates says, "The trunk show is a fantastic method to build retail traffic that is specifically not a 'sale' event."

Trunk shows take their name from the days of traveling salesmen who used trunks to carry the sample merchandise, which they wholesaled to merchants around the country. Starting in the 1980s, trunk shows turned into glossy retail events for stores such as Marshall Field's, helping them build a following for couture labels such as Bill Blass and Escada without having to devote much floor space to $2,000 suits and $10,000 gowns all year long. And the shows also helped attract men to the sometimes-intimidating world of $1,500 made-to-measure suits; Barneys New York regularly holds trunk shows for makers of upscale men's suits.

Though there's no official tally of trunk shows, a cross section of retailers say they are starting to employ the sales tactics more frequently. Primarily getting on board are independent retailers, Such as Village Sportswear, with a small, loyal clientele. But even bigger retailers are seeing increasing merit in them. Manhattan's Bergdorf Goodman, for instance, now uses trunk shows to introduce young designers to a new generation of affluent women in their 30s and 40s. And retail giant Saks Fifth Avenue is expanding its trunk shows to feature handbags and accessories, as well as women's and men's clothing.

The payoff for retailers can be significant, as illustrated by the trunk show at Village Sportswear put on by Lafayette 148 New York, a fast-growing clothing brand specializing in silk and linen separates priced at about $200 for blouses and $400 for jackets. In December, 60 or so stylish suburban women turned out via special invitation for the two-day trunk show at the small boutique situated in a ritzy Birmingham enclave of Tudor-style shops.

Once there, several women zeroed in on customized details they wanted, such as having their pants or skirts longer or shorter. Lafayette's traveling sales representative was ready to oblige. Meanwhile, Village Sportswear's six eagle-eyed saleswomen kept track of who was ordering what, hoping to prevent social-circuit clashes, such as two women

continued on page 30

Box 2.1 continued from page 29

wearing the same outfit to the same country club. Ultimately, Village Sportswear sold the women at the show about 10 spring wardrobe items apiece on average. All merchandise was sold at full price, with no advertising or markdown costs.

Still, for all its appeal, pulling off a successful trunk show is no shoo-in for designers or retailers. Many designer brands don't have a strong following they can count on every season, or they are overexposed at department stores, decreasing the cache they hold at trunk shows. Moreover, most designers manufacture abroad, making it difficult to execute a fast turnaround on special-order merchandise-something imperative for trunk shows.

For their part, retailers risk alienating customers if trunk show orders arrive too late. And if garments don't fit right, which is possible because trunk shows only offer a size 8 to try on, it undermines the whole exercise of customization.

Trunk shows let Lafayette 148 sidestep the costly fashion runway shows favored by bigger name designers on New York's Seventh Avenue. Although Lafayette sells to a few up-scale department stores, including Saks Fifth Avenue, Neiman-Marcus and Nordstrom, its core business comes from 250 independent specialty shops in cities like Birmingham and Oklahoma City where Lafayette does 200 trunk shows throughout the year. Since the trunk shows at small shops kick in about a third of Lafayette's business, Lafayette is guaranteed a healthy chunk of full-priced business, without paying for advertising allowances and markdown rebates the big chains require.

Trunk shows turned Lafayette into Village Sportswear's top-selling brand after only three years. The shop holds the shows twice a year for four other brands-which is vital to Village Sportswear's strategy of giving shoppers exclusive merchandise they can't get at department stores.

The final tally for the trunk show in Birmingham this day is heavy on pants, suits in linen and many wrap blouses. The 413 garments the women ordered from Lafayette will start arriving at the store two months later.

Source: Agins, T. (2001, February 5). Trunk-show chic. *Wall Street Journal*, p. B1, B4. © *Wall Street Journal*, Eastern Edition. Reprinted with permission.

continued from page 28

sales floor of a retail store. Consumers are given the opportunity to see the original manufacturer's runway show or an action view of how to wear the merchandise. **Instructional videos** are created for in-store training of sales personnel, and may also be presented to the store's customers. They show the current information on fashion trends in addition to the special features of the products. The **documentary video** focuses on the designer or behind-the-scenes activities of the manufacturer. These may be used for training company employees, produced for television shows, or used at a retail store for point-of-purchase entertainment.

Contemporary fashion show videos take their cue from the music and electronic media. These videos combine all of the theatrical elements from the entertainment industry. The modern consumer has grown up with television and expects a highly sophisticated video presentation.

In addition to videos, runway fashion shows are often digitally produced and delivered to manufacturers, retailers, and consumers on CD-ROMs or DVDs. Two CD-ROMs of an entire Fashion Week fashion show can be delivered to a designer, two days after the show for approximately $200 (Braunstein, 1999). Pierre Garroudi has used a mini CD-ROM as an invitation and sampler to his collection shows. Additionally, manufacturers and designers who do not have Web sites can place their collections on CD for distribution to industry members and consumers.

In a 1970s textbook on fashion show production, it was stated that fashion shows had not yet become major television entertainment (Corinth, 1970). Wow, have things changed! In the 21st century, not only are fashion shows major television entertainment, but also, as introduced in Chapter 1, they are emerging on the Internet as both entertainment and business tools. It started with Helmut Lang.

Lang made history when two months before the Fall 1998 New York shows he announced he would forgo his show in favor of an Internet presentation (Foley, 2001). This was the first time a fashion designer used the Internet as a medium to show runway fashions to a global audience. Designers and retailers have followed this trend using the Internet to bring footage from runway shows to online audiences. For example, kennethcole.com allows the viewer to see the looks presented at the Kenneth Cole Company's most recent Fashion Week runway show. The company is dedicated to bringing online video coverage to Internet audiences. According to a company spokesperson, [Kenneth Cole] does not want coverage of fashion shows to be exclusive to fashion insiders, but allow all interested parties to share the experience (Braunstein, 1999).

Web sites such as nytimes.com, style.com, and fashionwindows.com feature online viewing of the New York shows during and after the presentation of fashions each fall and spring. Some sites are password protected, while others are free.

Many domestic and international Web sites exist to offer fashion show coverage including londonfashionweek.co.uk, modemonline.com, and firstview.com (Fig. 2.6).

Chaiken clothing broadcasts an entire runway show for the viewer. The first time Chaiken presented fashions on the Internet, they uploaded two distinct versions of their 2001 spring collection show. The first version was unedited, geared to retailers and buyers. It was placed on their site a few days after the fall shows, password protected with access limited to press and the industry only (Braunstein, 1999). The site was password protected to prevent knockoffs appearing. In November, closer to the spring shipping dates, Chaiken put an edited version on their Web site geared toward consumers, to present more items in a more rapid fashion to their consumers.

In this section we have introduced the different types of fashion shows used by professionals and amateurs to sell merchandise and create entertainment. In the next section, we will focus on specialized fashion shows used by designers and manufacturers to introduce new lines to retail buyers, the fashion press, and in some specific instances exclusive customers. All of the shows discussed in the next section are formal runway shows. In certain instances, some elements such as musical and theatrical ambiance, used in a production show are also used in formal production shows to create excitement for the shows. However, these shows are

Figure 2.6 Home page for firstview.com. Italian, French, and American fashions can be viewed over the Internet. *Courtesy, © Firstview.com.*

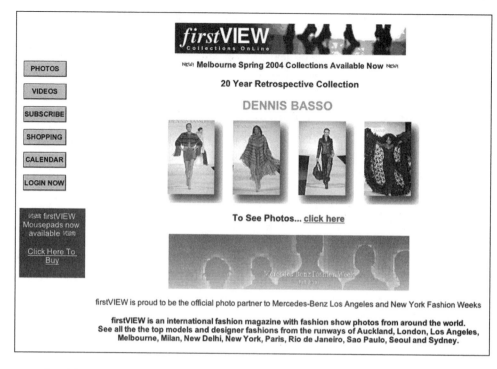

considered formal runway shows because of the sequential use of models presenting trends in a parade format. Additionally, some of the specialized presentations are also digitally recorded for use to broadcast fashion shows on video, CD-ROMs, DVDs, or the Internet.

Specialized fashion presentations

Each market level of the fashion industry utilizes fashion shows to present the latest trends in fashion apparel and accessories to their potential customers. Fashion shows have developed into specialized fashion presentations aimed at specific target markets within the industry. These specialized presentations included:

- Haute couture shows
- Ready-to-wear shows
- Trade shows
- Trade association shows
- Press shows

Most of the specialized presentations are produced by manufacturers or designers to show retail buyers or the fashion press new trends. In the case of haute couture shows, exclusive customers are also invited to the runway shows to view the latest designs. Trade association shows may also incorporate a broader audience and include consumers. In the case of press shows, manufacturers, designers or retailers may sponsor the show to create publicity for the business.

Location plays an important role in specialized fashion presentations. Haute couture shows are only presented in Paris. Ready-to-wear shows, trade shows, and press shows can be seen around the world. Throughout this section we will highlight the global nature of these specialized presentations.

Historically, Paris, Milan, London, and New York have been the major international cities where fashion trends are presented, analyzed, purchased, and worn. However, in the 21st century, many other international capitals are making a name in the fashion world including Hong Kong, Madrid, Australia, São Paulo, Oslo, and Los Angeles by producing designer lines. An apparel designer may produce up to five lines a year, one for each season: fall, holiday, resort, spring, and summer. More than 50,000 fashion professionals and fashion followers visit these fashion capitals at least twice a year (for fall and spring) to view the dazzling fashion presentations.

Fashion is presented to the retail trade and fashion press approximately two to six months before consumers see the merchandise in the store. During the spring season (January/February/March/April) fall fashion collections are introduced while spring collections are shown in the fall months (July/August/September/October). Shows are held far in advance to allow manufacturers ample time to produce the merchandise in time to meet the demands of the retail stores. The more fashion forward the merchandise, the earlier it will be shown. Haute couture fashion is shown first. Most haute couture is designed for, and sold to, individual clients who hand pick items from the line to be custom fit and adapted for one-of-a-kind looks. Retail buyers view the haute couture shows to identify the earliest inspirations and trends of the season. These trends will be repeated in the ready-to-wear lines where buyers will select items for their representative stores.

Haute couture shows

Haute couture is the French word for high fashion and the name of the French industry that produces high fashion garments. Couture shows are the source of fashion leadership and innovation supporting the trickle-down theory of fashion. Highly detailed and sophisticated items are presented first at higher prices to a limited audience and later are adopted at lower prices, with less sophistication and detail by a larger audience. These innovations serve as inspiration for mainstream fashion houses.

Because haute couture is considered the height of fashion, it must be innovative. The innovativeness of some haute couture has often led to controversy over the appropriateness of the fashion themes. In 2000, John Galliano, designing for Christian Dior, was accused of going too far with his "wet world" couture line (Fig. 2.7) that was themed around tramps and hobos (Foley, 2000). While the collection received some strong press, politicians and journalists considered it trivializing a human tragedy. Critics considered it an example of a designer tossing out responsibility for hype. Other controversial themes of the 1990s included Alexander McQueen's Highland Rape line (showing bloodied models with slashed clothing) and Jean Paul Gaultier's Hasidic collection (models wearing side locks) (Foley, 2000). Although not an haute couture designer, Calvin Klein has also been controversial from time to time including his Heroin Chic theme (dark-eyed makeup and ashen skin paints to create a gaunt, burned-out look) for ready-to-wear. Haute couture designers past, present, and future will always push the edge and use the runway show to reflect their concept of beauty and fashion.

Figure 2.7 Innovation or trivializing a tragedy—these shredded garments were part of an haute couture line designed by John Galliano. *Courtesy, Fairchild Publications, Inc.*

The **Chambre Syndicale de la Couture Parisienne** is France's governing body of fashion. The body organizes the Paris fashion shows and represents the French fashion industry abroad. The Chambre has a 16 member executive committee that includes the following fashion houses: Emanuel Ungaro, Chloé, Thierry Mugler, Yves Saint Laurent, Chanel, Kenzo, Issey Miyake, Jean-Paul Gaultier, Lanvin, Sonia Rykiel, Jean-Charles de Castelbajac, Hermés, and Pierre Cardin (Murphy, 2001).

In order to be recognized as a member of the haute couture the company must meet the following qualifications:

1. A formal written request, with the sponsorship of two current members is presented and voted on by the entire organization.
2. Workrooms, providing quality workmanship, must be established in Paris.
3. The designer or an employee of the house must design the collection. Garments are individually made to a client's measurements.
4. Collections must be presented twice annually in January and July during the times set by the Chambre Syndicale.
5. At least 75 designs must be included in the collection.
6. The house must have three models employed throughout the year.
7. The house must employ a minimum of 20 sewing workers in the workrooms.

Many of the major couture houses take their collections to other countries after the Paris shows. Some of the most important looks are flown to New York, Tokyo, and the Middle East and shown to potential customers.

Ready-to-wear shows

While haute couture is the highest, most exclusive work a fashion house produces, the bread and butter for the fashion house is **ready-to-wear**, mass-produced fashion. Ready-to-wear is produced in many countries throughout the world. The highest price-point ready-to-wear is considered the **designer** category. This category consists of ready-to-wear from successful designers who own their own business or have a "signature collection" with their name on the label. All haute couture designers also create a designer ready-to-wear line (Frings, 2002).

Designer collections are generally introduced immediately following the haute couture shows in September and February. Many countries, including the United States, bring together designer ready-to-wear vendors for Fashion Week in London, New York, and Australia. **Fashion Week** is designated as a time when many designer collections are brought together and shown as a series of fashion shows. During Fashion Week each designer has one opportunity to show his or her line. Fashion shows are presented daily on the hour, scheduled so buyers might attend as many as six or eight shows each day. Notice in Figure 2.8 that no signage, props, or staging elements other than lighting are used because many different designers will use the same stage with limited time between shows to setup and strike. Often, more than one show will be scheduled for the same time so retailers and journalists must decide which show they will attend. Typically 75–100 garments are presented in approximately 30 minutes leaving audience members little time to move onto their next appointment. As many as 100 or more fashion shows are produced during a typical Fashion Week. While designers are allowed only one showing of their lines, they may videotape or digitally produce their show for later viewing on CD-ROM, DVD, or the Internet.

Each year the schedule is tenuous as countries jockey for the first position to introduce the latest ready-to-wear lines. Historically, the ready-to-wear shows began in Europe and concluded in New York. However, in 1999, in an attempt to gain stature as a fashion capitol, New York scheduled the American shows before the European shows (Horyn, 2001). American designers want to stake claim on trends at the beginning of the season. However, this is in direct

Figure 2.8 Staging is minimal for Fashion Week shows where many designers use the same stage and have limited time to set-up and strike the show. *Courtesy, Fairchild Publications, Inc.*

conflict with retailers who want to see the New York shows last for the sake of convenience and their ability to sum up the unreachable dreams of Paris and Milan fashion into tangible trends ("New York," 2001). Fashion Week presentations in February and March of 2003 continue the trend with collections showing first in New York, followed by London, Milan, and concluding in Paris.

Paris **Prêt-à-porter** is the ready-to-wear fashion industry in Paris. The **defiles des createurs** are the designer runway shows featuring the newest creations from France as well as other international designers. The ready-to-wear shows are scheduled by the **Fédération Française du Prêt-à-porter Feminin**. Paris fashion shows have been presented at a variety of venues such as tents, the Tuileries, the Bois de Boulogne, the Palais de Congres, and the Louvre.

Rome and Milan The **Camera Nationale della Alta Moda Italia** governs Italian fashion. The organization oversees activities of the couture designers and ready-to-wear, shoe, and accessory manufacturers. The Camera provides organization for group events including the ready-to-wear shows in Rome and Milan. The Italian ready-to-wear industry has been gaining international significance. Much of the high fashion industry and design activities take place in Rome. However, due to the aggressive nature of Paris couture and the confusion over show dates, many Italian designers show their couture collections in Paris.

The semi-annual fashion shows featuring Italian ready-to-wear are held in Milan just prior to the designer shows in Paris. Italy is primarily known for knitwear, sportswear, and accessories by such designers as Giorgio Armani, Missoni, Fendi, and Valentino. The fast-paced Milan ready-to-wear shows are presented at the Fiera, a three-story convention center on the outskirts of Milan.

Laura Biagiotti is typical of the Italian ready-to-wear producers. Mrs. Biagiotti lives and designs in Rome, but her international showroom and sales force are located in Milan. She shows only two collections a year, put together in Rome but shown in Milan. A complete collection may consist of as many as 500 pieces. During the approximately 40 minute show, approximately 160 pieces, representing her entire collection are shown on 35–40 models.

London   London, the city associated with the 1960s fashion revolution of Mary Quant, Carnaby Street, and the Mod Look, remains the center of innovation and classic British fashion. Twice a year London hosts London Fashion Week organized by the **British Fashion Council**. The 5-day event includes nearly 50 fashion shows for buyers and international press (CNN.com, 2000). In recent years London has reveled its growing reputation for cutting edge, wearable collections. Designers Zandra Rhodes, Stella McCartney, Caroline Charles, and Vivienne Westwood are just a few leading talented British designers. Young experimental designers continue to spark in London as a fashion center.

New York   Fashion Week is the most important fashion event held in the United States (Horyn, 2001). Fashion Week is held in New York each February and September. The 10-day event is a marathon of fashion shows with nearly 100 designers showing their latest lines to retailers and journalists. Mercedes-Benz is the official sponsor of Fashion Week, which has renamed the event Mercedes-Benz Fashion Week. Previous sponsors included General Motors and 7th on Sixth.

The Council of Fashion Designers of America (CFDA) originally created **7th on Sixth** in 1993 as a non-profit organization. The mission of 7th on Sixth was to organize, centralize, and modernize the American runway shows and provide a platform for American designers to present their collections to a worldwide audience of media and buyers. Several thousand buyers, retailers, and members of the national and international press from around the world come to New York each season to review the latest American designs. Since it's inception, 7th on Sixth has produced 25 seasons totaling over 100 shows. In 2001, CFDA sold 7th on Sixth to IMG, a sports management and marketing company. IMG purchased the fashion shows because of their ability to generate sponsorship and provide more televised fashion events, commercial development that concerned some critics (Horyn, 2001). With one exception, each year 7th on Sixth has been held in a series of tents at Bryant Park.

The economic impact for New York of fashion shows twice a year is estimated to be $247 million spent on goods and services by those attending the shows (Horyn, 2001). For the Fall 2001 season, 1,650 members of the news media registered and 503 foreign journalists registered, an increase over the previous year. Although the number of retailers attending is not recorded fashion executives say the number has steadily increased.

For the first time in 2001, organized delegates from Hong Kong, Portugal, and Africa staged fashion shows in Bryant Park (Feitelberg, 2000). Figure 2.9 lists the up-and-coming featured designers. Hong Kong chose to show in New York because the United States is the largest market for Hong Kong clothing, accounting for about 35 percent of the total export value. Previous to New York, Hong Kong designers have shown their lines in Australia, Japan,

Figure 2.9 Featured designers from Hong Kong, Portugal, and Africa at the first annual International Fashion Day at the Mercedes-Benz Fashion Week in 2001. *Adapted from* Women's Wear Daily, *Fairchild Publications, Inc.*

Hong Kong Designers
- Vivian Lau of Blanc de Chine
- Barney Cheng
- Flor Cheong-Leen
- Joanna Liao

Portuguese Designers
- Anabela Baldaque
- Ana Salazar
- Manuel Alves & Jose Manuel Goncalves
- Inspiro by Marco Morgado & Helder Pinto
- Luis Buchinho
- Bruno Belloni by Pedro Mourao
- Maconde by David Shaw
- Joao Tome & Franciso Pontes

South African Designers
- Deola Sague
- Bonga Bengu
- Tracey Lee
- Julian
- Bongiwee Walaza

Source: Feitelberg, R. (2000, September 6). Foreign imports [Section II]. *Women's Wear Daily,* pp. 24, 57.

and Singapore. In addition to the merchandise from Hong Kong, organizers arranged to have a few Hong Kong-based models walk the runways in their shows.

Portugal designers operate under Portugal Fashion International, which introduced its designers to Brazil and Paris before New York. The Portuguese fashion industry produces quality, creative and innovative fashions (Feitelberg, 2000).

Mark Eisen, a native of South America, served as a juror to help select five designers to represent South Africa. Designers traveled from 42 of Africa's different countries within the continent to participate (Feitelberg, 2000). The designs showed artistic creativity and referenced Africa's heritage. In addition to the designs, African models competed in Faces of Africa modeling contest sponsored by M-Net, South Africa's largest subscriber-TV service.

Los Angeles In Spring 2002, Los Angeles hosted the first ever L.A. Fashion Week (Jones, 2001) complete with official schedules, corporate sponsorships and consecutive fashion shows held in tents. Los Angeles Fashion Week was developed to highlight California designers and the lifestyle they project which is quite different from New York. Organizers of the event compared the 21st century L.A. fashion industry with that of the London industry during the 1980s, full of creativity and ready to explode. In April 2003, Mercedes-Benz Shows L.A. was launched to feature the Fall 2003 collections and put Los Angeles on the world's fashion schedule.

Other emerging countries Many other countries are adopting the fashion week concept to show their latest designer collections to the world. Australia hosts a fashion week each May in Sydney. Featured Australian designers include Akira Isogawa, Charlie Brown, Easton Pearson, Michelle Jank, Nicola Finetti, Peter Morrissey, and Todd Robinson.

Vancouver, British Columbia hosts the Vancouver International Fashion Week each April. The event is held at the Vancouver Convention and Trade Centre and features designers from Canada, Mexico, Indonesia, and China. More than 18,000 fashion professionals and journalists attended in Fall 2001. Featured designers included Anne Hung, Cheri Milaney, Feiza Virani and Neto Leather, and French Laundry among other designers. The week was kicked-off with an opening night gala runway show.

During Fashion Weeks, fashion shows are the primary promotion tool used by designers to show their latest lines. In the next section, we will discuss trade shows and apparel marts. Fashion shows are also used to promote lines during trade shows and at apparel marts but on a more limited basis.

Trade shows

The term **trade** refers to any activity aimed at distribution of fashion and related products within the industry. **Trade shows** are groups of temporary exhibits of vendor's offerings for a single merchandise category or group of related categories (Rabolt & Miler, 1997). Trade shows are produced to sell raw materials to manufacturers, or manufactured goods to retailers. The advantage to a trade show is the ability for buyers and journalists to view many different vendors' offerings in one location.

Trade shows differ from Fashion Weeks. At a Fashion Week, much of the viewing of lines takes place at orchestrated fashion shows. At a trade show, much of the viewing of lines take place at temporary booths with a limited number of fashion shows presented during a day or week. Trade shows may be held once or several times during the year. Some shows are exclusive to one product category such as Ski Industry America, while other trade shows, such as Style Industrie and the International Fashion Boutique Show, may involve several categories of merchandise.

Trade shows generally show merchandise from bridge, contemporary, missy, junior, men's, and children's wear categories. The **bridge** category features less expensive alternatives to designer fashions often created by the same designers who have designer lines. The **contemporary** category features merchandise that is more fashion forward than the missy category, but at a price point between bridge and budget. Conservative looks available at the better, moderate or budget price-point make up the **missy** category. The **junior** category features styles appropriate for a younger figure (Frings, 2002).

MAGIC (Fig. 2.10) is a bi-annual trade show held in Las Vegas each February and August. Originally conceived as a market for the upcoming men's wear season, vendors at MAGIC also provide fill-in merchandise for the current season. MAGIC generally runs for four days at the Sands Expo and Convention Center. The show runs concurrently with three other trade shows: MAGIC International men's wear show, WWDMAGIC Kids, and The Edge, a women's and men's streetwear event (Malone & Ellis, 2000). The four shows collectively draw approximately 91,000 visitors, including buyers and industry representatives. Buyers from regional chains and specialty stores work the show to get a sense of what trends are likely to be important for the next season.

Market calendars publicize the dates for trade shows. These dates are generally termed **Market Weeks** and correspond with manufacturer's seasonal delivery dates. Market Weeks

Figure 2.10 Daily fashion shows feature current trends at WWDMAGIC in Las Vegas. *Courtesy, Fairchild Publications, Inc.*

and the corresponding months include: Summer shown in January, Fall I shown in April, Fall II shown in June, Resort shown in August, and Spring shown in October.

Sellers and buyers conduct business at trade shows. Existing facilities are temporarily used to house a trade show. Convention centers, hotels, and apparel marts are common locations for trade shows. In the next section we will discuss the relationship between trade shows and apparel marts.

Regional **apparel marts** are wholesale centers located in major cities throughout the United States. Marts lease space to manufacturers who are able to offer their lines closer to the retailer's geographic location so retail buyers do not have to travel to New York City to purchase merchandise. These fashion centers offer the convenience of many manufacturers in one location.

Many small store buyers have found the regional centers to be very responsive to their needs. In addition to the convenience and reduced expenses, the regional marts sponsor retailing seminars and fashion shows for participants.

The major apparel marts are located in Los Angeles, Dallas, Chicago, and Atlanta. Other regional market centers include the Miami International Merchandise Mart; Denver Merchandise Mart; Carolina Trade Mart in Charlotte, North Carolina; San Francisco Mart; Northeast Trade Center in Woburn, Massachusetts; Radisson Center in Minneapolis; and Trade Center in Kansas City, Missouri among others. These centers make vendors accessible for many small retailers who find it difficult to visit major market centers. The convenience and generally lower cost associated with visiting a regional center are adding to their popularity.

Regional apparel marts introduce the new lines of merchandise through fashion trend shows held for the retail buyers at the start of a market week. According to Yvette Crosby, former fashion director for the California Apparel Mart, she had approximately 48 hours to pull together a fashion show for the center. This involved selecting merchandise to be shown from the various showrooms, coordinating into scenes the diverse themes of goods being presented, hiring and training the models, and staging the show in the apparel mart theater. Although it was hectic, the show was pulled together at the last minute. Commentary was not used. Music was selected to coordinate with the looks being featured. Dramatic lighting emphasized the changes in groups or themes.

At apparel mart fashion shows fashion buyers are given an opportunity to sort the themes being presented by the manufacturers prior to visiting individual showrooms. These fashion trend shows help the retailers pinpoint the merchandise and trends that would meet the needs of their particular customers. These shows are an entertaining and uplifting start to the chaotic buying process.

Other fashion shows produced by the apparel centers might include specialty shows for back-to-school, men's wear, or individual categories of merchandise. These fashion shows generally follow a pre-planned format. Music, clothing, and accessories are changed to meet the current trends.

Regional apparel marts and trade shows   Los Angeles is the home of the CaliforniaMart (Fig. 2.11). The California Mart (CalMart) hosts the Los Angeles International Textile Show and EKN International's Pacific Champions among other trade shows and special events (Ellis & Bowers, 2000). The Los Angeles International Textile Show is a three-day event that features 350 domestic and international exhibitors. Typical attendance is between 5,000 and 6,000 buyers. EKN International's Pacific Champions is held twice a year in April and November and offers accessories, contemporary and designer sportswear, sweater resources and bridge lines from over 50 exhibitors. Although not a regular feature, fashion shows are occasionally staged with major retailers such as Burdines, Rich's, Bloomingdale's, the Bon Marche, Macy's West, Charming Shoppes, and Carson Pirie Scott in attendance (Ellis & Bowers, 2000).

The International Apparel Mart is located in Dallas. More than 12,000 apparel lines are showcased, including women's designer, missy, junior, contemporary, intimate apparel, bridal, accessories, footwear, activewear, outerwear, plus sizes, petites, maternity, special occasion dresses, children's, and Western. Additionally, the Mart houses all categories of men's wear, young men's, and unisex urban lines (Haber, 2000). Fashion shows and special event sites include the Great Hall, the West Atrium, and the Fashion Theatre.

A strong target market for Dallas is the midwest. In 2000, 150 midwest retailers were introduced to manufacturer lines housed at the International Apparel Mart. The International Apparel Mart is part of a larger Dallas Market Center (DMC) complex. Covering more than 100 acres, the DMC is composed of the World Trade Center, Trade Mart, International Floral Design Center, and Market Hall in addition to the International Apparel Mart.

Figure 2.11 One of California's regional apparel marts. *Courtesy, Fairchild Publications, Inc.*

Atlanta is the home of AmericasMart Atlanta, which was originally the Atlanta Merchandise Mart developed in 1959 to establish a wholesale trade industry in the southeast. It currently consists of three buildings totaling over 4.2 million feet of exhibit space. The Mart hosts 17 shows each year and the largest in terms of attendance and product variety is the Atlanta International Gift and Home Furnishings Market held in January and July.

Bridal is an up-and-coming niche market for Atlanta (Lee, 2000c) with shows in October and April. The same retailers who purchase prom, pageant, and special-occasion apparel are being cultivated. Atlanta has also attracted Canadian companies. Each October it hosts Montreal Collective featuring approximately 70 vendors, of which approximately 80 percent have permanent showrooms. Having constantly sought out higher-end lines over the past decade, AmericasMart Atlanta is primarily made up of better-to-bridge-priced apparel. To promote the all-betterwear concept, multiple fashion shows have been consolidated into one Friday night event featuring trend segments and fashion direction segments.

The Merchandise Mart in Chicago holds exhibits for the following industries: bridal, casual furnishings, commercial furnishings, gift and home accessories, men's wear, residential furnishings, women's apparel, and children's apparel. StyleMax™ (Fig. 2.12) is a women's and children's apparel and accessory trade show held on October at the Merchandise Mart in Chicago featuring over 3,000 resources. The first StyleMax™ show was held in October 2000. The next year a second show in March was added due to the success of this trade show (Brumback, 2000). StyleMax™ was created to attract retailers from a 13-state area in the Midwest, from Ohio to Nebraska and Minneapolis to Kentucky. Two fashion shows are held as part of the event.

Miami hosts Fashion Week of the Americas, a four-day event promoted as a showcase for Latin America's considerable design talent (Lee, 2000a). The event held in South Beach highlights nearly 25 designers from 11 countries in South America and the Caribbean in continuous individual and collective fashion shows. Total weeklong attendance is approximately 10,000, including 350 registered media. Different from other trade shows, the public is invited to attend this show for a $25 day pass. Previous years' events have culminated with an appearance by Oscar de la Renta, a native of the Dominican Republic.

Although, this show is not held at the Miami International Merchandise Mart, many other trade shows are held at the facility which houses over 300 permanent wholesale showrooms featuring apparel, jewelry, and home furnishings. The Miami Cruise 2001 swimwear show is held at the Miami Merchandise Mart and Radisson Center with an estimated 2,000 buyers, 300 exhibitors, and 1,000 swimwear lines (Lee, 2000b). In a departure from past years, the fashion show that was always held in a tent at the mart has moved to a new venue, the Loews Miami Beach Hotel. The event draws more than 1,200 people and extra tables have been brought in for the overflow crowd. This show highlights a trend in trade show fashion shows. The event has transformed from a formal runway show to a production show type. The event included a live auction, a sit-down-dinner, after-dinner entertainment by comedian David Brenner, and a post-show bash at the Level nightclub.

International trade shows and trade centers The Fashion Week of the Americans trade show is an example of international designers being showcased in the United States. However, trade shows are not limited to the United States. Many international cities host trade shows showcasing international designers for American and international press. In the past few years, Australia, Russia, India, Iceland, and Brazil have each promoted a Fashion Week (Kerwin, 2000). Many attribute this to a growing global economy, ease of travel and the Internet. While the term *Fashion Week* is used here, many of these events are more characteristic of a trade show, with business taking place at booths and limited fashion shows, versus the continuous fashion shows used to promote designer collections. In the United States, we commonly use the term *trade show*; however, in other countries the term **trade fair** is more common.

Annually, Paris hosts prêt-à-porter scheduled at the Porte de Versailles exhibit center (Fig. 2.13). Milan hosts many trade shows each year including Milano Freestyle, a trade show featuring urban clothing and sportswear.

Brazil hosts Morumbi Fashion, their version of 7th on Sixth. The show was first held in 1996. During the 1990s, trade regulations were lifted allowing Brazil to grow their industry and show off their unique talents to their American and European peers (Kerwin, 2000). Models including Gisele Bündchen, Caroline Ribeiro, Ana Claudia, Renata, and Mariana Weichert, all from Brazil, have walked the runway to support their fellow designers. Alexandre Herchcovitch, Zoomp, and Ellus, headed by Nelson Alvarenga, are among popular Brazilian designers. Brazil is an up-and-coming international city showing its ready-to-wear lines to the world.

In Spain, both Madrid and Barcelona host trade shows for the fashion world. La Semana Internacional de la Moda de Madrid (SIMM) is a twice yearly ready-to-wear fair featuring approximately 750 exhibitors and over 22,000 visitors including nearly 1,500 from outside Spain (Barker, 2001). According to organizers, the Madrid fair is becoming a springboard to Latin America and Portugal.

Figure 2.12 StyleMax™, a regional trade show for women's and children's apparel is held in Chicago twice a year. *Courtesy, Fairchild Publications, Inc.*

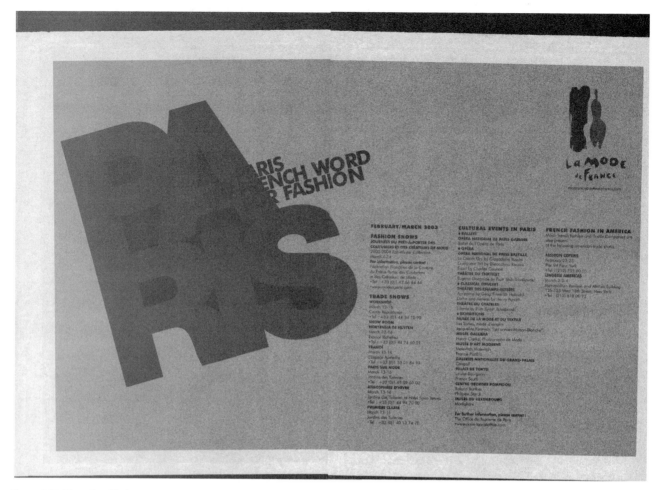

Figure 2.13 Here is a listing of popular events, which showcase French fashion to the media and retailers.

Pitching itself as a window to the emerging Eastern European market, Poznan, Poland is an up-and-coming city vying for attention of an increasingly global fashion industry (Beckner, 2001). Poznan hosts a Fashion Week in late August. The fair showcases men's and women's clothing, underwear, footwear, accessories, leather goods, and textiles. Forums, seminars, and fashion shows are part of the activities with underwear and footwear shown on the runway in addition to apparel. The fair also grants numerous awards for innovative products and designs and among the winning products in 2000 were antibacterial socks.

Not to be left out, Scandinavia also hosts several fashion related trade shows. The BellaCenter in Copenhagen, Denmark, is the largest mart in Scandinavia and hosts, among other events, the Copenhagen International Fashion Fair each February organized by the Federation of Danish Textiles and Clothing. Over 7,000 exhibitors show over 2,250 collections to approximately 19,000 buyers including footwear, bags, and leather goods for Denmark and around the world. As with many trade shows fashion shows are part of the event.

The above listing is only a sample of the many domestic and international trade shows held around the world each year. *Women's Wear Daily* publishes a complete listing of American and international trade shows twice a year. Additionally, a search on a Web browser using the country name and the term *trade show* as key words is likely to identify trade shows in the apparel and related industries. Before we leave this section on specialized fashion presentations, it is necessary to discuss two other show types: the trade association show and the press show.

Trade association shows

Trade associations are groups of individuals and businesses acting as a professional, non-profit collective in meeting their common interests. Membership in trade associations provides a means for information exchange and political action to benefit the public opinion and legislative concerns. Trade associations represent almost every division of the fashion industry. These associations may be very specialized such as the *Jewelry Industry Council*, *Cotton Incorporated*, or the *Cosmetic, Toiletry and Fragrance Association*. Other associations focus on a broad or more generalized representation such as the *American Apparel and Footwear Association* and the *National Retail Federation*.

Many ready-to-wear runway shows tend to demonstrate silhouettes and color. However, many fiber trade association shows concentrate on the fiber content of the garments featuring many different manufacturers. Tencil, Incorporated sponsored a fashion show during the 2001 New York shows to get retailers excited about its lyocell brand (Malone, 2000). Men's and women's wear was featured from Brazilian, French, English, Italian, Japanese, and U.S. designers. According to Ellen Flynn, director of textile marketing at Tencil®, the goal of the fashion show was to show the company's lyocell fiber could work in clothes outside the weekend-casual arena with which it is commonly associated.

Press shows

Press shows are held specifically for members of the media prior to presenting the fashion story to the public—consumers. Members of the media represent magazines, newspapers, radio, television, Internet services, and wire services. Buyers, specially invited guests, or important customers also may be invited to press shows. Stores may give a press show when a new department is opened, a designer visits the store, or a major promotion is launched. Manufacturers may invite the press to view a new line or product.

A press show must present new and exciting merchandise, since the press is in the business of reporting newsworthy events and products. The press show must be timed before the customers have seen the merchandise. One important reason for the press show is to create interest about the product or event beforehand.

Members of the press are routinely provided information about the merchandise, designer, or event in the form of media kits, press releases, and photographs. Some reporters will bring their own photographers for exclusive pictures.

Consumer shows

This chapter concludes with a section on consumer shows. As the name implies, **consumer shows** are directed toward consumers. They may be sponsored by a retailer to introduce consumers and employees to the latest fashions, or they may be sponsored by a civic or school organization as an entertainment and/or fundraising special event.

Consumer shows are popular in the United States and international cities. Retail department stores in Paris have a reputation for presenting fashion shows to international guests. The two large department stores in Paris, Printemps and Galeries Lafayette, both produce weekly fashion shows for their international clients. At Galeries Lafayette a special weekly or twice weekly fashion show is presented specifically for international visitors. Figure 2.14 shows promotional material for the fashion shows at Galeries Lafayette.

The Galeries Lafayette fashion show was created in 1987 to entertain visiting dignitaries and attract foreign visitors to the department store. Approximately 150 people attend each show. The shows are promoted using brochures and advertising on airlines and in hotels, the Internet and through the French tourism industry. A staff of about 40 people are involved in the production of the Galeries Lafayette International Fashion Show.

The crew includes models, dressers, technicians, hostesses, and the commentator. The commentator simply announces the designer or manufacturer name to avoid multiple translations for the multinational audience.

The show is typically divided into scenes with an audio-visual presentation used to highlight Paris and emphasize various themes. The show has six segments:

- Lingerie—pajamas, robes, bustiers
- Avante Premiere—very young trend-setting fashions
- Couturiere —exclusive designer and classic fashions
- Cocktail—short evening wear

Figure 2.14 Promotional material for the Galeries Lafayette fashion shows.

- Dinner—long dresses
- Wedding—finale with wedding apparel

The producers do not attempt to change the clothing each week. The show is formulated to emphasize looks and tendencies rather than specific garments. Clothing and accessories are changed four times a year, with new items added regularly to freshen the show between major seasonal changes.

The show at Galeries Lafayette is an example of a fashion trend show. **Fashion trend shows** are produced to introduce consumers to the latest trends in silhouettes, fabrics, colors, and themes for new seasonal merchandise. Fashion directors and buyers identify trends by attending haute couture shows, designer collection and trade shows. Upon returning home these professionals identify the specific trends that will be represented in the merchandise buys for their company. Finally, the identified trends must be shown to the consumers so they will get excited and want to buy the new merchandise. Fashion trend shows are presented to consumers at the beginning of the season and each show segment features a major trend.

In order for retailers to successfully sell new trendy merchandise to consumers, it is important to educate sales associates about trends and related promotions intended to highlight new merchandise. **In-store training fashion shows** may be used as the training tool for store associates. These shows may be live or videotaped and may use store employees as models. The in-store training show enables employees to see the trends and adapt the look to all departments from apparel to accessories and to all price points from designer to budget.

New store openings provide a good excuse for retailers to host fashion shows for consumers. The retailer may use a fashion show to introduce a new location, new store personnel or new merchandise lines to the public. As a created publicity event the fashion show can generate excitement about the products and people associated with the new environment.

Manufacturers and retailers will sometimes join together to present a **cooperative fashion show** in which both parties share in the production costs of the show. Major fashion publications such as *W*, *Glamour*, and *Vogue* present fashion shows to consumers as **magazine tie-in** events. This is a cooperative fashion show because the retailer and magazine publisher share the cost of producing a show. These events are generally designed to improve fashion awareness, build loyalty for the brand, or increase the consumer's knowledge of the publication. Many publications have monthly columns dedicated to telling consumers the cities and retailers they will be visiting. *Vogue*'s Haute Stuff is an example of such a magazine feature.

The *Ebony* Fashion Fair (Fig. 2.15) is the world's largest traveling fashion show and a well-known magazine tie-in event. The show travels to nearly 200 different cities in the United States, Canada, and the Caribbean each year. The models, commentators, and crew routinely travel from one city to the next setting up and striking the show on a nightly basis. The magazines' fashion staff visits many different European and American designers and selects trend merchandise for the traveling show. The show changes merchandise twice a year with season changes. The traveling event is a cooperative venture between the magazine and hundreds of local charities serving as a fundraising event.

Many consumer shows are presented for a specific target market. Niche markets that might benefit from the promotion of a fashion show are endless. The last section of this chapter

Figure 2.15 Model Rud Fuller walks the runway during the *Ebony* Fashion Fair fashion show.

highlights some of the more popular consumer show possibilities. Examples of many specialty market and special interest fashion show ideas are listed in Figure 2.16. **Specialty market shows** highlight trends from a specific product category or a certain body type. **Special interest shows** are presented to consumers that have a special affinity with each other or a unique vocation that can be represented through fashion.

Bridal fashion shows always generate lots of consumer interest and are an example of a specialty market, product category show. Bridal fairs are often presented in the spring and feature wedding dresses, tuxedos, and wedding party attire. The fair may also display wedding gift ideas such as flatware, crystal, and china, and have representatives such as caterers, photographers, and florists on hand to contract services.

Other specialty market product categories include footwear, lingerie, and skiwear or other sporting activity clothing, among other merchandise groups. A popular product category that holds special interest to college students is career wear. As many students reach their last semester, they realize the need to dress for a job interview or the job they want after college. Many university student organizations sponsor fashion shows. These shows provide professional, economically affordable business fashions that are available in the community. Résumé workshops, beauty tips, and stress reduction workshops may also be part of the career fashion show event.

Special sizes for both men and women are rapidly expanding specialty markets. Retailers are increasing their merchandise selection in petite, plus size, tall, and big and tall offerings. Fashion shows are used to promote non-traditional sized merchandise and celebrities are participating in the events to show enthusiasm for the products. In Figure 2.17, Camryn Manheim, Emmy-award winning actor on *The Practice*, is a featured model for retailer Lane Bryant.

Specialty market and special interest fashion show ideas		
Product Categories	**Body Types**	**Special Interests**
• Athletic wear	• Big and Tall men's wear	• Ethnic influences
• Back-to-school	• Children's	• Hair designs
• Bridal wear	• Juniors	• Holiday fashions
• Career wear	• Petites	• Lifestyle clothing
• Cosmetics	• Plus-sizes	• Local designers
• Footwear		• Wearable art
• Intimate apparel or lingerie		
• Prom dresses or special occasion dressing		
• Skate wear		
• Skiwear		
• Swimwear		
• Unisex urban wear		
• Western wear		

Figure 2.16 Specialty market and special interest fashion show ideas.

Figure 2.17 Camryn Manheim models for Lane Bryant. *Courtesy, Fairchild Publications, Inc.*

Wearable art by local designers is an example of a special interest fashion show. Artists often use fibers and fabrics as media to express their art. A fashion show is a creative way to show off these designs which often look better on the human form than hanging two-dimensionally in an art gallery. Fashion shows are also a great venue to show off high school or university art or design student creations. Other special interest fashion shows may include highlighting fashions popular with ethnic groups, holiday fashions, or lifestyle apparel such as garments made from organically grown cotton.

Fashion shows are big business within the fashion industry. At every level of the distribution channel, fashion shows are presented to show trends to retailer buyers, exclusive customers, fashion press, or consumers. Fashion shows can be extremely lavish or somewhat minimal. But all are effective in creating excitement and promoting fashion awareness. This chapter has highlighted many show types used by designers, manufacturers, retailers, and consumers to promote fashion trends. As readers you are now encouraged to use these show types as inspiration as you plunge into producing your own fashion show. The remaining chapters in this text guide you through the specific details of producing a fashion show.

Key fashion show terms

7th on Sixth

apparel mart

bridge

British Fashion Council

Camera Nationale della Alta Moda Italia

Chambre Syndicale de la Couture
    Parisienne

consumer show

contemporary

cooperative fashion show

defiles des createurs

designer

documentary video

fashion trend show

Fashion Week

Fédération Française du Prêt-à-porter
    Feminin

formal runway show

haute couture

informal fashion show

in-store training fashion show

instructional video

junior

magazine tie-in

mannequin modeling

market calendar

Market Week

missy

point-of-purchase video

press show

prêt-à-porter

production show

ready-to-wear

special interest show

specialty market show

tea-room modeling

trade

trade association

trade fair

trade show

trunk show

video production

References

Barker, B. (2001, May 23). Spain's Latin link [Section II]. *Women's Wear Daily*, p. 22.

Beckner, A. (2001, May 23). Not so quiet on the eastern front [Section II]. *Women's Wear Daily*, p. 7.

Braunstein, P. (1999, September 15). Fashion week on the web. *Women's Wear Daily*, p. 19.

Brumback, N. (2000, December 13). The next step for StyleMax {Section II]. *Women's Wear Daily*, p. 11.

CNN.com. (2000, September 28). *British designers' look for 2001: Sexy, colorful, fun*. Retrieved September 29, 2000, from http://www.cnn.com/20.../britian.fashionweek.ap/index.html

Corinth, K. (1970). *Fashion showmanship*. New York: Wiley.

Daswani, K. (2000a, April 5). British are coming. *Women's Wear Daily*, p. 9.

Daswani, K. (2000b, June 13). Hannant's Hong Kong trunk show sells $120K. *Women's Wear Daily*, p. 5.

Ellis, K. & Bowers, K. (2000, December 13). Niche going in L.A. [Section II]. *Women's Wear Daily*, p. 5.

Feitelberg, R. (2000, September 6). Foreign imports [Section II]. *Women's Wear Daily*, pp. 24, 57.

Foley, B. (2000, January 26). Dior: The saga continues. *Women's Wear Daily*, pp. 8–9.

Foley, B. (2001, April 4). Going back to Paris? Helmut Lang ponders leaving NY runway. *Women's Wear Daily*, pp. 1, 3.

Frings, G. (2002). *Fashion from concept to consumer* (7th ed.). Upper Saddle River, NJ: Prentice Hall.

Haber, H. (2000, December 13). Roaming therapy [Section II]. *Women's Wear Daily*, p. 8.

Horyn, C. (2001, February 17). Fashion week fizzles under the tents. *New York Times*. Retrieved February 17, 2001, from http://www.nytimes.com

Jones, R. (2001, April 2). L.A. Fashion Week. *Women's Wear Daily*, p. 11.

Kerwin, J. (2000, July 11). One haute samba. *Women's Wear Daily*, p. 14.

Lee, G. (2000a, April 20). Fashion week with a Latin beat. *Women's Wear Daily*, p. 16.

Lee, G. (2000b, July 20). Miami stages a real variety show. *Women's Wear Daily*, p. 12.

Lee, G. (2000c, December 13). Atlanta's revival [Section II]. *Women's Wear Daily*, p. 9.

Malone, S. (2000, September 6). Present Tencel [Section II]. *Women's Wear Daily*, p. 54.

Malone, S. & Ellis, K. (2000, March 1). So long somber, here comes color. *Women's Wear Daily*, pp. 12-13.

Murphy, R. (2001, June 15). Power play brewing for Chambre control. *Women's Wear Daily*, pp. 2, 21.

Naughton, J. (2001, January 21). Sephora to climb on the catwalk. *Women's Wear Daily*, p. 6.

New York date debate: Designers say 'first,' audience disagrees. (2001, April 19). *Women's Wear Daily*, pp. 1, 4-5.

Rabolt, N. & Miler, J. (1997). *Cases and concepts in retail and merchandise management*. New York: Fairchild.

Socha, M. (2000, April 7). Galliano gets home at Saks. *Women's Wear Daily*, p. 11.

Wilson, E. (2001, May 21). New YLS logs $1M at trunk show. *Women's Wear Daily*, p. 3.

Young, K. & Saeks, D. (2000, September 18). Passport check. *Women's Wear Daily*, p. 35.

THE PLAN

3

Fern Mallis, Executive Director for 7th on Sixth and veteran fashion show organizer, says the real headaches happen months before the actual event. According to Mallis, "It starts with our agreement with Bryant Park" (Nolan, 2000, para. 5). Then, permits are requested from the City Parks Commission and the Department of Transportation. Even with past cooperation from the mayor's office, his approval is sought. With these permits, 7th on Sixth producers are able to close streets near the event to refuel their generators, which have the capability of providing power for a town of 35,000 people. Just imagine the logistical problems of putting on such an event. Figure 3.1 shows the entrance to the tents at 7th on Sixth.

Event sponsors for the Spring 2001 collections, including E! Style, Sephora, and Evian, were involved with the planning process too. Evian had a large presence at the show, providing approximately 96,000 bottles of water to participants over the course of the events, as estimated by 7th on Sixth planners.

Planning for fashion shows starts well in advance of the production. Event planning involves so many variables, from the selection of the show location to the number of water bottles needed by participants. This chapter, The Plan, profiles the planning and organization techniques that make a fashion show fun and rewarding. After the purpose of the show is determined, the fashion show director can evaluate audience characteristics, appoint a fashion show staff, develop a theme, find a location, prepare a budget, and put the plan into action. Problems are anticipated and contingency plans are considered. Planning and budgeting in advance of the show helps to make everything run smoothly.

Planning involves all aspects of preliminary preparation necessary to present a well-executed show. Planning must be appropriate to the purpose of the show and the abilities of the group producing the show. A back-to-school fashion show should focus on fall school clothes, using children as models and attracting parents and children as the audience.

Figure 3.1 Much of the success of such large-scale fashion shows as 7th on Sixth is due to advance planning and attention to every detail before the start of the shows. *Courtesy, Fairchild Publications, Inc.*

Planners for charity shows should keep in mind the purpose to raise money when planning an event, but should not over-price the show tickets for the intended audience.

Working out the many details starts with selecting the appropriate leadership. The leaders, in turn, delegate responsibilities, foresee problems which may occur, and continually review the progress of the show. Figure 3.2 illustrates fashion show leadership. The size of the show may determine the location. The lifestyle of the audience may dictate the theme. A service organization may have a guaranteed audience but no theme or location. A retail store may have a planned storewide theme, but it may need to concentrate on finding an appropriate target market.

Without advance planning, unexpected problems occur which could easily be avoided. Communication is very important to advance planning. Lines of communication among the fashion show producers must be well defined and functional or planning will be of no benefit.

Targeting the audience

Planning a fashion show must include determining who the audience will be. Many times the audience will shape the purpose of the event. The audience may consist of fashionable, conservative, or career oriented individuals (Fig. 3.3). The merchandise selected for the show must match the audience in order to promote appropriate trends.

The audience may take two different forms—guaranteed or created. An audience that is established before the show is organized is considered a **guaranteed audience**, individuals who will attend the show regardless of the fashions displayed. A show that is presented at an annual meeting of an organization with an existing membership list is considered a guaranteed audience.

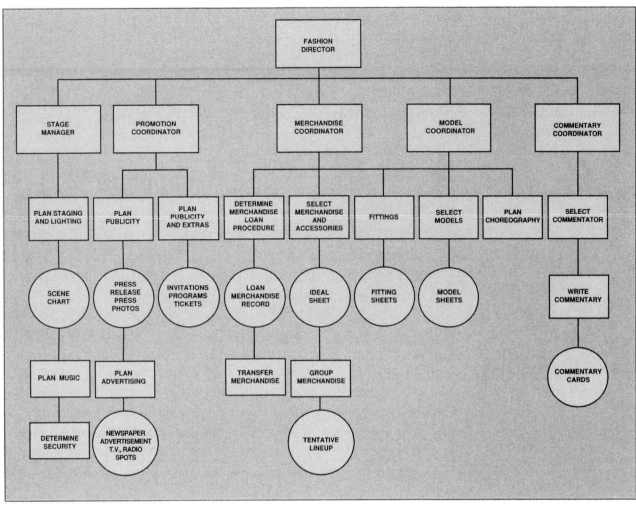

Figure 3.2 An organization chart illustrates fashion show leadership and responsibilities. Key: Boxes are used to designate the people involved with a fashion show activity; circles represent an action executed with written evidence.

An audience which is established after the show is planned as a result of publicity and advertising is considered a **created audience**. A retailer may use a fashion show to attract an audience for the premiere of a new department. The retailer is creating a new audience by producing a show that meets the needs of the audience. This audience is very concerned with the type of fashions displayed.

An audience may be gathered from many different sources. Department stores may use customer mailing lists. Communities with local business or social organizations may share their membership lists. Fashion students from universities, colleges, and high schools are always an eager audience. Fashion shows are generally more successful when a specific audience is attracted rather than promoted to the general public. The size, age, gender, income, and career of the targeted audience must be appraised. Other considerations are the interests and lifestyles of the audience, and the occasion and/or season for which the show is being held.

Audience size

The size of the audience often determines the type of show, although, the type of show can in some instances determine the size of the audience. All members of the audience need to be able to easily view the fashions from a comfortable location. A production or runway show

Figure 3.3 Determining audience characteristics is essential to the planning process, enabling fashion show producers to target the products and theme to those individuals who will be attending the fashion show. *Courtesy, Christopher C. Everett.*

may be required if the audience is large, filling a grand ballroom or an auditorium. Small audiences allow a more intimate environment between the models and the audience, therefore an informal show setting within a retail store or restaurant as the location may be appropriate. If it is necessary to limit the number of people attending a fashion show, reserved tickets or RSVPs may be required.

Audience age

The age of the audience should be considered when planning a show. Young audiences need to be entertained with plenty of action. It is also necessary to have louder, more contemporary music with a faster beat for a younger crowd. A more mature crowd is usually more interested in the merchandise than a younger audience is, and wants very explicit, detailed commentary. The music must be softer and non-distracting if commentary is used. If the audience is mixed, the show theme should appeal to many age groups, not offensively loud to turn off people, or slow to the point of boredom for the younger population.

Audience income

If selling merchandise is the primary reason for producing a show, then it is important to be aware of the income of the audience. Through database management, retailers know the approximate spending habits of their customers, and this should be reviewed before selecting the merchandise (Fig. 3.4). Merchandise that is too expensive, or has the appearance of being too expensive, will intimidate customers, and they will feel embarrassed that they cannot afford to purchase anything. On the other hand, merchandise that is inexpensive in the eyes of the audience will be overlooked as nonstatus items. Fashions ill-matched to the audience will lose both immediate sales and future sales because the audience will not return to the store.

Audience gender

Consider whether the audience will purchase the displayed merchandise for themselves or for others. Specialty stores, featuring gift merchandise, may offer a men's night before Christmas or Valentine's Day. These fashion shows can be very successful promotion tools. Men, who might be uncomfortable entering a lingerie store, might welcome an invitation to a pre-holiday intimate apparel fashion show.

Audience occupations

Fashion show planners should review the careers of the audience members. Are members of the audience looking for career clothing or recreational clothing? Some customers may feel they can spend more money if the garments will be used for business instead of pleasure, while others might be looking for apparel to wear on vacation.

It is important to review all of the points discussed above regarding the audience when planning a show. Forgetting one element can change the atmosphere of the show and decrease the opportunity for ticket and merchandise sales.

Figure 3.4 A *Glamour* editor commentates this show. The advance planning for the event is accomplished by the local retailer and the store's fashion director. *Courtesy, Christopher C. Everett.*

Developing leadership

Professional designer runway shows, which are produced for such events as 7th on Sixth in New York, London Fashion Week, or the Prêt à Porter in Paris, typically rely on the designer's public relations officer to assist the designer in hiring a show producer. Whereas, retailers, fashion schools, and charitable organizations more typically use the skills of a fashion director or fashion show coordinator to direct the production of the show. Both types of shows require leaders with strong organizational and managerial skills. We will look at both types of leadership styles.

Designer show's production team

According to Widdows and McGuiness (1997), the public relations representative from the designer's company, depending upon the wishes of the designer, may put together or make recommendations on the composition of the show production team. This team includes the show producer, stylist, makeup artist, hairdressers, models, and the behind-the-scenes stage crew.

Show producer   The **show producer** is the individual hired to bring all of the fashion show elements together, translating the designer's vision into a three-dimensional live show. These responsibilities include, but are not limited to, casting the models, overseeing the design and construction of the set, and directing the lighting and music crews. The show producer is in charge of a large staff that takes the initial plans and translates these ideas into the actual show.

In addition to organizational and communication skills, the show producer must be creative. The show producer sets ideas, which enhance the designer's image through set design, choreography, music, and lighting, in motion. With good industry contacts and positive working relationships with model, hair, and makeup agencies, staging firms, and media representatives, the show producer can hire the best team for the job.

The show producer works with the designer and stylist to decide which models will wear which outfits. By choosing the best models to wear the most significant outfits, the interest from the major fashion editors can almost be guaranteed. Understanding what helps or hinders the fashion press is also part of the show producer's responsibilities.

Stylist   The stylist is the unsung hero of many fashion shows. It is the responsibility of the **stylist** to provide creative input to the designer and show producer, and present the clothes immaculately. The stylist supervises the wardrobe mistress and dressing team. His or her responsibilities include planning how to highlight key pieces of the collection through editing and accessorizing.

The stylist must understand the designer's target audience and help to interpret the look with attention to detail, appropriate model fit, and use of suitable props. The smallest loose thread or the most insignificant crease becomes exaggerated on the runway with bright lights.

After the stylist has seen the collection, he or she plans the accessories. Shoes, jewelry, handbags, and millinery are borrowed or commissioned from another manufacturer, if these items are not part of the designer's regular collection. These accessories are borrowed for a promotional credit, hired for a fee, or commissioned and paid for. Whichever method is used, the stylist sources these items and makes sure the designer approves their use.

Stylists also work on the garment order and which garments are coordinated to form an outfit, strongly influencing the overall impact of the merchandise. These fine details give the collection its feel, from sexy to casual, or formal to modern. With up to 100 outfits per show, each garment is considered as an individual item as well as a part of a collection. This can make the stylist's job quite intense.

In addition to runway work, stylists do work for magazines, newspapers, advertising campaigns, and videos. They also work for celebrities as they prepare their wardrobes for award ceremonies and other high profile events. Stylists have become Oscar power figures, commanding record fees for their work and becoming recognizable names. The best-known stylists, including Phillip Bloch and Jessica Paster, may charge up to $2,000 per day for bringing celebrities and designers together (Ginsberg, 2001). An event like the Oscars, with a worldwide audience in the billions, might require a good three to four weeks of work.

Fashion show director's leadership team

Retail stores, fashion schools, and charitable organizations may be able to hire a fashion show producer, but more frequently they use their own fashion director, special events director, or fashion show director. These directors or coordinators are employees of the store or school, or possibly advanced students or graduates of the program. They may also be volunteers for the school or charitable organization, who have modeling and fashion show backgrounds and an interest in fashion show production.

A retail store **fashion director** or **special events director** is an individual responsible for creating the fashion image for that particular retailer. The fashion director, in cooperation with the store's buyers, is responsible for selecting silhouettes, colors, and fabrics for the upcoming seasons and establishing a sense of fashion leadership for the store to the public. Fashion show production plays a major role in the job of a fashion director.

A school production or civic organization may have a fashion show director or co-directors. A **fashion show director** is the individual charged with the responsibility of producing the show, planning all arrangements, delegating responsibilities, and accepting accountability for all details. In school productions and civic organizations the coordinator may be elected or appointed by the group members.

A fashion show director must have several traits. The director must be able to communicate with all parties involved both verbally and in writing. Verbal information may not be enough communication. Written communication must be stressed. Information should be put in writing so that individuals are aware of details. People often give directions verbally in a hurried manner only to forget the directions later; written communication allows both parties to refer back to what directions were assigned. Additionally, the director must keep a written **diary** or record of all plans for the show. This diary serves as a reminder to the director of tasks to be completed, follow-up dates, and future needs of the show. The diary may also be a helpful tool if an organization decides to produce another show in the future.

The show director must communicate planning activities to all concerned individuals. A retailer should inform all salespeople far in advance about the details of the show so they may promote the event to their customers. A school group or civic organization must pass information to all members so that they may invite other people.

A fashion show director must be able to foresee show problems and be flexible to work around these problems and/or inconveniences. Many problems occur during critical moments of the show and must be dealt with in a professional and timely manner. Common problems include models not showing or merchandise exchanges right before the show causing changes in commentary and lineup.

The fashion show director must continually review the progress of the show, making sure the show is running smoothly and deadlines are met. Many people are involved in the show and it is important for the show director to know everything that the others are doing.

The show director must also assign tasks to other coordinators. Each fashion show director will divide responsibilities differently depending on the size and complexity of the show. Production shows may require many area coordinators with specialized responsibilities, while a trunk show may only require one or two area coordinators with several responsibilities.

Model coordinator   One area of responsibility that a show director often delegates is the organization of models. A **model coordinator** is responsible for selecting and training the models, and coordinating activities that involve the models. Additional areas of responsibilities for the model coordinator may include supervising a female and a male model coordinator, a model workshop coordinator for inexperienced models, and makeup, hair, or other beauty technicians.

Stage manager   Most large shows require the services of a **stage manager** who oversees use of the stage and runway, organizes equipment, and supervises people providing services behind the scenes, such as a properties manager, stagehands, music, microphone, and lighting technicians. Some facilities, such as city auditoriums, have a stage manager on their staff and require that they be hired by the group when the location is rented.

Promotion coordinator   Most fashion shows require promotion. Show coordinators may delegate these responsibilities to the advertising department of a retail store if one is available or select a promotion coordinator and a program editor. The **promotion coordinator** is accountable for the creation and distribution of promotional materials for the show including press releases, press photographs, tickets, invitations, commercials, signage, table decorations, and other forms of promotion. The promotion coordinator may also supervise an assistant or hostess to fulfill these obligations. The promotion coordinator may additionally perform public relations activities. This coordinator may hire photographers and a video crew for services before and during the show.

A **program editor** is responsible for all activities related to creating a program. This includes the design and printing of the program, distribution of the program, and the solicitation of advertisements to pay for the program.

Merchandise coordinator   The **merchandise coordinator** is in charge of the selection of merchandise for each scene and the entire show. As we learned earlier, this is the responsibility of the designer with the assistance of the show producer and stylist, if the show launches the designer's collection. Fashion shows done for retail stores, charity, or training allow the merchandise coordinator to pick clothing, accessories, and props to pull each segment of the show into a harmonized event. The merchandise coordinator also works very closely with the model coordinator to facilitate fittings prior to the rehearsal.

Commentary coordinator   All of the show oratory, written commentary, and selection of announcers and/or commentators, are the responsibility of the **commentary coordinator**. Since many shows no longer use commentary, the role of the commentary coordinator might be limited to finding an appropriate announcer to open and close the show, or the job of locating an announcer may be delegated to another show coordinator.

When delegating responsibilities, all available resources, personnel, and services should be considered. A show director must have a sense about people to determine how well they will follow through with assigned work. Sometimes the best available people are volunteers rather than individuals paid to perform a task. However, there are volunteers who will not take their responsibilities seriously. Enthusiasm must be proven in actions not words. The fashion show staff meets regularly (Fig. 3.5) to make sure all elements come together.

Responsibility documentation

A **responsibility sheet** is a helpful tool in planning a show and delegating responsibilities to all participants (Fig. 3.6). The show director records each delegated task on the responsibility sheet, then distributes copies of this form to coordinators so that all individuals may know who is accountable for each task. Figure 3.7 shows a time line of responsibility, which gives a rough guideline for task completion prior to the day of the show.

Figure 3.5 Once the leadership team is determined, planning meetings, such as this one back stage at the fall Gucci show, help the personnel in organizing the event. *Courtesy, Fairchild Publications, Inc.*

Figure 3.6 The Responsibility Sheet is a documentation of each coordinator's task and contacts, which also serves as a report about task completion.

RESPONSIBILITY SHEET

Show Theme _____

Location_____

Day_____

Date _____

Time _____

Confirmed by _____ Phone_____

Contact Person at Location _____ Phone_____

MERCHANDISE

Merchandise Coordinator_____ Phone_____

Specific Categories   Category Titles

1. _____

2. _____

3. _____

4. _____

5. _____

6. _____

MODELS

Model Coordinator _____ Phone_____

Number of models _____

Model Resources _____

Contact Person at Agency_____ Phone_____

PROMOTION

Promotion Coordinator _____ Phone_____

Type of Promotions Used   Completion Dates

1. _____

2. _____

3. _____

Designer _____ Phone_____

Printer _____ Phone_____

STAGE

Stage Manager _____ Phone_____

Type of Production _____

Supplies Needed _____ Completion Date _____

Props Needed _____ Completion Date _____

Music Selection _____ Completion Date _____

Commentator _____ Phone_____

	Time Allotment Before Show	
Responsibility	Earliest Planning	Latest Planning
Select Show Director	6 months	5 weeks
Decide Show Theme, Location, Audience	5 months	5 weeks
Plan Budget	5 months	5 weeks
Select Show Co-Chair	5 months	5 weeks
Reserve Location	5 months	5 weeks
Plan Seating Arrangement	1 month	week of show
Technical Run-Through	1 week	1 day
Dress Rehearsal	1 week	day of show
Strike Show	day of show	
Evaluation	1 day after show	1 week after show
Model Committee		
Select Models	3 months	3 weeks
Prepare Tentative Lineup	1 month	2 weeks
Set Choreography	1 month	week of show
Merchandise Committee		
Plan Merchandise Groupings/Scenes	4 months	3 weeks
Review Merchandise	3 months	2 weeks
Prepare Tentative Lineup	1 month	2 weeks
Fittings	2 weeks	week of show
Pull Merchandise	week of show	
Prepare Final Lineup	week of show	
Transfer Merchandise	1 week	day of show
Return Merchandise	day of show	1 day after show
Commentary Committee		
Prepare Filler Commentary	5 months	2 weeks
Write Commentary	1 month	week of show
Staging Committee		
Begin Music Selection	4 months	3 weeks
Prepare Set	3 months	2 weeks
Publicity Committee		
Send To Printer: Program Cover, Flyer, Invitation, Tickets	3 months	3 weeks
Plan Advertising	3 months	2 weeks
Write Press Release	2 months	3 weeks
Send Press Release	6 weeks	2 weeks
Distribute Flyers	6 weeks	2 weeks
Run In-Store Advertising	6 weeks	week of show
Send Invitations	1 month	2 weeks
Send To Printer: Program Contents	1 month	10 days
Run Newspaper Advertising	1 month	week of show
Write Thank You Notes	1 day after show	1 week after show

Figure 3.7 The time line of responsibilities helps coordinators and staff members stay on schedule with their various jobs.

Creating fashion show themes

Fashion shows should have a **theme** and a creative title, which will tell the audience the nature of the fashion show. These should be selected during the planning stages. The theme can be developed around the targeted audience or around the merchandise selected. It allows the publicity, merchandise, and other planning elements to be joined to show continuity.

Show themes

Probably the easiest show theme will come from a season or a holiday. Lingerie shows are always popular around Valentine's Day, just as back-to-school shows are the hit in August and September. Special occasion, holiday, and resort wear shows are common in November and December.

If a holiday has been overused then current events can be used to create a theme. Current music or art trends may lend themselves to a theme, particularly if the music or art is popular with the selected audience. Spring always brings about travel ideas with themes centering around geographic locations. "Get Away" shows, exhibiting tropical paradises with casual resort clothing, always attract large audiences. Specific color themes or a special interest of the audience may also be an easy theme to develop. The outdoor atmosphere may be perfect for a sporting goods fashion show attracting a certain audience to the event. *Rock the Runway*, *Wear to Go*, or *The Professional You!* are examples of fashion shows with creative themes.

Fashion show themes relating to the type of merchandise or sponsor being presented might include *Bridal Gala*, *Symphony Fashion Jubilee*, or the *Junior League Soiree*. Themes could also be related to the designer presenting the fashions. The *Geoffrey Beene Collections* or *Breakfast with Donna Karan* reflect designer themes. When a fashion show is sponsored by a vendor, publication, or organization, it is often a courtesy to include their name in the theme. It not only promotes the vendor but can also pull in a larger audience if the vendor is well known.

Scene themes

Fashion shows are divided into scenes or segments depending on the type of merchandise selected. After a show theme has been developed each segment or scene can be created to coordinate with the chosen title.

Victoria's Secret Cannes 2000 Lingerie Show, which was seen by nearly two million international viewers as a Web cast, featured three merchandise segments. The first part of the show was called "Angels in Heaven." This opening scene, with heavenly clouds and dramatic blue lighting as part of the stage design, featured dresses that were mostly white or blue. The second segment was called "Inferno," depicting fallen angels. The stage set was transformed into a realistic image of blazing flames, with exotic lingerie. The final scene symbolized joining together heaven and earth with gold dresses and gold background images ("Review," 2001).

Rock the Runway was a fashion show, which featured the fusion of fashion trends with musical styles, produced by merchandising students at Northern Arizona University. The show was divided into five scenes, each with a distinctive apparel category and complementary musical type. The show opened with the theme, "Oops...I wore it again," which featured denim and casual clothing. The second scene, "Wild Wild Dress," was developed to show the western apparel trends of the season. The western influences were followed by the third scene, "To Glam or Not to Glam," highlighting dressier garments that would be worn on dates. Scene four, which was titled "Suit Suit Riot," was the segment devoted to business apparel. "Classical Couture," the final scene, concluded the show with the most dramatic holiday and evening merchandise. Musical selections and dance routines helped to emphasize the various merchandise and musical trends. A discussion of the music selected to coordinate with the fashion show theme and scene themes will follow in Chapter 7.

Finding a venue

Will the audience travel a long or short distance to view the show? Production shows are often used when the audience has to travel a longer distance. The audience may feel they are getting "more for their money" for the distance traveled if they view a production show rather than an informal show. Many variables will influence where to hold the show. Are you holding the show in a hotel, restaurant, or auditorium? On the retail floor? In the manufacturer's showroom?

Working with a hotel

The member of the fashion show committee responsible for working with the hotel should make an appointment to speak with the hotel representative as soon as possible. The individual in charge of hotel sales may have such titles as Sales or Marketing Manager, Coordinator, or Director. Depending upon the size and type of hotel there may be one or more people directly involved in the services relating to banquets and catering or sales and marketing.

It is best to have some simple qualifying questions ready prior to the first meeting. Some qualifying questions include:

1. Is there a specific date when the show is to be held or is the date somewhat flexible?
2. What is the size of the audience?
3. What type of seating arrangements will be needed?
4. Will food service take place in the same location as the fashion show?
5. What sound and lighting systems, staging, and dressing area facilities are available?

The sales directors will assist fashion show producers in every aspect of planning as it relates to room rental and food and beverage service. Other services may include setting up, serving, and cleaning up.

There are additional concerns in relationship to the physical facilities. The number of people that are able to attend may be limited by the size of the room. However, show planners should work with the type of hotel that can offer the services desired by the group. If a room for an audience of 250 is needed, but the hotel can only handle 100 people, it does not make any sense to waste the time of the hotel personnel. The hotel should be able to provide tables, tablecloths, serving dishes, plates, glasses, flatware, and napkins. Some hotels, particularly in larger cities may be able to provide various seating arrangements from theater style to luncheon style. Extra amenities might include runways and skirting, stages, public address systems, audio-visual projection systems, and technicians to run the media.

Hotels rarely permit people to use outside caterers or to "self-cater" events. Outside food service preparation has generally been a hassle for hotel personnel and health regulations or state laws may prohibit this type of activity.

Alcoholic beverages may also be served to a fashion show audience. If the hotel has a liquor license, the hotel can set up a cash or hosted bar. If alcohol is to be served, some states require that tickets state who is eligible to drink the beverages. Depending upon the state laws, a special permit may be obtained for serving wine for a fundraising activity.

When the arrangements are finalized, a contract should be written. Fashion show planners should be suspicious if a contract is not required as it protects both the hotel and the organization using their services.

Working with a campus venue

Many high school or college campuses have ballrooms and/or auditoriums that can be used for staging fashion shows. Arrangements to use these venues should be made well in advance, particularly when the popular locations are scheduled for many different school activities. The ballroom on the campus of one university is generally booked every night of the week, especially near the end of the fall semester with the Thanksgiving and Christmas holidays. That location may require reserving the space six to nine months in advance of the show.

Fashion show planners can expect school venues to have strict guidelines and restrictions for use. These guidelines can regulate and limit hours of room availability, the type of food and beverage service, a minor's participation, and participants' willingness to sign liability waivers. Planners can also anticipate regulations regarding ticket sales. In some places, tickets may only be sold through a campus ticket office or company, such as Ticketmaster, increasing expenses due to set up fees.

Despite some of the limitations and regulations, there are many benefits to using campus facilities. Benefits might include such things as a built-in sound system and stage lighting, a portable runway, campus liability insurance, licensed food service, and an experienced staff to set up and take down the seats and runway. The venue might also have the capability of advertising and promoting the event through on-site video screens and signs.

A contract established between the school venue staff and the fashion show leadership clearly states the expectations and expenses for both parties in the rental agreement. The contract approval process can also provide an outline of the steps required for student organizations in their event planning.

Working with a restaurant

Many of the concerns relevant to working with a restaurant are similar to those discussed when working with a hotel. One of the main differences is in regard to a contract—a restaurant may not require a contract.

Restaurants or cocktail lounges may allow fashion show producers to use their facilities as long as the show does not interrupt normal business activities. Owners and managers of such establishments recognize that a fashion show may increase traffic to their site.

A common use for a restaurant is for informal modeling provided by a local retailer during the lunch hour. This would not require the use of a commentator, specialized music, or a large technical staff.

Problems to consider before using a restaurant or lounge for a fashion show might include health regulations and the age of the participants. Dressing rooms cannot be placed in or near kitchen areas as required by state health officials. Fashion show staff under legal drinking age may not be allowed at the facility during certain business hours.

Serving food and beverages

Food served to the audience depends upon a number of conditions including the type of show being presented and the budget. Service may be as simple as providing beverages or as elaborate as a multiple course meal. Figure 3.8 shows the audience enjoying fashion show refreshments.

Retail organizations trying to attract the customer interested in business apparel have tried breakfast and box lunch shows. These shows feature a simple and attractive breakfast or lunch during the time this customer traditionally shops or prior to going to the office. Tying meal time to the entertainment of the fashion show, has proven to be a popular approach to attracting this type of client.

Charitable organizations like to include a social element with the formal fashion presentation. A cocktail hour before and/or a meal after the presentation are a preferred methods of combining food and fashion.

Figure 3.8 The audience enjoys the fashion show refreshments, which were planned to make the event more pleasurable. *Courtesy, Christopher C. Everett.*

Most restaurants, hotels, or other facilities require using their food and beverage services. When selecting the location for the fashion show this limitation should be discussed. If there are no such restraints from the location management, it may be appropriate to work with any caterer.

Working with catering services

A retail store or a manufacturer presenting a fashion show at their own location is more likely to work directly with a caterer. A runway may be set up on the retail sales floor where the merchandise is located or in a special room reserved for fashion shows. A manufacturer may show the collection right in the showroom. A caterer should be able to provide the fashion show planners with samples of their work and information about the type of clients and food served in the past. Photographs of prior parties or events should be able to give the fashion show planners an idea of how previous events were handled. Generally caterers will provide the names of patrons who have used their services. It is a good idea to check some of the references or check with other people who have used a particular caterer.

A contract should be prepared to protect both the caterer and the fashion show producers. It should explain what will be served, the costs, and any other obligations of the caterer.

Timing the show

While planning a fashion show, timing certain activities of the show is crucial and often done poorly. Poor timing will cause havoc as the show draws closer.

Show schedule

First, the day, date, and time of the show must be set. This must be established when the location is being determined so as to coordinate all efforts. A location which is accessible only during business hours should not be chosen if the show must be held in the evening. Time of the show must be set so that all participants and audience members can allocate traveling time to and from the show. Check for possible conflicts with other events. Avoid selecting a day that is already filled with other community activities.

Some shows are developed six months in advance while others are prepared days in advance. A timetable should be created with deadlines so all individuals can work together (Fig. 3.9).

Individuals within the fashion industry are familiar with the **Fashion Calendar**. This weekly calendar serves as a guide for retailers, manufacturers, and the press to keep industry insiders aware of market weeks. It provides a clearing house for dates and relevant information regarding key national and international fashion events, helping to avoid potential conflicts.

Length of the fashion show

The length of the fashion show should also be established. Usually this is determined by the number of outfits in the show. A show within a retail store should last no longer than 45 min-

October 2002

Sun	Mon	Tue	Wed	Thu	Fri	Sat
		1	**2** Decide on show theme, audience, location, budget, and director	**3**	**4** Select coordinators and reserve venue	**5**
6	**7** Plan show scenes and appropriate merchandise groupings	**8** Hire technical staff and stage crew	**9** Write press releases and schedule press photo session	**10** Plan advertising and cover art for print materials	**11** Audition models and select model for press photo shoot	**12**
13	**14** Meet with music technicians and begin music selections	**15** Press photo shoot Model training and practice	**16** Finalize cover art and copy for flyers, programs, ads, and invitations	**17** Take copy ready artwork to the printer	**18** Arrange for security Plan decorations and hospitality	**19**
20	**21** Send press releases and photos to media Confirm advertising	**22** Model practice Establish tentative lineup	**23** Review merchandise selections Send ads to media	**24** Send invitations	**25** Prepare commentary for the opening and closing of the show	**26**
27 Run newspaper advertising in Sunday paper	**28** Start pulling merchandise Put up store signage and hand out flyers	**29** Model practice	**30** Reconfirm venue and hospitality	**31** Gather props and accessories		

November 2002

Sun	Mon	Tue	Wed	Thu	Fri	Sat
					1 Finalize merchandise selection and prepare the copy for the printed program	**2** Send program inside sheets to the printer
3 Run newspaper advertising in Sunday paper	**4** Model fittings Build set RSVPs due: Plan seating	**5** Model fittings	**6** Prep dressing room, set stage, move merchandise to venue	**7** Dress rehearsal Finalize seating chart	**8 SHOW DAY!** Strike the show and prepare merchandise for return	**9** Return merchandise and accessories to sales floor
10	**11** Complete show evaluation, update show diary. Write thank you notes	**12**	**13**	**14**	**15**	**16**
17	**18**	**19**	**20** Watch the video of the show with show producers and models	**21**	**22**	**23**
24	**25**	**26**	**27**	**28**	**29**	**30**

Figure 3.9 A fashion show planning calendar helps staff to accomplish tasks in a timely and organized manner.

utes to keep the audience interested in the show. If the audience is more fashion forward they may be able to view more clothes in a shorter period of time, and absorb more fashion trends. A younger audience dictates a faster paced show. Some trade shows last 20 minutes or less.

Protecting people and things

The security of merchandise and equipment are big concerns when producing a fashion show and should not be overlooked in the show preparation. The security of the audience and show personnel must also be investigated to insure safety of the participants and protect the show against legal damages. Protection of people and materials should be reviewed as the show is finalized. To protect all individuals involved in transportation of merchandise, equipment, locations, or any other materials, agreements should be put in writing and signed by both show personnel and the leasing agent for the venue and the merchandise.

Merchandise security

Merchandise on loan from retailers for the rehearsals and the show is the responsibility of the show staff. It must be protected from damage while it is being worn and from theft or vandalism.

Consumer shows on location away from a retail store have special concerns regarding theft. The nature of fashion shows permits many individuals to have access to the stage and dressing areas where merchandise is located during the show preparation and performance. Consequently, merchandise while it is away from the merchant, should be protected from show personnel and others. Show personnel should always be aware of all necessary staff and question any unfamiliar bystanders. Hiring professional models and technicians may cause less concern than using amateurs.

One person or a merchandise committee should be assigned the responsibility for organizing, labeling, transferring, and securing the merchandise from the retail store to the show location. This committee should also know what personnel may have direct contact with the merchandise. Shows using amateur personnel, models, or dressers, may ask these individuals to sign waivers making them responsible for missing or damaged merchandise. This contract encourages and strengthens a sense of responsibility. Figure 3.10 is an example of a security contract.

Beyond merchandise security against theft or damage, couture or prestige merchandise must be protected against **design piracy**. Stealing designs and creating **knockoffs**, or copies of designer originals at lower prices, are so commonplace in the fashion industry that European designers hire security agents during collection openings. The agents do not allow any individuals to see the collection until it is presented on the runway. Timing is crucial in the presentation of these design ideas. They are so secret that a show can be ruined if the design ideas are leaked before the proper time.

Venue and equipment security

Show staff also have the responsibility of securing the location and any borrowed or leased equipment. **Lease agreements**, contracts between leasing agency and users, should be written before the show. If necessary, security personnel should be hired to keep watch of the equipment.

SECURITY CONTRACT

On (fill in date of show) a fashion show will be presented by (group) at (location). The show will display merchandise from local merchants and benefit the (fill in name of group/organization).

Upon departure from the retail store, the merchandise will be the responsibility of the Show Director. He or she will be accountable for the merchandise until it is returned to the retailer after the Show.

I, the undersigned, realize that I am responsible for caring for each garment carefully and professionally. If a garment or accessory is missing or damaged, it will be my responsibility to report the items to the Merchandise Chairperson immediately. I will be accountable for any unreported merchandise.

Signed _____

Date _____

Figure 3.10 A security contract may be developed to assure the responsibility of fashion show volunteers.

Hotels, auditoriums, restaurants, and other locations may provide insurance policies to cover show liabilities. The show coordinator should know where the responsibility for fashion show insurance lies, with the show personnel or with the venue. If insurance is provided show planners should make sure it covers the period of time when the merchandise is transported from the retail store or showroom to the show location. The policy should also cover the audience and personnel of the show against accidents or injury as a result of attending the fashion show. If the location does not provide insurance the fashion show committee may wish to take out a policy to protect merchandise, equipment, personnel, and guests of the show. It is better to have coverage than leave the show organization open to lawsuits that may be very costly.

Audience security

The audience must also feel safe at the location and be protected from equipment used during the show. Electrical cords used for sound equipment or lighting that crosses audience walkways should be taped securely to the floor. It is necessary for show personnel to make sure fire codes have been met at the location. Fire extinguishers and other safety equipment should be available. Entrances and exits should be marked for the audience in case of emergency. Aisles should be spaced properly to allow for easy access.

Staff security

In addition to being concerned about audience safety, fashion show planners need to assure the safekeeping of all the models, announcers, technicians, makeup and hair personnel, dressers, show coordinators and staff, and backstage guests. Care must be taken with garment steamers, electrical cords, merchandise fixtures, hair appliances, trash, and any equipment that might be dangerous.

Security should never be overlooked in show preparation. The show director is responsible for accidents or injuries of the audience and staff; professionally the director must assure the safety of the garments and accessories; personally, the director must show confidence to the staff and crew that safety will be assured.

Estimating the budget

Many inexperienced fashion show producers think fashion shows cost little or nothing to produce. Even informal shows can involve some substantial costs. As the show becomes more elaborate and complex the costs increase. The **budget** is an estimate of the revenues and expenses necessary to produce the fashion show. It is the best guess of what will be included in the costs and income from ticket sales or vendor cooperative financial support. The budget must remain flexible, an essential part of the forecasting and planning process, since there may be some unexpected or hidden costs. Budget revisions need to take place if circumstances change.

The type of show being produced, audience, location, and special features of the show are directly dependent upon the amount of funds available in the budget. The least expensive type of show to produce is an informal show presented right at the point of sale, the manufacturers' showroom or the retail sales floor. The most expensive shows are large benefit programs or specialized couture shows for private customers and the fashion trade. These shows require large numbers of support staff as well as hotel and equipment rentals. Some of the top designer fashion shows have been reported to cost over a half million and up to a million dollars. The 2002 Victoria's Secret fashion show was estimated to cost nearly six million dollars, making it one of the most expensive shows ever produced (Znaimer, 2002).

Regardless of the extravagance of a show, fashion show planners must evaluate all of the various expenses involved in producing the show during the initial stages of planning. In order to achieve the goals set for the production, the budget process must be approached in a methodical manner.

The fashion show plan

The **fashion show plan** is a schedule for a specific period of time, commonly six months or a year, for all of the fashion shows that a firm intends to produce. The fashion show plan includes the following information:

- Planning calendar
- Divisions, departments, products, or services targeted for fashion show participation
- Estimated costs

The planning calendar consists of the dates, times, and locations for fashion shows. As much detail as possible is used to outline the time frame necessary to plan and produce all fashion shows for a particular season (Fig. 3.11).

The fashion show budget

The fashion show budget is a projection of all of the expenses and anticipated revenues for each fashion show. Some shows, which are staged to raise money for charity, keep a close eye on both sides of the budget sheet. While other shows staged primarily for publicity or fashion image, may not plan a profit. It does not matter what the reason for the show, an accurate accounting of expenses and revenues is necessary.

Betsey Johnson started staging her fashion shows at 7th on Sixth in 1993, when the New York Fashion Week shows at Bryant Park began (Wilson, McCants, Fung, & Kletter, 2000). Johnson spent anywhere from $80,000 to $400,000 each season, depending upon the theme of her collection and her budget. She felt one the best things about showing at 7th on Sixth was her ability to stick to her budget.

The first step in planning the budget for a fashion show is to consider all of the possible expenditures. Figure 3.12 identifies possible fashion show expenses. The fashion show director or the person delegated this responsibility should get estimates for the various costs. Written estimates should be provided for large expenses such as site fees and catering. Each show will incur a specific set of expenses. For example, there is generally no site fee if the show is held in the retail store or manufacturer's showroom. The plan for expenditures should be updated

continued on page 76

April

Sun	Mon	Tue	Wed	Thu	Fri	Sat
		1 Restaurant Informal Modeling 11 to 1	2	3	4	5 Children's Department 2 pm Easter fashion show
6	7	8 Restaurant Informal Modeling 11 to 1	9	10 Spring Charity Show with Symphony Guild Guild Hall 7 pm	11	12 Breakfast with the Easter Bunny in restaurant 10 am until noon
13	14	15 Restaurant Informal Modeling 11 to 1	16	17 Launch of new plus size department with informal modeling 5-7 pm	18	19 Breakfast with the Easter Bunny in restaurant 10 am until noon
20 Store closed **Easter Sunday**	21 Career Week Liz Claiborne Special Events room at noon	22 Career Week Lauren by RL Special Events room at noon	23 Career Week Jones New York Special Events room at noon	24 Career Week Nine West Special Events room at noon	25 Career Week Sigrid Olson Special Events room at noon	26 Career Week Dana Buchman Personal Appearance Special Events Room 10 - noon Sales floor 3 to 5 pm
27	28	29 Restaurant Informal Modeling 11 to 1	30 Launch of new petite department with informal modeling 5-7 pm			

2003

Figure 3.11 A Retail Fashion Show Calendar makes everyone aware of the events happening at the store during each month.

Figure 3.12 Identifying possible fashion show expenses is one of the first steps in creating a fashion show budget.

POSSIBLE EXPENSES

1. Rent
   A. Show
   B. Rehearsal
2. Meals
   A. Set up/Rehearsal
   B. Refreshments for Show
3. Ushers
4. Gratuities
   A. Coat Room
   B. Rest Room
   C. Other
5. Models
   A. Fittings
   B. Rehearsal
   C. Show
6. Advertising and Publicity
   A. Invitations
      1) Design
      2) Printing
      3) Mailing
   B. Posters/Programs
   C. Tickets
   D. Photographs
   E. Broadcast Production Radio/TV
   F. Buying Media Time
   G. Press Release/Media Kit
7. Technical Aspects
   A. Photography/Video
   B. Lighting and Electricians
   C. Stage/Runway
      1) Runway Construction
      2) Props
      3) Painting
      4) Carpenters
   D. Public Address System
   E. Music
8. Behind the Scenes Crew
   A. Hair
   B. Makeup
   C. Dressers
   D. Alterations/Pressing
   E. Security
9. Transportation
   A. Clothing
   B. Equipment
   C. Celebrities
10. Hospitality
    A. Celebrities
    B. Guests
11. Depreciation of Merchandise
    A. Alterations
    B. Pressing
    C. Damage
    D. Shortage
12. Insurance
13. Taxes

Box 3.1
Fashion Shows that Make $$s and Sense

There appears to be a mindset prevailing in the retail industry that is so tightly woven in the fabric of our belief system that we fail to see the forest for the trees. The two fallacies I am about to explode will give a clearer picture of the fashion show potential for stores:

- Models must be professional and be size 10 or smaller, regardless of who is sitting in the audience (most of whom are size 10-22).
- Efficiency dictates that we quickly gather up the clothes after a show and whisk them out the back door to return them to an empty store. In other words, we just left an excited audience eager to see, touch, try-on, and yes-even buy our goods-empty handed. We are hoping they will visit our store, but we cannot depend upon:

1. The incentives we have given them, such as discount coupons and flyers, etc.
2. The hope that their enthusiasm lasts for more than 10 minutes after we are out of sight.

Fashion shows can be your biggest marketing tool for very little expense and some effort. But, you need to clear out those old notions first. It's so simple: organization and clear delegation are the keys to mounting a successful fashion show.

For a smooth show from start to finish, follow these guidelines:

1. The set-up. A 30-minute planning session, one month in advance of the show. In attendance at that time should be your show chairman—a representative of the church, club, business or retirement center where you are holding the show.
2. The Workshop. Demonstrate to participants from the above group, how to model,
3. Fittings. Allocate one half-hour to each "model" and give your undivided attention to her selections. Each model should receive a discount. (We suggest 15 percent.)
4. A Rehearsal. To be held on site, just before the scheduled show; duration 30 minutes.
5. The Show. Make it newsy, chatty, and comfortable for everyone involved. Give them information they can take home with them.
6. Backstage Boutique. After the show, invite the audience into the dressing room to make purchases and to sign up for your mailing list.

At a recent Dallas Market presentation, I gave to a group of 50 buyers; we were able to pinpoint some of the areas of pain and frustration associated with fashion shows. Here are some of the questions those retailers posed—and my responses to them:

Q. Can you give me new ideas for my fashion shows?

continued on page 76

Box 3.1 continued from page 75

A. You don't have to make your show a big stage production. My best success came from shows where the foundation is "teaching" even though the approach will vary depending upon the club theme. Help the audience learn something. Your fresh merchandise provides a new palette for each new show.

Q. How can I make my shows more profitable?

A. By selling clothes and accessories to the "models." We measure our success on what the models, not the audience, buy. Those models are then placed on our database, together with their birthday, size, and preference information. If the audience does buy, that is "icing on the cake," but it isn't the focus.

Q. Can you give me some hints of scriptwriting for the show?

A. I used to labor over a commentary for each fashion show, but once found myself in a situation where I had to come up with a spontaneous description of the clothes. So I now pretend I am at the mirror with one of my customers, telling her about the garment. It works!

Q. Where is the best place to get help with my presentation skills?

A. Unquestionably it's Toastmasters International. There are many such organizations around the country, and most cities have several groups. These groups help you gain confidence and oratory skills as well as to produce new material.

Peggy Johnson, owner of the Petunia Patch women's specialty stores in Jacksonville, Florida, wrote this article for *Women's Wear Daily A Special Report*. Johnson is a 28-year industry veteran, author, market seminar leader, and has created a unique fashion show system program that provides invaluable tips and guidance to help retailers maximize their fashion show potential.

Adapted from: Johnson, P. (2001, January). Retail success story fashion shows that make $$s and sense. *Women's Wear Daily Specialty Stores: A Special Report*, p.33.

continued from page 73

as the actual expenses are incurred. These records should be kept for a final accounting of the currently produced show, and they should be available for reference when planning for future shows (Fig. 3.13).

The fashion show director and staff should be aware of the following categories of expenses:

- Site rental
- Food or catering
- Models
- Advertising and publicity
- Photography and video
- Technical and support staff
- Miscellaneous expenses such as decorations, transportation, hospitality, depreciation of merchandise, insurance, and taxes

FASHION SHOW BUDGET

Name of Show _____
Date _____
Location _____
Time _____

	Planned	Actual
REVENUES		
Ticket Sales Qty___ x $_____	_____	_____
Vendor Coop Money	_____	_____
EXPENSES		
Physical Facilities		
Room Rental	_____	_____
Chairs	_____	_____
Tables	_____	_____
Food Service	_____	_____
Decorations/Flowers	_____	_____
Stage Set	_____	_____
Runway	_____	_____
Public Address System	_____	_____
Lighting	_____	_____
Technicians & Equipment		
Music	_____	_____
Electrician	_____	_____
Show Photographer	_____	_____
Video Crew	_____	_____
Makeup	_____	_____
Hair Stylist	_____	_____
Show Personnel		
Models	_____	_____
Dressers	_____	_____
Cue People	_____	_____
Transportation Staff	_____	_____
Hosts/Ushers	_____	_____
Publicity & Advertising		
Publicity Materials	_____	_____
Photography	_____	_____
Press Release/Media Kit	_____	_____
Invitations	_____	_____
Tickets	_____	_____
Programs	_____	_____
Advertising	_____	_____
Creative Production	_____	_____
Media Time/Space	_____	_____
Merchandise		
Damages/Repairs	_____	_____
Lost/Stolen	_____	_____
Insurance	_____	_____
Security	_____	_____
Hospitality		
Celebrity/Guest	_____	_____
Transportation	_____	_____
Hotel Room	_____	_____
Entertainment	_____	_____
Gratuities	_____	_____
Taxes	_____	_____
Emergency Reserve	_____	_____

Figure 3.13 This fashion show budget shows the planned revenues and expenses as well as the actual financial results.

Venue rental fees   One of the largest expenses associated with the cost of presenting a fashion show is renting the **venue**, which is the location where the show will take place. A charitable organization may ask for reduced or waived rental rates, but members of such groups must realize that hotels, restaurants and caterers are often asked for such gratuities. These companies are in business to make a profit, but some may be willing to throw in amenities to benefit the cause or charity.

Realistically most groups, whether they are nonprofit or profit-making, will have to lease the space for the event. A nonprofit organization has 501 c3 status as designated by the Internal Revenue Service. In order to be incorporated as a **nonprofit organization** the organization must have published articles of incorporation and have a board of directors. Additionally, no officer or staff member of the organization may make personal gain from the organization, and there must be no stockholders. All money earned by the organization is returned to the organization. A nonprofit organization may sell tickets and/or ask for donations, using money raised for operational expenses or charitable causes.

Costs for the site rental should include the time to set up the facility, present the fashion show, serve refreshments, and clean up. Some of the activities, such as room set up and clean up, may be handled by the employees at the venue. Depending upon the room and facilities, these activities may require outside help. Refreshments may be included in the room rental or an outside caterer may be used.

If a rehearsal is required, the estimated cost of using a rehearsal room or renting the site of the actual fashion show must be included in the expenses. If it is not possible to use the contracted space for a rehearsal, another room may be needed for planning choreography and practicing the show. Costs for renting all meeting rooms must be added to the budget.

One of the first questions the hotel's sales or marketing director will ask is about the date of the show. The season, day of week, and time of day will impact the price for the room. During the busy seasons, especially Thanksgiving through New Year's Eve and the traditional wedding period, hotel banquet rooms are solidly booked, as much as a year in advance. Saturday nights are more expensive than weeknights. Evenings are more costly than day times. The show planners should keep in mind that a hotel sales director may not be able to suggest alternatives if the date for the show has already been firmly established.

If a meal is served in one room while the show is presented in another meeting room, there will be additional charges for the use of two rooms. The hotel representative and show producers must consider where the models will change. One possibility is to use an adjacent meeting room. Another prospect is to use nearby hotel rooms. Costs for these services must be factored into the budget. Some hotels may be willing to waive the rental of the room if specified food and beverage expenditures are met. One rule of thumb used by a national hotel chain requires spending one and one-half times the cost of the room rental on food and beverages for the elimination of separate room rental charges. The fashion show planners should expect to pay a deposit for the hotel services.

Food or catering fees   There are two factors to be evaluated in relationship to food service budgets. Food and beverages to be served to the audience must be a foremost concern. However, it may be necessary to provide refreshments to the crew during rehearsal, set up and/or clean up. This would be an appropriate gesture if many of the people participating in the activity are volunteers. Union rules may require serving food to union members dependent upon the amount of time involved.

While an actual contract most likely will be negotiated, at minimum the fashion show staff should expect a written estimate regarding food and catering services. Most likely a deposit or prepayment may be required.

Model fees   The expense of hiring professional models varies from one city to another. Customarily, models are paid on an hourly basis, and this fee will include their time at fittings, rehearsals, and the show. Top international models may demand very high salaries.

Each year *Women's Wear Daily*, *Vogue*, and *New York Times* report the astronomical salaries paid to supermodels. Readers are dazzled to hear that a model is paid $5 million to pose for an advertising campaign or $25,000 per day to walk the catwalk shows. While model Gisele Bündchen's agency in New York quoted her fees at $7,000 per hour (Benoit, 2000), other models may earn as little as $75 per hour.

Professional modeling rates vary by experience, gender, city, and type of modeling job. According to Esch and Walker (1996), the highest paid models at the Wilhelmina Model Agency are editorial models working the **high board**, which is where **bookers** manage the proven and most successful models' schedules and fees. Each division of the agency has a **board** from which a model is promoted, her schedule coordinated, and her fees negotiated.

Throughout the United States, the highest paying modeling jobs are in print and commercial advertising. Print models are paid an hourly or day rate, usually in the range of $150 to $300 an hour or $1,200 to $2,400 per day. Catalog work, which involves photographic modeling for direct response promotion, may consist of 10 to 30 days of work at $1,000 or more per day (Preston, 1998). This is considered "bread and butter" money, allowing models to pay the rent while pursuing bigger jobs with higher fees and more recognition. Female models have traditionally been paid much higher salaries than male models.

Modeling rates for shows are dependent upon the type of show and its location. A typical mall, department store, or charity show at a hotel or restaurant might only pay models $150 to set up the clothing in the dressing room and then modeling in the show. If a show has independently scheduled fittings, a rehearsal, and required travel, models are normally paid $75 per hour (Preston, 1998).

Designer shows have the potential to pay the highest runway rates. For name models at the top of their career, agencies negotiate the highest possible rates. Modeling fees for top models at designer shows may run as high as $6,000 to $10,000 or more.

Despite aggressively working to attract new media coverage of their runway shows, the French fashion houses were threatened by the union representing many of the modeling agencies in Paris. Citing failure to keep pace with model fees in other cities, the Syndicat des Agences de Mannequins, the French Union of Modeling Agencies, demanded an additional payment from the Paris fashion houses that posted their fashion week shows on the Internet. This increased payment request, equal to 2.5 percent of the model's fee, was based upon a 1983 French law prohibiting media outlets from showing more than three minutes of a runway show. Union president Etienne des Roys said model fees in Paris were much lower than in other cities (Benoit, 2000).

Since amateur models are often used for retail or civic shows, it may be appropriate to offer a gift, discount or a gift certificate. The discount will be included as part of the store's markdown allocation and is not considered part of the fashion show budget. Costs for any gifts or flowers presented to amateur models, however, should be considered as part of the fashion show budget.

Advertising and publicity fees   Activities relating to advertising and publicity should also be included in the budget, including all duties from designing and producing to distributing these materials. Invitations, posters, programs, and tickets need to be designed and printed; invitations need to be mailed or printed in a newspaper or magazine. If tickets are used, there is a cost of buying printed coupons or designing special personalized tickets. The costs for all of these materials must be included in the budget.

To project a consistent look and prevent duplication of the printer's set up costs, one printer can print invitations, posters, programs, and tickets. Also a printer may prefer to bid on a package rather than individual items. Printing costs are determined by the types of services required. Each service increases the cost. There is a cost involved if the size of any artwork needs to be enlarged or reduced to fit on the different size products. Basic black ink is the least expensive color to reproduce. Colored inks and the use of multiple colors are more costly. The type, weight, and color of paper will also impact the overall printing cost.

Advertising must include the cost of creative production which involves any artwork, graphic design or layout for print materials. It also involves any photography, models, filming or videotaping, or studio rental. The creation of press releases and media kits may be the responsibility of someone working for the firm producing the show or an outside press agent. Those costs of developing press releases, photographs used in the press materials, and any additional materials used to publicize the event must be incorporated into the budget.

If advertising plans include buying spots on radio or television, the cost of producing the commercial becomes a budget item. Buying space in the newspaper or magazine must also be added to budget costs.

Photography and video fees   Photography expenses will need to be considered as part of the budget. The fashion show staff will need to determine the type of photography required. The staff may wish to include a photograph rather than artwork for invitations and advertising purposes. This would require hiring a photographer and model prior to the show far enough in advance to allow time for printing.

A photographic record of the show may be desired. Expenses relating to hiring the photographer and supplies will need to be figured into the budget. Supplies might encompass such things as film, paper, processing, and equipment. Press photographers from a newspaper or magazine are sent by their employers to record the event for their medium. Since press photographers are guests and often the target for fashion show publicity, their fees are not included in the budget.

A video of the show is frequently desired and commonly recorded. The video may be a simple start-to-finish documentary of the event or an elaborately edited video production. Manufacturers regularly record their fashion shows to use as an employee training tool, teaching sales personnel about the items in the latest line, or as a promotional strategy, playing the video in the retail sales area to educate customers about the styles being offered.

Educational institutions use fashion show videos as recruiting materials to attract new students to the school where the show is produced, or as a historical record. Students involved in fashion show production classes like to view the videos produced by previous classes and use them as a guide for creating their own assignment. Students also like to keep a copy of the video as part of their portfolio.

Technical staff fees   Salaries for any people hired to perform technical aspects of the show are also part of the budget. Examples of such technical staff include the carpenters hired to build, set up and paint the stage, runway, backdrops, or props. The services of electricians who work on the lighting and public address system may be needed. Musicians, recording personnel, or disk jockeys may be hired to provide the essential mood with background music.

Support staff fees   The support staff includes all behind the scenes personnel who facilitate the smooth and professional appearance of the show. These people are typically the unsung heroes of the show. The budget must cover the expenses for the hair stylists, makeup artists, dressers, alterations and pressing people, and security. For charity shows many of these indispensable participants may be volunteers.

The need for **hosts** and **ushers**, people in charge of greeting and directing the audience to their seats, increases as the show gets larger and more complex. Members of professional or charitable organizations may serve as volunteer hosts for charity shows. Commercial events may need to hire people or use company employees to help seat the audience.

Members of the audience will be impressed with the organization presenting the show when guests are handled courteously and professionally. Hosts or ushers may act as greeters. The hosts should have a detailed list of guests for shows that require reservations and/or special seating. Hosts and ushers then direct guests to refreshments and seats. Having pre-arranged seating makes the guests feel welcome.

Gratuities are the cash tips given to service people such as waiters or waitresses and attendants in the coat check and rest rooms. Tips may be included in the cost to the hotel, restaurant, or caterer and are negotiated at the time the location and services are reserved.

Miscellaneous expenses   Any expenses not previously discussed are considered miscellaneous expenses. Decorations and transportation are among the examples. Decorations for the physical facilities may be limited to the stage and runway set up. More elaborate scenes may include floral arrangements or specialized table settings. Adornment of the room is determined by the type of show, location, audience, and budget allocation. A fashion show with a nautical theme could include miniature ships and red, white, and blue table accessories. A southwestern theme could be decorated with coyotes, cactus, conchas, and brightly colored textiles.

Ideas for ornamentation are limitless. The theme of the show can be greatly enhanced by using decorative elements. Charitable organizations may use table centerpieces as additional fund-raisers by holding a raffle for these elements. The only constraint for decorating is budgetary limitations.

Transportation costs must be considered. Clothing may have to be moved from the store or manufacturer's showroom to the location of the show. Equipment such as runways, rolling racks, steamers, and furniture may have to be moved. Transportation of celebrities from another city or within the city may also have to be considered, thus, hiring a limousine for ground transportation may be necessary.

Hospitality includes arrangements for housing, food, or entertainment for special guests. A celebrity designer may be brought to a city to meet potential customers at a retail store or for a benefit show. The designer may request the participation of his or her favorite models. Additional personnel, such as a fashion show coordinator from the designer's staff, may travel with the designer to coordinate activities with the local retail store promoting the designer's appearance. Senior executives of the retail company may arrive from other parts of the country. Hotel rooms, meals, and transit must be provided for out of town participants. Any special activities before or after the fashion show for patrons of an organization must be included in the budget.

Damaged or lost merchandise occurs even though great care is taken in preserving the condition of the garments and accessories. Sometimes items break, seams fail, or merchandise is missing after the show. Costs of replacing or reconditioning merchandise to its original shape is another item that should be planned into the budget.

The value of the merchandise may require purchasing special insurance to guarantee the product in case of theft or damage. Insurance may be needed for such high cost items as jewelry, furs or designer clothes. The cost of the insurance becomes part of the budget.

Depending upon the geographic location, it may be necessary to be taxed for various services. Taxes may be as high as ten percent in some locations, which can greatly add to the expenses of doing a fashion show.

It is a mistake to overlook planning and budgeting, and therefore, not put a lot of effort into the preliminary stages of the fashion show. Often the excitement and enthusiasm of a fashion show overshadow the details necessary to produce a successful show. One such detail that cannot be ignored is the budget. Controlling costs will add to the profit if the show is intended to make a profit. Accurately projecting ticket sales will enable fashion show planners to set realistic expectations for spending money on such things as site and model fees, hospitality and staging expenses. In evaluating the success of a show, fashion directors and retail executives will always want to know if the show was within the budgetary estimates set prior to the show. If the show comes within budget the executives are more likely to look favorably on this type of promotion and be responsive to future fashion show productions. The more planning that goes into the show the more confidence the show director and fashion show staff will have when it comes time to present the fashions. Planning will not prevent all problems associated with fashion show production, but it will help to eliminate many concerns.

Key fashion show terms

board	gratuities	promotion coordinator
booker	guaranteed audience	responsibility sheet
budget	high board	show producer
commentary coordinator	host	special events director
created audience	knockoff	stage manager

design piracy	lease agreement	stylist
diary	merchandise coordinator	theme
Fashion Calendar	model coordinator	usher
fashion director	nonprofit organization	venue
fashion show director	planning	
fashion show plan	program editor	

References

Benoit, R. (2000, February 18). Paris models demand extra pay. *Women's Wear Daily*, 15.

Esch, N. & Walker, C.L. (1996). *The Wilhelmina guide to modeling.* New York: Fireside.

Ginsberg, M. (2001, March 23). The styling life. *W.* Retrieved June 27, 2001 from http://www.style.com/peopleparties/events/2001RCW/OSCAR/day3.html

Nolan, S. (2000, September 14). Logistics for 'fashion week' no small feat. *Fashion Wire Daily*. Retrieved September 14, 2000 from http://cnn.com/2000/STYLE/fashion/09/14/fwd.fashion.week/index.html

Preston, K. (1998). *Modelmania: The working model's manual.* Marina Del Ray, CA: Dog Gone Books.

Review. (n.d.). *Victoria's Secret Cannes 2000 Lingerie Show.* Message posted to http://www.indexo/pionexnet.co.uk/webbuk2/vs/vs.htm

Widdows, L., & McGuiness, J. (1997). *Catwalking: Working with models.* London: B.T. Batsford.

Wilson, E., McCants, L., Fung, S., & Kletter, M. (2000, August 24). Selling the shows: Would a new owner spoil a good thing? *Women's Wear Daily*, 1, 6-7.

Znaimer, M. (Executive Producer). (2002, December 7). *Fashion Television* [Television broadcast]. Toronto, Canada: Citytv.

THE MESSAGE

What do the following examples have in common?

- A designer whose career hangs in limbo requests a meeting with a journalist in the hope of receiving more "personal" attention.
- A press agent for a French house invites reporters to preview its collection, so the designer can explain his ideas; a few days later the reviews are full of those very ideas.
- In Milan, a publicist reacts to a bad review by scolding the writer for not attending a preview where she would have "understood" the designer's finer points.

All these, according to *New York Times* Fashion Editor Cathy Horyn, "are nothing more than attempts to spin a story-something political columnists and Hollywood reporters face every day, but with a difference: fashion spin doctors are better dressed and can pronounce "chic" without sounding like Farmer Brown going out to inspect the henhouse" (2000, p. 1).

Horyn continues that the need for spin control in the world of haute couture fashion shows is becoming greater because designers are reaching for wild ideas. The shows themselves are becoming forms of theater, and the houses are seeing unlimited potential for exploiting brands through new media (2000). Successful designers and sharp-eyed publicists know that catchy phrases are being passed out along with the facts. But they also know that well-placed words have the potential to become the dominant sound bite of the shows.

According to Horyn (2000), the practice of inviting a few senior writers to review the collections a few days before the show is not a new practice. It largely serves magazine editors who want a heads-up so they can plan photography sessions. It also serves the promotional interests of a fashion house, which can use the informality of a preview to get across obscure or controversial themes. And, to a lesser extent, "previews are also an undisguised attempt by a house to establish 'a more personal contact' with a journalist, especially one who has been critical. Think of it as an attempt to diffuse a bomb" (Horyn, 2000, p. 3).

This chapter, The Message, will discuss publicity and advertising among other promotion strategies. The message involves communication between the sponsoring organization, the media, and readers or viewers of the media in order to publicize a fashion show. The chapter begins with a general discussion about promotion and the responsibilities of a promotion coordinator. Then we will narrow our focus and talk about publicity and the role of public relations in promoting a fashion show. Spin, as Horyn refers to it, is one aspect of publicity. Next, we leave the editorial component of promotion and turn our attention to advertising. In the final two sections of this chapter we will concentrate on direct marketing strategies that have particular value to fashion show promotion. The chapter concludes with a few words about sponsorship.

Historically, the media has been a channel to pass the fashion message from the sponsoring organization to the public. In the 21st century, as public interest in fashion accelerates, increased media coverage is a contributing factor to the popularity of fashion. Previously, we have discussed the haute couture shows and the ready-to-wear shows including 7th on Sixth. These shows are extravagant promotion tools used to get the media, and other people, excited about the fashion messages of the new season. Consumer shows also depend on publicity and advertising efforts to assure an audience for their production. Without pre-show publicity and advertising to create excitement about the show, the 7th on Sixth audience shown in Figure 4.1 would be nonexistent.

Promotion

In Chapter 1, promotion was defined as a comprehensive term used to describe all of the communication activities initiated by the seller to inform, persuade, and remind the consumer about products, services, and/or ideas offered for sale. Common promotion activities involve fashion shows, personal selling, visual merchandising, special events, public relations, publicity, advertising, and direct marketing. Promotion may be **institutional**, enhancing store image, or **promotional**, selling specific products.

Personal selling is the direct interaction between the customer and the seller with the purpose of making a sale. It is one of the most successful forms of sales promotion. It enables the salesperson to promote the characteristics of the product and overcome any objections by the customer. Some customers see this personal attention as validating their selection of a product. **Visual merchandising** is the physical presentation of products in a nonpersonal approach. This may include window, interior, or remote displays.

Special events are planned activities intended to cause individuals or groups to gather at a specific time and place because of a shared interest (Swanson & Everett, 2000). The range of these activities is vast, from large-scale storewide celebrations, to singular product promotions in one department. Store image is differentiated through execution of special events. It

Figure 4.1 Publicity and advertising are necessary promotion tools to attract an audience to a fashion show. *Courtesy, Fairchild Publications, Inc. Photo: Angeli Photo News Agency.*

is becoming more important as a device to draw customers into the store during off peak selling seasons. Fashion shows may be a part of a special event.

Public relations (PR) is the interrelationship between service providers and the public as it relates to the image of the organization through all levels of communication. PR as it is also known, may analyze public opinion and create programs to improve relationships with the public. **Publicity** is non-paid, un-sponsored information delivered at the discretion of the media, whereas **advertising** is information paid for and controlled by the sponsoring organization.

Direct marketing is the marketing process by which organizations communicate directly with target customers to generate a response or a transaction (Swanson & Everett, 2000). The strength of this strategy is the direct communication used to attract a fashion show audience or sell fashion merchandise from a fashion show.

Sponsorship involves supporters who lend their name to an event and/or underwrite production costs of the event. Sponsorship is gaining importance in the fashion world and should be considered when planning a fashion show.

All fashion shows, regardless of the kind or size, require promotion to create interest in the show and attract an audience. But who is responsible for the promotion of a fashion show?

While ultimately the success of promotion lies with the show director, specific responsibility is often delegated to a promotion coordinator, introduced in Chapter 3.

Promotion coordinator

The promotion coordinator is responsible for the creation and distribution of all promotion materials associated with the show. Understanding communication in all forms-oral, visual, and written-is key to the success of a promotion coordinator. This person must have good interpersonal communication skills to interact with individuals and groups. Creative abilities to see and understand the visual elements of advertising and photography are an asset to a promotion coordinator. Finally, the promotion coordinator must be an excellent writer, both in developing his or her own pieces and in editing pieces from a committee or staff member. The promotion coordinator will also perform public relations activities. At times this person may be a spokesperson for the fashion show, the retailers, or the sponsoring organizations projecting a professional image to the media and various publics.

The promotion coordinator will oversee the creation and distribution of press releases, press photographs, media kits, television commercials, radio spots, direct marketing pieces, and other forms of promotion. Each of these tools will be discussed in detail later in the chapter. The coordinator is knowledgeable about publicity and advertising and is willing to ask questions of the media representatives. He or she should understand the nuances of promotion and select the most appropriate types of promotion for the intended fashion show rather than the least expensive or easiest method of production.

One of the first tools a promotion coordinator should generate is a media list. A **media list** is a list of all media outlets (local, regional, national, or international) that might be used to publicize the fashion show. All contact information should be provided on the media list: name of media outlet, contact person(s) and titles, mailing address, phone number, fax number, and e-mail address or Web site if appropriate. The forms of promotion most often used for consumer shows are advertising and publicity. In the next section we will discuss publicity and the tools used in producing publicity materials. As you read each section, use the media outlet examples to develop your own media list.

If the sponsoring organization is a nonprofit association, the promotion coordinator should consider using **Public Service Announcements** (PSAs) as a part of the promotion plan. PSAs are print or broadcast spots that run free-of-charge to charitable organizations (Swanson & Everett, 2000). Advertising and the other promotion tools discussed in the next sections have expenses attached to them. The only expense associated with a PSA is staff time to write and deliver the PSA to the media. The promotion coordinator should set as a priority the distribution of PSAs to all outlets on the media list.

Publicity

Publicity is non-paid, un-sponsored information initiated by the party seeking to tell others about the event, and delivered to the public at the discretion of the media. The sponsoring organization informs the media of the event through publicity materials; the media in turn informs the public of the event through print or broadcast outlets.

An article in a publication expressing the opinion of its editors or publishers is considered editorial. Publicity is considered **editorial content** because the media, not the paid sponsor, determines whether the piece will run. Paid announcements are considered **advertising content**. Readers or viewers of the media consider editorial content, representing the opinion of the media, to be more objective than advertising content. Fashion businesses achieve success in promotional efforts by balancing editorial content and advertising content. Businesses show support for the media outlet by purchasing advertising; in return, the media shows support for the fashion business by running publicity pieces.

Publicity is run at the pleasure of the editor of a print publication, or the news director of a broadcast show. Editors and news directors read many press releases every day and determine which, if any, will run in print or be broadcast on air. Therefore, the information must be presented to the media in a newsworthy manner so that the editor or news director will see the news value of the event and pass it on to the readers or viewers.

Publicists are the individuals hired to publicize a client or client's product in the media. They may work for a private business or public relations firm, or they may sell their services as a freelance consultant. According to Marin (2001), three types of publicists exist in the industry: personal publicists, spinmeisters, and event publicists. Personal publicists are gatekeepers to the stars. A spinmeister is a well-connected strategist who specializes in damage control. Event publicists promote events, encourage celebrity attendance, and identify corporate sponsors. The popularity of fashion worn by celebrities has thrust fashion shows into the event arena and corporate sponsorship, and celebrity audiences are now part of the promotion plan.

Publicity is released to the media through press releases, press photographs, and media kits. Common outlets for sending publicity include local print publications such as newspapers and magazines, TV stations, and radio stations. For national or international coverage, publicity may be sent to national print publications, national broadcast networks, and wire services. Newspaper options include daily or Sunday editions; living, style, or fashion sections within the daily or Sunday editions; and community weekly editions. At the national level, trade publications such as *Women's Wear Daily* cover fashion shows. Magazine coverage may include regional publications or national and international publications. Broadcast outlets include local or regional network affiliates, cable channels, and local radio stations. Additionally, in some communities, the Internet may be an outlet to share fashion show information. At the local level, many local newspapers are publishing an online version of the printed newspaper. At the national and international level, many of the fashion sites we discuss in this text may be outlets for fashion show coverage.

The promotion coordinator must be careful in his or her choice of communication channels. While 7th on Sixth is a large enough fashion show event to get coverage on *Good Morning America*, most local events should focus on local media. To get the message across, the channel must be one that the target audiences will receive and believe (Newsom & Carrell, 2000). Mass media such as newspapers, radio, and television are the best mediums for fashion show coverage. Magazines are also excellent channels for fashion show coverage, but they require a longer lead-time for publication than is available to many fashion show planners.

People are also channels for communicating messages. Person-to-person meetings or person-to-group interactions are very good channels to promote fashion shows, particularly within a local community or on a university campus. In addition to face-to-face communication, e-mail can be effective in delivering personal communication. And finally, another communication channel is direct marketing such as flyers, personal invitations, or other promotional pieces to get the fashion message across to the public.

Press releases

A **press release** is an article on a newsworthy event sent to editors or news directors for publication or broadcast in the media. The information includes all the details about the event, and is written to gain the attention of an editor or the news director. If the editor or news director finds the event interesting they will then run the narrative in their media.

To gain the editor's or news director's interest, the press release should not be long winded-usually limited to one or two pages. Longer press releases become redundant and lose the attention of the reader. Press releases should be hand-delivered, mailed first class, or e-mailed if the media outlet approves of this delivery method.

Press releases are not specific to fashion show publicity. Variations of style may occur, but they follow a general format and are used by any organization or individual wishing to publicize an event.

Guidelines for press releases Figure 4.2 illustrates some of the elements of a press release. When writing a press release the following guidelines should be used. A press release should be typed and submitted on 8 1/2″ × 11″, white or light colored paper using only one side of the page. The copy should be double-spaced with left and right margins at least one inch, and top and bottom margins at least two inches. Margins are wide to allow for editing or revisions from the editor. The actual copy of the release should start approximately halfway down the page. **Copy** is the actual material to be printed in the media, excluding headings and other material such as the *release date* or *special to* information used only by the editor. Paragraph openings should be indented five spaces with an extra line added to the double spacing between paragraphs. If the press release is more than one page, all the pages after the first page should be numbered in the upper right-hand corner and include a two- or three-word heading, repeating important words from the headline, in the upper left-hand corner. The word "more" should be used at the bottom of any page where copy is continued. Never break a paragraph from one page to another. At the conclusion of the press release the symbol #### appears in the center at the bottom of the page.

The press release should include the company name and address typed in the upper left-hand corner, followed by the contact person and phone number and/or e-mail address. If letterhead stationery is used, the company name and address can be omitted. The contact person may be the show director or the publicity chair, whomever wrote the press release. An individual should not be listed as the contact person unless he or she is informed about the event. A common error is to list organization presidents who are so far removed from the actual workings of the event that they can provide little information to a caller. A release date should be included to inform the editor when the release should run in the media. Editors prefer an actual date to the commonly used statement "for immediate release."

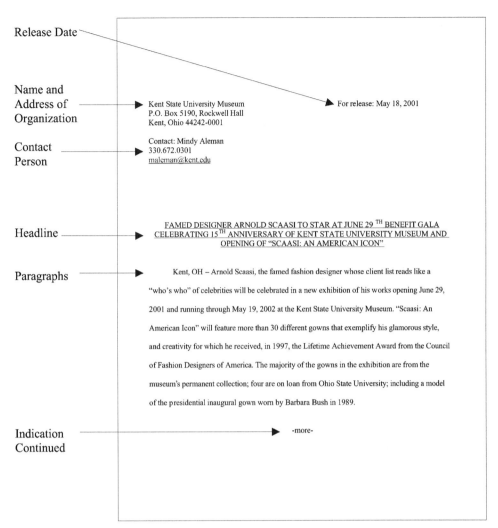

Release Date

Name and
Address of
Organization

Contact
Person

Headline

Paragraphs

Indication
Continued

Kent State University Museum
P.O. Box 5190, Rockwell Hall
Kent, Ohio 44242-0001

Contact: Mindy Aleman
330.672.0301
maleman@kent.edu

For release: May 18, 2001

FAMED DESIGNER ARNOLD SCAASI TO STAR AT JUNE 29 TH BENEFIT GALA
CELEBRATING 15 TH ANNIVERSARY OF KENT STATE UNIVERSITY MUSEUM AND
OPENING OF "SCAASI: AN AMERICAN ICON"

Kent, OH – Arnold Scaasi, the famed fashion designer whose client list reads like a
"who's who" of celebrities will be celebrated in a new exhibition of his works opening June 29,
2001 and running through May 19, 2002 at the Kent State University Museum. "Scaasi: An
American Icon" will feature more than 30 different gowns that exemplify his glamorous style,
and creativity for which he received, in 1997, the Lifetime Achievement Award from the Council
of Fashion Designers of America. The majority of the gowns in the exhibition are from the
museum's permanent collection; four are on loan from Ohio State University; including a model
of the presidential inaugural gown worn by Barbara Bush in 1989.

-more-

Adapted from: Kent State University Museum: Press Releases. (2001). Available:

http://dept.kent.edu/museum/pr/press.html

Figure 4.2 Elements of a press release. *Courtesy, Kent State University. Used with permission.*

The headline, lead, and amplification should also be included in the press release. The **headline** should be typed, centered, all in upper case letters and underlined, placed approximately one third down the page. The headline should be the title of the release including the news value of the story, using an action verb. It is not necessarily the title the publisher will use for the story.

The **lead** is the most important part of the press release. It is one or two sentences that summarize the news including who, what, where, when, and why of the event.

The **amplification** follows the lead and provides additional information and facts about the event. Amplification may be one or several paragraphs always written in diminishing order of importance. If there is limited space available to an editor, he or she may chose to omit some of the copy at the end of the press release. It is imperative to list the most important information first.

Press releases should be written objectively, not subjectively, from a third person point of view. Do not use *I*, *we*, or *you* when writing the release. The writer should not show biased interest in the event by using opinionated words when describing the event. Fill the press release with facts not opinions. It is important to follow the correct format so the press release will not be discarded before the content is read.

The distribution of press releases should be looked at as a strategy, not a mass distribution. Each medium should be considered separately and contacted in the most appropriate manner for that medium: mailed, delivered in person, delivered on disk, or in some instances sent by e-mail.

Some news people sign up for e-mail-delivered new releases (Newsom & Carrell, 2000). In a local or regional setting, it is necessary to find out how each targeted medium prefers to receive releases. Even within a specific outlet, each individual may have a preference.

During the development of a media list, media outlets should be contacted to verify information. This is a good time to get specifics about how the information should be sent. If the information can be sent by disk, verify that the computer formats are compatible. If the news outlet allows the press release to be sent by e-mail, send an e-mail message about the story tailored specifically to the recipient's interest in the story, with the press release itself as an attachment. Again, be sure e-mail software and attachment capabilities are compatible. Keep the file size of a press release small and put art or graphics in separate attachments to avoid slow downloading of the article or artwork.

Press photographs

Press photographs are photographs prepared specifically for use in print media to accompany press releases or to be included in a media kit. Photos are selected to emphasize a specific fashion, look, or person. Each photograph should communicate a message about the fashion or the trend and enhance the written communication of the press release. Avoid photographs that have busy backgrounds or those that do not convey a specific message about the intended subject.

Although press releases are prepared and sent to more than one publication, press photographs are exclusive to each publication. Therefore, the same photograph should not be sent to more than one publication. Just as press releases are prepared using a standard format, so are press photographs.

Guidelines for press photographs   Press photographs are a standard size of either 8″ × 10″ or 5″ × 7″. The acceptable size for portraits is 4″ × 5″. While black and white photographs are preferred, color photographs are becoming more widely accepted. If color photographs are available, inform the publication and ask if color shots are acceptable before submitting the photography. Today, more digital photography is being used, however no clear guidelines on submitting digital photographs have been established. Inform the publication that digital photography is available before submitting the work, and be sure that formats for data transfer are compatible and the resolution is of high quality to assure good reproduction.

Handle photographs carefully to avoid fingerprints on the image. When writing on the back of a photo, only use felt-tip pens with a very light touch to avoid pressure marks showing through to the front of the image. Photos can easily get separated from press releases or media kits, therefore, the image should be identified with the same contact information as the press release (company name, contact person name, address, phone number, fax number, and/or e-mail address).

Additionally, each photo should have a **caption** that describes and explains the picture to the audience. The caption should be typed and no longer than five or six sentences. Captions should be written using the same grammatical format as the press release. Although captions are offered, a publication may write its own caption for the photograph. Captions should be attached to the bottom of the backside of the photograph. Use rubber cement to adhere the caption so it can be removed if necessary.

Photographs that emphasize people should have names of all individuals listed in the caption. People should be identified from left to right with full name, title, and firm affiliation. A model release should be obtained for all models or individuals in photographs. All syndicated or stock photographs must be credited with the photographer's name. Other photographers may be credited as required by the publication. A common fashion show photograph may show a model in apparel by a featured designer or retailer. In this instance, the caption may or may not include the name of the model. If the model's name adds to the newsworthiness of the photograph then include it.

Fashion photographers (Fig. 4.3) come from many sources. A staff or committee member may have skills in photography and can take the necessary shots. Freelance photographers are also available on a fee basis to shoot press photographs and other necessary photography. Some publications may offer a staff photographer to take fashion show pictures, based on the newsworthiness of the fashion show event.

The press release and photographs should be sent to the media for publication as close to the event date as possible. The publicity writer should give plenty of time to the editor to review the materials. They should be delivered at least two weeks before the event is staged. Successful publicity is often delivered to the editor a full month before the event is held.

Media kits

If the proposed fashion show is a large event in which many media outlets are going to be invited, the use of a media kit may be a better promotion solution, compared to press releases and press photographs alone. A **media kit** (Fig. 4.4) is a collection of materials delivered or mailed to the press in a colorful folder with pockets. The folder or envelope is usually graphically illustrated to present the theme of the event and reinforce the importance of the event to the editor or director.

Media kit is a term of the 21st century replacing the term press kit. A press kit implies the materials included are only for newspapers or the press. Media kit is a more inclusive term that suggests the prepared materials are appropriate for any media (Newsom & Carrell, 2000). Keep in mind the media kit should be prepared for an intended media outlet. A media kit prepared for a broadcast media outlet should not include press photographs. A media kit that is prepared for a newspaper should not include video and sound on a CD.

Figure 4.3 Press photographers waiting to shoot at a haute couture show. *Courtesy, Fairchild Publications, Inc.*

Media kits developed for fashion shows may include a combination of any of the following elements: facts sheets, program of events, list of participants, biographical information, a page of isolated facts, a straight news story, a feature story, and press photographs. A cover letter telling the media why the event deserves attention in the medium should be included with the media kit.

The media kit may include two fact sheets. A **basic fact sheet** offers details about the fashion show and explains its significance in a factual manner. This fact sheet should include contact phone number and address because it may become separated from the rest of the kit, as well as the date and time of the show, the participants, and sponsoring retailers or organizations. An additional **historical fact sheet** may also be included. This fact sheet tells when the show was first held, where, who attended and their significance, milestones in the events history, and other historical facts about the show. When discussing historical facts, always make clear the significance of each fact (Newsom & Carrell, 2000). For universities or organizations that host annual fashion shows, the historical facts sheet may be particularly valuable.

A **program of events**, sometimes called a schedule of activities, is a detailed description of the time data of the show. Broadcast media frequently rely on this information and may also want to have a script if one is available. A complete **list of participants** highlighting their contributions to the event and their relationship to the organization may be part of the media kit. Supplemental to the participation list is **biographical information** of the principals, including headshots if available. Refer to press photographs for proper formatting of photog-

Figure 4.4 Left: Media Kit announcing the *Ebony* Fashion Fair. Below: The caption for a press photo uses the same basic information and format as the press release.

```
KARL LAGERFELD
144 AVENUE DES CHAMPS ELYSEES
75008 - PARIS
TEL. : 43.59.57.50

PRINTEMPS - ETE 1991

VESTE LEGEREMENT CINTREE EN NATTE DE
COTON MARINE A DOUBLE COLSUR BLOUSE
COMBINAISON ET COLLANT CORSAIRE.

NAVY BLUE COTION BASKETWEAVE FITTED
JACKET, DOUBLE COLLAR OVER TUNIC AN
CAPRI LEGGINGS.

COIFFURE : GERALD POUR ALEXANDRE DE PARIS
MAQUILLAGE : PIERRE MARIE HUMEAU

MENTION OBLIGATOIRE : KARL LAGERFELD
OBLIGATORY MENTION : KARL LAGERFELD

EKTA SUR DEMANDE
EKTA ON REQUEST

PHOTOGRAPHE : KARL LAGERFELD
```

raphy. A **page of isolated facts** about the current fashion show and past fashion shows if the show is an annual event, should be included. These facts are often picked up by broadcasters to use if they broadcast the event and may be included in print copy if a reporter covers the fashion show.

Two news stories should be included-a straight news story and a feature story. A straight **news story** gives basic information about the fashion show in an announcement news approach. For print media, this story should be approximately a page and a half, double-spaced on a 60-space line. For broadcast media, the article should be one or two short paragraphs triple-spaced (Newsom & Carrell, 2000). If presenting the information to a broadcast outlet, include the print story also, so that more information can be gained about the fashion show. A longer general news story that ties the background information may be as long as three double-spaces pages for print media and one full page for broadcast media. A **feature story** is a an article that provides insight to the event. It may focus on one particularly interesting aspect of the show. Two stories can be included if appropriate. This story is written only in the format for print media (as long as three double-spaced pages) but may be included in the broadcast media kit.

Press photographs should be included but are often difficult to develop if the fashion show is a first-time event. Only use photographs of people if the individuals can be identified. If photographs from past events are included, they should be labeled as such to not mislead the audience. Also, any photographs included in advertising copy should not be used in publicity. Follow labeling procedures for all press photographs.

If you are considering including more than text materials in the media kit, you might develop a CD-ROM. However, you should first assess how many of your targeted media are likely to use this technology. Additionally, it is important to determine the platform that the media outlets use, PC-compatible or Macintosh-compatible computer systems. Some sophisticated systems allow cross-platform CD-ROMs that will run on either system (Newsom & Carrell, 2000).

It is important to match the publicity with the event. If the show is large with great fashion influence, publicity should be preplanned to reach national magazines and online channels among other media. If the show is smaller in nature, organizers should take advantage of local media opportunities, creating a newsworthy event for a local audience.

In this section we have discussed publicity as editorial content in a publication or broadcast. In the next section we turn to advertising content. As a promotion coordinator, committee member, or staff member, it is important to understand the difference between editorial and advertising content. When working with media professionals, requests for publicity and advertising should be clearly defined.

Advertising

Advertising is information paid for and controlled by the sponsoring organization notifying the public about an event. Advertising should supplement publicity. As long as standards are acceptable for publication or broadcast, advertisements or commercials run as submitted by the sponsoring organization.

To use advertising for a fashion show, sponsors will buy space in print media, buy time in broadcast media, or buy space on online media. Advertising can be purchased in newspapers and magazines, broadcast on network television, cable television, and radio, or purchased on online publications such as a banner ad. Banner advertising has only proven successful for fashion shows in limited situations. Victoria's Secret was successful in using banner advertising on the online version of the *Wall Street Journal* to publicize an online fashion show.

The cost of advertising is based on specific rates of a publication or network. Rates for advertising units are published for all media on **rate cards**. The costs are based on specific rates of time, frequency of the advertisement or commercial, and special requirements of the publisher or network. Rate cards are available to the public by calling or writing to the media outlet. Many media outlets post their rate cards on the Internet.

Newspapers

The most common form of advertising for a retail or consumer-oriented fashion show is through newspapers. Newspapers reach a local audience efficiently and are more cost effective than magazine or television advertising. Advertising in newspapers is commonly sold by **standard advertising unit** (SAU). An SAU is 2 1/16″ × 1″. Ad prices are based on 1 SAU. The basic rate of a newspaper advertisement allows the advertiser to run an ad at a **run-of-position** (R.O.P) rate. This means the newspaper can choose to run the advertisement on any page in any position within the paper. If the advertising budget is large enough, it may be beneficial to pay a slightly higher rate called a **preferred position** and specify the page or position where the advertisement will be placed within the paper.

The *St. Petersburg Times*, Tampa Bay's largest newspaper, provides comprehensive daily coverage of Florida's west coast. The newspaper has a circulation of 335,167 copies Monday-Thursday, 360,473 on Friday and Saturday, and 434,604 copies on Sunday. Readership during the week (Monday-Thursday) is 700,500; Friday and Saturday readership is 753,400; on Sunday the newspaper has a readership of 899,600. This newspaper is typical of many national and regional newspapers with readership growing throughout the week and peaking on Sunday.

The *St. Petersburg Times* provides a good example of a rate card (Fig. 4.5). Payment terms are listed at the top of the page. All rates are net cash unless prior arrangements for credit have been made. Advertisers are invoiced monthly. Businesses may advertise over a 12-month contract period or on a non-contract basis (*St. Petersburg Times* Advertising Rates, n.d.). If a local retailer is sponsoring a fashion show, the newspaper advertising may be part of an annual contract. If the fashion show is being sponsored by an organization, the non-contract rate may be a better option.

The *St. Petersburg Times* offers advertisers full-run or zoned editions. **Full-run** means advertising will run in all editions of the newspaper. **Zoned editions** means advertising can be selectively run in only one or a few geographically selected editions. Looking at the full run table in Figure 4.5, an advertiser who contracts 100,000 column inches per 12-month contract, running Monday-Wednesday, will pay $81.71 per column inch as compared to an advertiser purchasing only 50 inches who will pay $106.16 per column inch for advertising. Typically, one-time events such as fashion shows will be more costly for fewer column inches. A review of the Neighborhood Times/Wednesday table in Figure 4.5 indicates that each zone has a slightly different rate. Full-run prices are higher but the trade off is a larger readership to view the ad.

The *St. Petersburg Times* offers "Taste," a weekly section that includes fashion, food, and lifestyle articles, and many newspapers have a similar weekly section. Preferred position fashion show advertising may be particularly beneficial in a section such as this.

Figure 4.5 *St. Petersburg Times* rate card. *Courtesy, St. Petersburg Times 2001 Retail Rates.*

3. *Payment Terms*

The St. Petersburg Times - Tampa Bay's Largest Newspaper

All rates are net cash with order unless credit has been approved. Where credit is extended, invoices are payable on terms stipulated. Advertisers will be invoiced on a monthly or cash basis depending on financial condition and known credit data. No prompt payment discount.

Accounts past due will be charged 18% annual interest and may incur additional expense should the use of a collection agency, attorney or both be required. Claims for errors in billing must be made within 30 days of date of invoice to be considered. Rates can be revised with 30 days written notice.

5. *Retail Rates*

5A. *Retail Advertising Rates*
12-Month Contract and Non-Contract Rates

Full-Run/Zoned Editions
Black & White ROP Per Inch Rates

Introductory Contract Rates
The introductory program allows new advertisers to run four ROP advertisements within four consecutive weeks at the discounted introductory rate. Contracts must be signed in advance.

FULL RUN				CITY & STATE		
Contract Sizes	Mon-Wed	Thurs-Sat	Sunday	Contract Sizes	Mon-Tues	Thurs Fri-Sat
100,000*	81.71	89.88	117.85	100,000*	53.85	54.91
75,000*	84.12	92.53	121.33	75,000*	54.31	55.38
50,000*	86.53	95.19	124.81	50,000*	54.77	55.84
25,000*	88.94	97.83	128.29	25,000*	55.23	56.31
10,000*	91.35	100.49	131.76	10,000*	55.68	56.78
5,000*	93.76	103.14	135.25	5,000*	56.15	57.24
2,500*	96.17	105.79	138.72	2,500*	56.59	57.71
1,000*	98.58	108.44	142.19	1,000*	57.05	58.71
500*	100.99	11.09	145.67	500*	57.51	58.65
200*	101.44	11.58	146.31	200*	57.97	59.11
100*	103.80	114.17	149.71	100*	58.43	59.58
50*	106.16	116.78	153.11	50*	61.11	62.31
Intro	116.77	128.46	168.43	Intro	67.32	68.64
Open	158.70	174.57	228.90	Open	96.13	98.01

*Full Run Rates apply when Regional Buy exceeds full run rate

NEIGHBORHOOD TIMES/WEDNESDAY					
Contract Sizes	Northeast	St. Pete	Beaches	Northwest	Seminole
100,000*	12.80	13.20	10.13	10.83	8.96
75,000*	12.91	13.31	10.21	10.93	9.04
50,000*	13.02	13.43	10.30	11.01	9.11
25,000*	13.12	13.54	10.38	11.11	9.19
10,000*	13.23	13.64	10.47	11.19	9.26
5,000*	13.34	13.75	10.55	11.29	9.34
2,500*	13.45	13.87	10.64	11.39	9.41
1,000*	13.56	13.98	10.72	11.47	9.49
500*	13.67	14.09	10.82	11.57	9.57
200*	13.78	14.21	10.91	11.65	9.64
100*	13.89	14.32	10.99	11.75	9.72
50*	14.53	14.98	11.49	12.30	10.16
Intro	16.00	16.49	14.05	13.53	11.20
Open	22.84	23.56	20.06	19.33	15.99

NEIGHBORHOOD TIMES/SUNDAY					
Contract Sizes	Northeast	St. Pete	Beaches	Northwest	Seminole
100,000*	17.63	17.82	12.44	13.71	11.13
75,000*	17.78	17.97	12.55	13.82	11.22
50,000*	17.93	18.12	12.65	13.94	11.32
25,000*	18.08	18.28	12.77	14.05	11.41
10,000*	18.23	18.43	12.86	14.18	11.51
5,000*	18.38	18.58	12.98	14.29	11.61
2,500*	18.53	18.73	13.08	14.41	11.70
1,000*	18.68	18.88	13.19	14.52	11.80
500*	18.84	19.04	13.29	14.63	11.89
200*	18.99	19.19	13.40	14.76	11.99
100*	19.14	19.33	13.50	14.87	12.07
50*	20.02	20.23	14.12	15.56	12.63
Intro	22.04	22.28	16.96	17.13	13.91
Open	31.48	31.80	24.22	24.47	19.87

TASTE/WEDNESDAY				
Contract Sizes	Southern Pinellas	Northern Pinellas	North Suncoast	Tampa
100,000*	35.00	26.35	20.86	6.17
75,000*	35.30	26.57	21.03	6.22
50,000*	35.60	26.80	21.19	6.28
25,000*	35.90	27.03	21.36	6.33
10,000*	36.19	27.25	21.53	6.37
5,000*	36.50	27.47	21.70	6.43
2,500*	36.79	27.69	21.86	6.48
1,000*	37.08	27.92	22.04	6.53
500*	37.38	28.15	22.19	6.59
200*	37.68	28.37	22.37	6.64
100*	37.98	28.59	22.70	6.69
50*	39.72	29.91	24.00	7.00
Intro	43.76	32.94	24.65	7.72
Open	62.48	47.04	37.15	11.01

LARGO TIMES			
Contract Sizes	Mon-Wed	Thurs-Sat	Sunday
100,000*	12.81	13.29	16.86
75,000*	12.92	13.40	17.01
50,000*	13.03	13.52	17.14
25,000*	13.13	13.63	17.29
10,000*	13.25	13.74	17.43
5,000*	13.36	13.86	17.58
2,500*	13.47	13.97	17.72
1,000*	13.57	14.08	17.86
500*	13.68	14.20	18.01
200*	13.79	14.31	18.14
100*	13.89	14.42	18.29
50*	14.54	15.09	19.14
Intro	16.01	16.62	21.07
Open	22.87	23.73	30.09

CLEARWATER TIMES			
Contract Sizes	Mon-Wed	Thurs-Sat	Sunday
100,000*	17.96	18.50	23.51
75,000*	18.11	18.66	23.71
50,000*	18.26	18.82	23.91
25,000*	18.42	18.97	24.10
10,000*	18.57	19.14	24.31
5,000*	18.73	19.29	24.51
2,500*	18.88	19.45	24.71
1,000*	19.03	19.60	24.91
500*	19.19	19.77	25.10
200*	19.34	19.92	25.31
100*	19.49	20.08	25.51
50*	20.39	21.00	26.69
Intro	22.45	23.13	29.39
Open	32.06	33.03	41.96

Sunday circulation and ad rates will apply to the following holidays: Memorial Day, July 4, Labor Day, Thanksgiving Day, Christmas Day and New Year's Day.

For additional information please see the Advertising Rate Card shell, contact your sales representative or visit our website at www.sptimes.com/ratecards
Retail Rates - page 1

Effective 7/1/01

St. Petersburg Times 2001 Retail Rates

When reading a rate card it should be noted that prices quoted are for for-profit businesses and organizations such as retailers. Some civic or school organizations may be considered nonprofit organizations. Often publications will give nonprofit organizations a break on the cost to run advertising. However, the price breaks will not be published on the rate card. Always tell the publication if you represent a nonprofit organization. Publications often lessen the cost per column inch for advertising for nonprofits, but do not expect the advertising to run at no cost. Common arrangements may be for the nonprofit organization to buy a certain amount of inches as quoted on the rate card and the publication will match the number of inches for a reduced rate. For example, a nonprofit may buy 100 column inches and the publication gives them an additional 100 inches at a reduced cost.

Published rates are for black and white advertisements. Color rates are also available but for a higher price. Figure 4.6 shows the color rates for the *St. Petersburg Times*. When color is

3. *Color Rates*

The St. Petersburg Times -
Tampa Bay's Largest Newspaper

7A. *St. Petersburg Times and Regionals*

You can run your color ad any size you choose. Artwork charges are not included. Companion tabloid pages are charged at the single-page rate. Standard-size ROP facing pages, as well as front and back cover pages in a special section, will be charged at the double-truck rate. If your color is not available, a 10% discount will be given if you agree in advance to use the publisher's designated color.

Single-Page Units or Less

Cost per edition	Black * One	Black * Two	Black * Three
St. Petersburg Times			
Full Run Mon-Wed	$1,365	$1,596	$1,995
Full Run Thrus-Sat	$1,430	$1,672	$2,090
Full Run Sunday	$1,610	$1,869	$2,340
Largo Daily	$179	$257	$331
Largo Sunday	$199	$284	$362
Clearwater Daily	$373	$520	$662
Clearwater Sunday	$394	$567	$725
North Pinellas Daily	$152	$226	$299
North Pinellas Sunday	$163	$247	$326
Pasco SW Daily	$179	$257	$331
Pasco SW Sunday	$199	$284	$362
Pasco NW Daily	$179	$257	$331
Pasco NW Sunday	$199	$284	$362
Pasco C\E Daily	$121	$184	$242
Pasco C\E Sunday	$131	$199	$268
Hermando Daily	$152	$226	$299
Hermando Sunday	$163	$247	$326
Citrus Daily	$152	$226	$299
Citrus Sunday	$163	$247	$326
Neighborhood - St. Pete Wed	$209	$289	$357
Neighborhood - St. Pete Sunday	$231	$315	$394
Neighborhood - Northeast Wed	$209	$289	$357
Neighborhood - Northeast Sunday	$231	$315	$394
Neighborhood - Northwest Wed	$209	$289	$357
Neighborhood - Northwest Sunday	$231	$315	$394
Neighborhood - Beaches Wed	$209	$289	$357
Neighborhood - Beaches Sunday	$231	$315	$394
Neighborhood - Seminole Wed	$152	$226	$299
Neighborhood - Seminole Sunday	$163	$247	$326
North of Tampa** Daily	$278	$441	$551

For additional information please see the Advertising Rate Card shell, contact your sales representative or visit our website at www.sptimes.com/ratecards
Retail Rates - page 7

Double Trucks or Companion Pages

Cost per edition	Black * One	Black * Two	Black * Three
St. Petersburg Times			
Full Run Mon-Wed	$2,076	$2,210	$2,604
Full Run Thrus-Sat	$2,175	$2,316	$2,728
Full Run Sunday	$2,444	$2,570	$3,065
Largo Daily	$304	$420	$540
Largo Sunday	$331	$457	$593
Clearwater Daily	$520	$662	$814
Clearwater Sunday	$567	$725	$893
North Pinellas Daily	$226	$299	$373
North Pinellas Sunday	$247	$326	$405
Pasco SW Daily	$305	$420	$540
Pasco SW Sunday	$331	$457	$593
Pasco NW Daily	$305	$420	$540
Pasco NW Sunday	$331	$457	$593
Pasco C\E Daily	$184	$242	$305
Pasco C\E Sunday	$199	$268	$331
Hermando Daily	$226	$299	$373
Hermando Sunday	$247	$326	$405
Citrus Daily	$226	$299	$373
Citrus Sunday	$247	$326	$405
Neighborhood - St. Pete Wed	$331	$441	$551
Neighborhood - St. Pete Sunday	$362	$483	$604
Neighborhood - Northeast Wed	$331	$441	$551
Neighborhood - Northeast Sunday	$362	$483	$604
Neighborhood - Northwest Wed	$331	$441	$551
Neighborhood - Northwest Sunday	$362	$483	$604
Neighborhood - Beaches Wed	$331	$441	$551
Neighborhood - Beaches Sunday	$362	$483	$604
Neighborhood - Seminole Wed	$226	$299	$373
Neighborhood - Seminole Sunday	$247	$326	$405
North of Tampa** Daily	$520	$662	$814

**Total cost for both days - Friday/Sunday combination.

Color Off-setting
When scheduling double-truck or facing pages keep in mind that large areas of dense/multi-color coverage may cause set-off of color or image to the facing page during the folding process. Color usage or weight of color coverage should be a consideration when planning these types of ads.

Effective 7/1/01

St. Petersburg Times 2001 Retail Rates

Figure 4.6 *St. Petersburg Times* rate card for color advertisements. *Courtesy, St. Petersburg Times 2001 Retail Rates.*

applied to a printed page, the entire page must be run through the press. Therefore, if advertisers are willing to pay for color, they may choose any size for the ad. Color ads are sold as black + one (a black and white ad with one color), black + two, or black + three. In the *Times*, a full-run ad running Monday-Wednesday, black + one will cost an advertiser $1,365, black + two will cost the advertiser $1,596, and three colors added to black and white will cost the advertiser $1,995. As we will discuss later, these costs do not include artwork charges.

Newspaper advertisements may be created by fashion show personnel or by the newspaper advertising department. The layout costs are similar with either option. Ask the newspaper what is preferred and be ready to create the advertisement if necessary. One account executive stated her newspaper prefers whatever works best for the advertiser, and that approximately 90 percent of her clients who had the newspaper staff create the advertisements found the advertisements to be acceptable with only minor changes. An advertising designer stated that on a limited fashion show budget the newspaper should create the advertisement to save costs rather than paying a freelance designer to create the advertisement. Generally newspapers have advertisements prepared two weeks in advance of when they will be run in the newspaper.

Many newspapers have **fashion editors** whose exclusive responsibility is fashion. This is the best person to contact at a newspaper regarding fashion show advertising or publicity. The fashion editor often knows the angle from which to direct the publicity or advertising to best expose the event to the public. Small newspapers might not have a fashion editor, but frequently feature or community editors will be the best contacts.

Preparing newspaper advertisements   A newspaper advertisement is composed of copy, art, and white space (Fig. 4.7). The text within the advertisement is designated as **copy**. Illustrations or photography are **art**, and space between the copy and art is designated as **white space**.

The shape of the white space is determined by the size of the advertisement. The size of the advertisement is based on the cost of the spot. Review the dimensions of the advertisement to ensure accuracy before preparing the ad. Two points should be considered when planning an advertisement. First, white space, copy, and art should balance proportionally. Advertisements with too much white space are considered boring by the reader and advertisements with too little white space are overlooked by the reader because they are hard to read. No rules determine the balance of white space to art or copy but ultimately it should be pleasing to the reader. Secondly, consider the viewing center of an advertisement. Readers will naturally place the center of the advertisement five-eighths from the bottom. An advertisement should not be divided in equal halves top and bottom, creating a top or bottom heavy spot.

Copy may include one or several of the following components: headline, subheadline, body, slogan, or logo. **Headlines** attract the attention of the reader and create interest in the advertisement and may contain the words *fashion show* or the show theme. **Subheadlines** are used to further explain the headline. They may inform the reader of the intended audience or promote the sponsoring retailer. **Body** includes the important details needed in the advertisement, such as the day, date, time, location, and price of the fashion show. The body pants (in that order) on one rack. Are they telling us something? You bet. This is the way this younger customer shops.

Banana Republic certainly is no newcomer to suit separates, or dressing up for that matter. A few summers ago I marveled at the store's Italian linen suit separates, so I wasn't surprised last week to find an elegant, two-button, dark-gray flannel jacket ($298) and nearby, the matching plain-front pants ($118). Same S-M-L sizing, but unfortunately, that was the only suit hanging.

There were, however, knockout cotton/Lycra dress shirts ($58) in checks,

they were only $39 per and, even in euros, a great buy to take home. They did.

When I returned to the office, I called a few retailers. "They're eating your dinner!" I said. "They're stealing your customer right from your nose!"

But they put me in my place.

Jim Giddon at Rothmans, New York, which sells to a pretty hip gang of young guys, said: "They're just training them to come to us." And then Kent Gushner in Philly added, "They're not our customer ... today."

Good point. Just give the 34th Street shoppers a few years—and a few raises. ■

should further stimulate the reader to want to attend the event. The **slogan** is usually a catchy phrase which is appealing when spoken or viewed in print. The theme of the fashion show may be used as a slogan. The slogan should be easily remembered by the reader. If the fashion show is produced in cooperation with a retailer or organization the company **logo**, a copyright protected symbol or phrase, may be incorporated in the advertisement. Repeating a logo in an advertisement creates immediate identification to the reader and increases interest in the event.

Line drawings, photographs, and halftones are considered artwork in the advertisement. A **line drawing** is created by pen, pencil, brush or crayon, as illustration for a printed advertisement. **Photography** is the reproduction of prints created by a camera. **Halftones** are reproduced photographs or drawings using screens to convert the design into a series of dots, making shaded values possible. Artwork must effectively create a visual message promoting the fashion show and attracting the reader's attention. The reader should first be aware of the artwork; the copy should serve to complement the artwork.

Reproduction quality is best achieved in newspapers by using line drawings. Line drawings consist of only lines to create shapes and shading. Halftones rely on tones of

Figure 4.7 This newspaper advertisement appeared in *DNR*.

watercolor such as crayon, chalk, or pencil to create the illustration. Halftones reproduce better than photographs but require skill beyond the amateur level to achieve the desired effect. If photography is used, follow the guidelines for press photography stated previously in this chapter. Examine your local newspaper to determine what is used most frequently for publication.

Clip art, prefabricated illustrations, generated on a computer or purchased in clip art books, is popular when creating advertising artwork. Time and expense are reduced by finalizing the artwork in the correct size from the computer before delivering it to the newspaper. Many local businesses have computers for the general public to use. Check with local copy centers and computer stores for information.

Copy, art, and white space must be arranged within the boundaries of the advertisement layout. Rough sketches of a layout are presented to the advertising representative of the newspaper. The representative will in turn have the art department of the newspaper reproduce the rough draft. The reproduction is called a **paste-up** and returned to the sponsor for review before final production is run. When both the sponsor and the newspaper have approved the advertisement, the newspaper will put the spot into production. Upon final production the newspaper will deliver a tear sheet to the sponsor. The **tear sheet** is the advertisement, torn directly from the newspaper, to show proof of publication to the advertiser. The tear sheet should be saved and included with other items submitted for evaluation after the show.

Depending on the type of fashion show and newspaper it may be advantageous to buy space in the classified section. These sections are often less expensive than other advertising and may have a large readership. If the target audience includes a college age group, classified sections of school newspapers are a good choice for advertising.

Magazines

W, Women's Wear Daily The Magazine (Fig. 4.8), *Vogue*, *InStyle*, and *Elle* are just a few of the national and international magazines that cover haute couture and ready-to-wear fashion shows. Publications such as *Women's Wear Daily* and *Vogue* have premiere positions at the end of the runway for fashion show photography. Magazines, as compared to newspapers, have excellent reproduction qualities that make fashion photography pop off the page. The excellent reproduction quality also makes this medium more expensive to produce than newspapers.

Magazine advertising is generally used to reach a national or international market. Very little advertising for fashion shows appears in national magazines except advertising for magazine tie-in shows as discussed in Chapter 2. Advertising in magazines for fashion shows may be achieved in city or state magazines that inform a local audience about happenings.

While fashion trends, looks, and themes present well in magazines, the lead time necessary to get specific events published inhibits the widespread use of this medium for fashion show promotion. Magazines are usually published monthly, so advertising or press releases must be delivered six weeks to two months or longer before the publication date. This is termed the **closing date**, the date when all ad copy must be received by the maga-

Figure 4.8 *WWD The Magazine* devotes much of each edition to fashion show coverage. *Courtesy, Fairchild Publications, Inc.*

zine for inclusion in the next issue. If magazine advertising is part of the promotion plan, it should be coordinated earlier than other media advertising to allow adequate lead-time for publication.

Magazines sell space by the page or portion of a page, and similar to newspaper advertising, rates are published on rate cards. *Glamour* magazine sells advertising space in the following page portions: 1 page, 2/3 page, 1/2 page, 1/3 page, or 1/6 page. A one-page advertisement in black and white costs $76,240 (*Glamour* 2001). A 1/6 page advertisement in black and white costs $15,480. For a two-color advertisement, 1 page is priced at $94,360 and the 1/6 page is $29,390. As with newspaper advertising, magazine advertising generally allows discounts if a certain number of pages are guaranteed over a 12-month period. *Glamour* gives a 3 percent discount for 3 pages up to a 19 percent discount for 48 pages over a 12-month period. As with most magazines, *Glamour* has an early closing date. For example, the September issue, which typically has more advertising pages than other issues, has a closing date of June 20, and the magazine will go on sale August 18. This means there is nearly a three-month lead-time to publicize a September event. Most fashion shows are not planned this early in advance, causing magazine advertising to be excluded from the promotion plan.

Many fashion magazines have a presence on the Internet, for example, *Vogue* offers a Web site in addition to the print magazine. Chanel and vogue.com planned the first "virtual trunk show" broadcast on the Web (Lockwood, 2000a), jointly presenting the Chanel 2001 cruise collection designed by Karl Lagerfeld, on the Internet. Chanel customers and Web viewers were able to view runway coverage that took place several weeks before in Paris, and reserve looks for future purchase. Once items were reserved, Chanel boutique sales associates followed-up with a phone call to customers to answer questions and place the order. According to Lockwood (2000a), it was the first time a major design house made its apparel available for advance order in cyberspace. *Vogue* was excited to be the first magazine to partner in such as way with a major design house. To publicize the event, Chanel sent out a mailing to customers; *Vogue* did an online campaign and mailed to subscribers, and Chanel advertised in newspapers.

Network and Cable Television

Television is the most influential type of advertising available and the most expensive. Only the largest fashion show budgets are able to afford television advertising. The costs of television advertising are based on the length of the advertisement-15-, 20-, 30-, or 60-second, and the specified time the advertisement will run. Prime time, from 7:00 to 11:00 P.M., will have the highest rates and the most viewers. The rates to advertise on television should be carefully evaluated before deciding on this type of advertising for fashion shows.

To advertise on television the sponsor must buy time as network advertising, spot advertising, or local advertising, local advertisements being the most economical. **Network advertising** is time bought on one of the major networks during a specified show. The network produces the shows and the commercials, and sends the package to network affiliates. Costs are the greatest for network commercials because they are produced nationally; $100,000 or more is not uncommon for a network budget for 60-second commercials.

Time bought on independently owned stations is considered **spot advertising**. Advertising is purchased by quantity and generally run in a specific time frame rather than during a specific show. Commercials on these stations are produced both nationally and locally, and can service a specific geographic area. Spot advertising is less expensive than network advertising but still may range in the thousands of dollars.

Local advertising is time purchased on local television stations by businesses or organizations. Advertising costs at these stations more readily fit into fashion show budgets because the shows are produced in and for the immediate area. If merchandise used in the fashion show is borrowed from a local retailer, it may be wise to ask the retailer to share in the cost of the commercial, since both parties will benefit from the advertising. Some advertisers will participate in creating the commercial while other advertisers leave it to the station. One advertiser may produce the photography and select the music, participating in about 75 percent in the production of the ad. A second advertiser may only participate by writing copy, contributing approximately 25 percent of the production time. A 30-second commercial should have approximately 70 words and photography should be in the form of videotape. Groups are encouraged to advertise on television but they should be highly organized with one person making decisions. If the decisions need to be discussed with all the members, too much time is wasted and production engineers may lose their patience.

The fashion show as entertainment has been a theme throughout this text. Cable television has encouraged this trend. Premiering with the Fall 2001 collections, several upstart cable outlets broadcast Fashion Week as part of regular programming (Marks, 2001). *The Style Network*, a spin-off of *E! Entertainment Television*, is a 24-hour network devoted to style, fashion, and design. At the beginning of the century, it signed a three-year agreement with the 7th on Sixth and the Council of Fashion Designers of America to broadcast all the fashion shows, parties, and behind-the-scene activities taking place during Fashion Week (Lockwood, 2000b). The network broadcast the Fall 2001 shows for two hours daily from Bryant Park, and ran a two-hour live telecast spotlighting the Sean John Combs show (Marks, 2001).

Additionally, *Metro Channel*, a channel committed to weather, sports, traffic, and culture of the New York area, dedicated the entire week to *Full Frontal Fashion*. It has become the network-of-record for the fashion industry, devoting 250 hours to Fashion Week (Marks, 2001). While neither network is available on basic service, their high-profile presence shows the cable television industry's commitment to bringing high fashion to a mass audience.

Radio

Radio is considered to be a cost effective medium compared to other broadcast media. Radio advertising is sold in 10-, 20-, 30-, and 60-second spots. Portions of shows may also be purchased and sponsored by the advertiser. Prime time is considered drive time in the morning and the evenings, from 6:00 to 9:00 A.M. and from 4:00 to 7:00 P.M. When advertising fashion shows it may be best to use only local or regional radio. Different fashion show audiences will listen to different radio stations so it is important to match the show to the station. Check with local stations to determine rates.

Radio commercials Because of the many varieties of radio stations, on-the-air radio commercials must target specific audiences more than print media. Commercials must be brief but they must get the message across. A 60-second commercial should be limited to 125 words. Shorter commercials should be planned accordingly. Radio commercials can be prepared in two forms: they can be read live on the air or taped in advanced and played on the air. If the fashion show budget does not include a prepared radio commercial, press releases should be delivered to all radio stations in a community two to four weeks before the event. Like other media, PSAs will be broadcast if the event is perceived by the news director as noteworthy. Figure 4.9 is an example of a radio advertisement script.

A promotion coordinator who is considering television or radio advertising should seriously evaluate the use of a professional advertising agency to produce the commercial. Professional agencies have studio space, equipment, and design talent not available to the layperson. Commercials, to be effective, must be of the highest quality to retain listeners.

Publicity should always be used; advertising should be used as the budget allows. Because publicity is non-paid promotion it requires careful planning to ensure an editor or news director will choose to publish or broadcast the information. Although publicity is non-paid promotion, there are still costs associated with developing and distributing the materials. Printing and the development of visual materials such as photographs, along with staff time

---

Radio Script

Page 1 of 1

ROCK THE RUNWAY
60 seconds

MUSIC:	ROCK MUSIC
ANNOUNCER:	What do you get when you mix your favorite tunes and your fashion trends in an exciting atmosphere with all of your friends? Rock the Runway, a fashion show produced by Northern Arizona University merchandising students. Join us for an evening of music, fashion and fun, November 17th, at 7:00 pm in the Du Bois Ballroom on the NAU campus. Tickets are $5.00 in advance or $7.00 at the door. All proceeds will benefit the NAU Merchandising Leaders of the 21st Century Scholarship Fund. You can't miss with music, fashion and friends. Call 9-2-8 – 5-2-3 – 5-5-5-5 for more information.
MUSIC:	ROCK MUSIC
SFX:	APPLAUSE
ANNOUNCER:	Sponsored by Northern Arizona Merchandising Associates and the School of Communication.

Figure 4.9 Example of a radio advertisement script.

are all costs that should be considered when planning publicity. Advertising is paid for, with the guarantee that it will run, but is often too expensive to be used extensively.

In the next section, we look at direct marketing strategies. Direct marketing strategies are also costly. In some instances, these tools are more important to the fashion show production than advertising and should have priority when developing a promotion campaign.

Direct marketing, as a promotion strategy is very old, beginning with catalog shopping in the late 1800s. However, technological advances in the 1990s such as the Internet and database management have reinvented direct marketing as a major promotion tool. Direct marketing has a newfound importance in promotion strategies and some of the strategies discussed next have particular value in promoting a fashion show.

Direct marketing

Direct marketing is the marketing process by which organizations communicate directly with target customers to generate a response or a transaction. The goal of direct marketing is to go directly to the consumer with the message to generate a response, in our case, attend a fashion show. Direct marketing often relies on **direct response**, which is the distribution method that requires a direct reply, for example an RSVP to an invitation. Direct response print media such as signage, posters, and direct mail are valuable tools in the promotion of a fashion show.

Direct response print media

Direct response print media are printed materials that require a direct reply from the consumer. Direct response print media takes two forms, mailed or delivered by other means instead of mail. **Direct mail** is all direct response communications delivered through the mail. Printed materials left on the counter at a retail store and posters mounted on a bulletin board are examples of non-mailed direct response print media.

Posters, flyers, and invitations   Often, the first place to start in developing a direct response promotion package is with a poster. Posters (8 1/2″ × 14″ or 11″ × 17″) are easy and effective ways to promote a fashion show. Posters can be read easily and quickly from a distance and the elements can be modified for use on tickets, the program, and other printed materials. Posters can also be placed at store entrances, near elevators, or used as in-store signage.

The keys to an effective poster are eye-catching visuals and easy to read information. Visuals should be large and have appeal when being viewed from a distance. Generally one visual element is enough when text is being included on the poster. Fonts should be large and easy to read from a distance, and according to accepted design rules, no more than three fonts should be used on one poster (including any fonts within visual elements). It is better to stay with one or two fonts and change the point size to create variety. A border can be used to tie all the elements together and create unity between text and visuals.

The poster should include a prominent design element or a logo for the show as well as the following information:

- Show title reflecting the theme of the show
- Day, date, and time
- Location
- Ticket information and costs
- RSVP if necessary
- Sponsoring organization
- Any other information useful to the viewer such as refreshments or door prizes

The best piece of advice for creating a poster is to *simplify*. Information should be stated as simply and specifically as possible. Proof reading by multiple committee or staff members is a must and as the poster is proofed, extra words should be eliminated. Figure 4.10 is a poster for *Rock the Runway*, a student produced fashion show.

Flyers (often a smaller version of the poster) are excellent for reaching general audiences such as a student body or mall shoppers. Standard sizes for flyers are 8 1/2″ × 11″ or half sheets, 5 1/2″ × 4 1/4″. Flyers can be folded in half or thirds and mailed. Flyers can also be distributed in person or used as a newspaper insert.

Invitations include the same textual information as the poster, but are printed on high quality paper with a more elegant look (Fig. 4.11). Invitations are more expensive to produce and should be sent to a more specific, identified mailing list, such as the sponsoring retailer's customer list. When developing an invitation, work with a printer who is familiar with standard invitation sizes. The minimum size for first class mail is 5″ × 3 1/2″. Certain sizes are considered irregular by the U.S. postal service and will require additional postage to be mailed.

When considering direct response print media, printing and postage costs should be evaluated. These costs are usually better accommodated by a fashion show budget than other types of promotion such as advertising. The addressee should receive mailed flyers or invitations at least two weeks in advance of the event. This gives the potential audience member enough time to make plans for the event. Plan ahead to accommodate for the necessary days the mailed pieces will be in route. It is not uncommon for pieces to be in transit for two-three weeks during peak mail times. Mail a sample to a committee or staff person to verify delivery time before planning a large mailing.

Mailing lists are an important tool when using direct mail. Membership lists and customer lists should be used whenever possible to generate an audience. When developing a mailing list it is extremely important not to duplicate mailings. An item mailed twice to one address aggravates the recipient and is costly to the organization. Many computer programs are available that can generate a database list and eliminate duplicates. A computer savvy committee member should take on this responsibility as part of the show preparation.

Tickets and programs   When planning the poster and other printed materials, it is easy to design tickets and programs at the same time. Tickets serve many purposes. For the show committee, they are a good way to control the number of attendees. For the attendee they serve as a reminder for the event. Mailing lists for future events can be generated from tick-

Figure 4.10 Promotional poster for *Rock the Runway* fashion show. *Courtesy, Promotions Committee, Rock the Runway Fashion Show. Sponsored by Northern Arizona University Merchandising Program.*

ets, if the voucher has a space for the attendee to write their name and address, or other contact information. Tickets can also be prepared with a perforated section so part of the ticket can be returned and part held by the audience member to use for door prizes (Fig. 4.12).

It is always an issue whether to sell or give away tickets. There are advantages to both free and sponsored shows. Shows free to the public are often common in retail stores. The cost of producing the show is usually recovered in retail sales after the show. With free shows many tickets are distributed with attendance ranging from a very low to a very high percentage of the total tickets distributed. Response rates increase if the show is specialized such as a bridal show, and if tickets must be picked up at a certain location, such as at the information booth of the retail mall.

Figure 4.11a and b a) the front and b) back of an invitation to the ChanPaul fashion show. *Courtesy, Mao and Chan Paul.*

a

chanpaul
fall 2003

Thursday, Feb 13
11 am

MAO SPACE
260 Fifth Ave
(between 28th and 29th Street)

r.s.v.p. MAO Public Relations
212.226.6196
www.maopr.com

RSVP by Feb 9th

Section_____ Row_____ Seat #_____

This invitation is non transferable · Invitation must be presented at door

CREATIVE

b

A minimal charge lends a degree of exclusivity to the show, causing it to have greater importance to the ticket holder. When tickets are sold, the number of tickets distributed will be lower but the percentage rate for those who attend will be greater. Plan for a 15 percent no-show and print that many extra tickets. Tickets can be printed at local print shops or purchased in rolls at stationery or office supply stores. If the show is being produced at an auditorium or a theater, the cost of printing the tickets may be part of the rental fee. Check with the management; do not assume the cost of the tickets is included.

Tickets should be carefully proofread to make sure day, date, time, and location are correctly printed. When these errors are not caught in time, the fashion show staff must either hand mark the tickets or spend additional money to reprint them. If reserved seating is used then tickets must be marked with the seat number. Tickets can be designed to complement the rest of the printed material, contributing to a well-coordinated package.

Printed programs serve as an outline or guide of the merchandise being presented. Programs may or may not be used depending on the type of show. Mail shows with audiences filtering in and out may not need programs. Programs for special event shows may help the audience keep track of the garments they intend to try on after the show.

In most cases, the program will list the garments in show order with a brief description of each ensemble. Model's names may or may not be used in the program, depending upon the type of show. Price is seldom listed unless the audience is very budget minded. Most people will investigate the garments they like regardless of price. Programs may also acknowledge the designers, models, manufacturers, retailers, or staff who volunteered their help to produce the show. This not only thanks those people who helped, it provides some publicity for businesses such as printers, photographers, hair stylists, cosmeticians, or technicians that have provided assistance. It can also serve to reinforce the charity and group sponsoring the show.

As with all printed materials, the design of the programs should emphasize the established theme, not detract from the show. It is better to have no program than a program which was slapped together at the last minute. Advertising space may be sold in programs. Rates are usually determined by the sponsoring organization. This is a way to increase profits of the show or cover advertising expenses.

Figure 4.12 Audience tickets may be used for gift drawings. The anticipation adds an element of excitement to the event. *Courtesy, Christopher C. Everett.*

Direct response online marketing

Direct response is not limited to print media. Direct response online marketing is also a tool being tested for fashion show promotion. **Direct response online media** includes all advertising communications done via a computer (Swanson & Everett, 2000). Online advertising is becoming a popular way for sponsors to communicate their message to consumers. **Online advertising** includes sponsored messages that appear on the Web sites of third-party vendors. These advertisements may also be called **banner ads**. As previously mentioned, Victoria's Secret used a banner ad in the *Wall Street Journal* to promote an online fashion show. This example is used primarily because it is the only company to date that has successfully used a banner ad to promote a fashion show.

The New York Times has a large number of banner ads. Banner ads are available in different sizes based on the number of pixels in the image. A **pixel** is the smallest image-forming unit of a video display. *The New York Times* online version sells 6 ad sizes. Banner ad costs are based on the cost per thousand impressions. For example, 500,000 impressions cost $40 compared to 14,000,000 impressions that cost $15 (*New York Times*, n.d.). Figure 4.13 shows common pixel sizes used for banner ads.

Figure 4.13 Banner ad dimensions based on pixels.

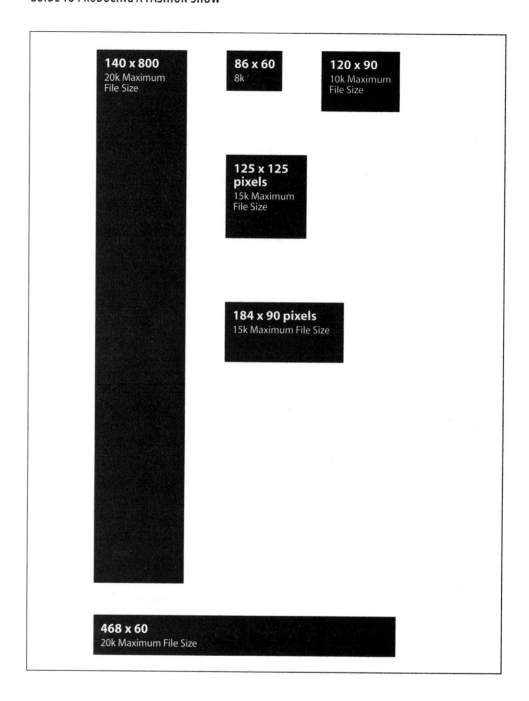

Online advertising of fashion shows is still in its infancy. However, it may be an economical way to advertise if the targeted audience can be identified. Local online newspapers may be a medium to investigate for local fashion show promotion.

The Internet is a common direct response online marketing medium used to promote fashion shows. Previously, we have talked about Internet advances including Helmet Lang as the first designer to show his line on the Web, Victoria's Secret use of online fashion shows to sell product, and Chanel partnering with vogue.com to be the first design house to pre-sell fashions in an online trunk show. There are many other examples of how the Internet has become a tool to promote fashion shows. Box 4.1 introduces us to two companies that have been producing the video footage that we see when we view an online fashion show.

Many fashion houses are developing Internet strategies to entertain viewers, and more importantly to increase sales. Ralph Lauren Media is one example. The company has two Web sites, each focusing on a different strategy. The Web site polo.com offers a broad overview of the Polo Ralph Lauren Company, its offerings, and e-commerce of iconic items such as polo shirts and chinos (Wilson, 2001). The second Web site, runway.polo.com, is designed to be more experiential in nature. This Web site is focused entirely on the designer's upscale collection with a comprehensive look at Lauren's take on trends of the season and runway shows online. David Lauren, chief creative and marketing officer for Ralph Lauren Media, believes the runway Web site is a resource for style to convey luxury in an exciting new way. According to Lauren when a designer sends a look down the runway, they are making that statement. Magazines then select the trend based on seeing it at five other shows. Sometimes the designer's point of view comes across very clearly, but at a company like Ralph Lauren that statement must be continually reinforced and it can be with a Web site (Wilson, 2001).

Publicity, advertising, and direct marketing are all necessary tools for promotion of a fashion show. And, as we have discussed, all three promotion types have associated costs. The final section of this chapter looks at sponsorship as a way to lessen costs associated with event planning. Regardless of the show size, promotion coordinators should consider sponsorship.

Sponsorship

Sponsorship involves supporters who lend their name to an event and/or underwrite production costs of the event. Sponsorship is gaining importance in the fashion world. In 2001, The Council of Fashion Designers of America sold the American fashion shows to IMG, a sports management and marketing company whose clients include Tiger Wood, Derek Jeter, and Wimbledon, and models Gisele Bündchen and Alek Wek (Horyn, 2001). One of the reasons IMG acquired the 7th on Sixth shows was to generate opportunities including global television and sponsorship with the shows.

In 2000, the Junior League of San Jose raised a record-setting $180,000 in corporate sponsorships for its annual *Avenues of Style Fashion Show* and Fundraiser (Junior League, 2000). This was the largest sum ever raised for the fashion show fundraiser. According to organizers, the corporate dollars directly translated into more funds available to support nonprofit agencies in Santa Clara County. Over the last ten fashion shows the League raised more than $1.5 million in funds that aided the local community. According to a corporate sponsor, the company donated to the League because it felt it was an investment in the community (Junior League, 2000).

continued on page 116

Box 4.1
Strutting the Cyber Catwalk

NEW YORK-Given the wall-to-wall coverage of New York's Fashion Week by MetroChannel's *Full Frontal Fashion*, *E!* and the *Style Network*, one would think that viewing runway footage on the Internet would have suddenly become passé. As it turns out, online coverage of 7th on Sixth suffered no shortage of providers or spectators, as footage of the shows turned up in more places than bootleg Hannibal videos-From fashionista hubs like www.virtual.runway.com and www.style.com to subscriber networks for industry insiders and video-on-demand services.

When it comes to shooting runway footage of Fashion Week collections, all roads somehow lead to B Productions, which has been filming, producing, and packaging videos of the shows since its inception in 1983. The company is headed by Bill Marpet, who began his videography career in the 1970s by shooting documentaries in two of the world's scariest hot zones-the Middle East and New York's East Village.

"I traded a hand grenade for a hemline," said Marpet, whose earliest fashion industry clients were Bill Blass and Calvin Klein. Still, Marpet found the transition from cinema verité to the catwalk chronicles less glaring than one would expect. "It's great to shoot live because you get the rush that either you catch the moment or it's gone forever," he said. "Each fashion look flows by very quickly and you have to capture the designer's aesthetic, the silhouette and as much detail as possible in less than half a minute."

In intervening years, B Productions has become the point of origin for much of the runway video footage seen on TV, the Internet, and by designers themselves. "We work with a wide range of clients." Vicky Bugbee, B Productions' director if marketing, told *Women's Wear Daily*, "one designer commissioned us to make 15,000 videotapes of a show to be sent out to clients and buyers. In previous seasons, we supplied footage to www.vogue.com. We also work with Intertainer, an online video-on-demand service, where you can literally order up whatever show you're looking for."

Every season brings special requests. Kenneth Cole commissioned B Productions to do a HDTV shoot of his Grand Central Station show. "Usually shows are shot horizontally, but Kenneth Cole had his show shot vertically, head to toe," says Bugbee. "He's planning to show the footage in his stores on giant, vertical HDTV plasma screens."

Bugbee feels that, given fashion's rate of mainstreaming among consumers, runway footage can find a home both on television and online. "I like the way the Web has opened things up, especially for people living outside New York City," said Bugbee. B Productions currently has two fashion-related television shows in development with Lifetime television.

Another major purveyor of runway and fashion footage is New York-based Global Fashion Village (GFV), which shoots shows (often in collaborations with B Productions) and then syndicates various video packages to such online entities as www.newyorktimes.com, www.bostonherald.com, www.elle.com, and subscription-based www.WWD.com.

continued on page 115

Box 4.1 continued from page 114

Global Fashion Village president and chief executive officer Ross Glick has no doubts about the long-term viability of online fashion video content. "The Web provides an interactive component to viewing fashion footage that you can't get on TV," he said. "But the biggest draw is video-on-command: viewing the collection you want, when you want, in the way that you want."

Global Fashion Village's runway packages tend to fall into two groups. While the company produces unedited, run-of show footage for such designers as Chaiken, Nautica, and BCBG, it also specializes in more compressed, abbreviated formats that intersperse runway footage with editorial. "One format is the runway highlights program, which runs one to three minutes and includes commentary by the designer," said Glick. "We also have another format, in which runway is intercut with commentary by editors, giving their reaction to the collection. It's more trend-oriented."

Cognizant of the variation in access speeds and plug-in formats by users, GFV video can be accessed at 56K, 100K, and 300K speeds, in Real Player, Windows Media Player, or QuickTime. Global Fashion Village has some other projects in the works, "In Milan we'll be shooting 50 shows, and doing an Italian version of our editorial packages, suitable for Italian Web sites," said Glick.

Global Fashion has also stumbled upon archival treasures of sorts: "Fashion Flashback" footage from the 1950s and 1960s, generally one-minute features with Movietone News-style voice overs that originally were shown in movie theatres. "We got the footage from a place called Fashiondig.com and we're hoping to offer it to online Web publishers," said Glick.

When deciding how to package and broadcast runway footage, both Web sites and television producers have to choose between the "purist" format-unadulterated, unedited run-of-show coverage without editorial-and the more commercial, editorial format that gives select runway coverage intercut with commentary. WWD.com opted for the latter model. The site features two to three minute runway segments, covering 20 to 25 shows in New York, Paris, and Milan, intercut with commentary from *Women's Wear Daily* editors.

Another repository for runway footage online is www.style.com, which previously used B Productions as its video provider but has since contracted its own crew to shot the shows, "We're an editorial site, so in our video coverage of the shows we try to be inclusive without being encyclopedic," said Mark Ganem, editor in chief of style.com.

For a recent season, www.style.com reviewed 35 shows from the New York collections and featured video from 18 of them. In Milan, 18 shows were reviewed and 10 were taped; in Paris, 25 shows were reviewed and 10 videos featured. Ganem believes that the viewing of runway footage on the Internet will continue to take root, and operate in tandem with growing television coverage of the shows, "Video-on-demand is just more convenient than television coverage when you need to see a particular collection at a particular time," said Ganem, who noted that style.com users tend to view runway footage throughout the season and not just during show week. "I find that television and the Web are very com-

continued on page 116

Box 4.1 continued from page 115

plementary, I mean, aside from running this site, I also appeared as a commentator on Metro's Full Frontal Fashion."

Web coverage of the shows has acquired a crucial foothold in parts of the United States as well as overseas, where television coverage is scant or nonexistent. Given that MetroChannel's *Full Frontal Fashion* was only available in the tristate area, and the Style Network reaches a mere 95,000 homes via Time Warner's DTV digital service, it's not as if fashionistas nationwide currently have access to wall-to-wall television runway coverage. One Web site that helps fill the gap is the Houston-based www.virtualrunway.com which provides insider fashion industry news and trend coverage for "Techno-hip and ready-to-wear obsessed, sophisticated women over 25," according to founder and president Janet Hobby.

The web site, which originally launched in 1999, features runway footage from approximately 50 shows, acquired from the designers themselves, available in Media Player format. According to Hobby, burgeoning fashion coverage on television and the Web can only help the industry. "I think mainstreaming and increased availability of runway footage is a huge boon to fashion," said Hobby. "When we launched I was frustrated as a couture-conscious woman that couldn't see the collections live and get inspired by them, since back then, there was practically no video coverage available anywhere online. Now I receive letters from people around the world commenting on our video coverage, and it's obvious that people are using the Web to learn more about their favorite designers. I think this kind of exposure can only add to fashion's bottom line."

Of course, proliferation of runway video only begs the question-Fashion Week footage will be available round-the-clock, in ever-improving video formats, on the Web and television, will more people start sitting out the actual shows? Or will Fashion Week become a total consumer, tourist-oriented event?

"That could happen," muses Ganem at style.com. "or it could work in the other direction and the shows will once again be attended just by professionals. That would be even better."

Adapted from: Braunstein, P. (2001, February 26). Strutting the cyber catwalk. *Women's Wear Daily*, p.18.

continued from page 113

When a company sponsors an event, it generally contributes through monetary and/or in-kind contributions. As in the San Jose example, corporations use sponsorship as a public relations strategy to enhance image. Other reasons corporations sponsor events are to improve customer relations, increase employee moral, or fulfill civic responsibilities (Swanson & Everett, 2000).

Businesses can sponsor an event in several ways. They can lend their name to the event such as the Mercedes-Benz Fashion Week. This enhances the image of both the event and the sponsoring organization. Along with name recognition the company also contributes financially to ensure the event will be successful.

Contributing door prizes and giveaways or providing refreshments are two other ways companies can sponsor a fashion show. Door prizes are gifts awarded by a drawing, to thank audience members for buying a ticket, as previously shown in Figure 4.12. Giveaways are items given to every member of the audience. A perfume sample left on each chair is an example of a giveaway, and the sponsoring fragrance company or retailer is acknowledged as a sponsor.

Door prizes and giveaways are used to build interest in the show and thank the audience for attending. Depending on the type of show, few or many of these presents may be used. Gifts may be large items such as weekend getaways, DVD players, or diamond jewelry, or small items such as cosmetics, tote bags, water bottles, t-shirts, accessories, or other mass-produced premiums. At fashion shows, it is also common to see gift certificates for manicures or hair cuts as part of sponsorship.

Sponsors may directly buy the gifts, or contribute money and allow the fashion show committee or staff to buy appropriate gifts. Often gifts with the corporation's logo are part of the giveaways, reinforcing brand recognition with the company.

Providing refreshments is also a way for corporations to sponsor events. Again, the company may provide actual product or provide money to buy the food and beverages. Local soft drink bottling companies often sponsor refreshments by contributing beverages for the event.

Not all shows will have refreshments. Refreshments can detract from a show if they are not located in an appropriate place. They should be located away from the staging area to minimize traffic and noise. Also, some venues may not allow refreshments, or, if they do the refreshments must be purchased from the venue's food service provider.

Promotion is a necessary element of all fashion shows. Although personal contact is one of the best methods to communicate a message, it is not always possible. A successful promotion plan will incorporate both editorial content (publicity) and advertising content to assure communication between the sponsoring organization, the media, and readers or viewers of the media. Not all shows will include all the promotion tools that have been discussed in this chapter. It is up to the show director and the promotion coordinator to plan a promotion campaign that will best fit the needs of the targeted audience and the sponsoring organization.

Key fashion show terms

advertising	media list
advertising content	network advertising
amplification	news story
art	online advertising
banner ad	page of isolated facts
basic fact sheet	paste-up
biographical information	personal selling

body
caption
clip art
closing date
copy
direct mail
direct marketing
direct response
direct response online media
direct response print media
editorial content
fashion editor
feature story
full-run
halftones
headline
historical fact sheet
institutional
lead
line drawing
list of participants
local advertising
logo
media kit

photography
pixel
preferred position
press photograph
press release
program of events
promotional
public relations (PR)
public service announcement (PSA)
publicist
publicity
rate card
run-of-position (R.O.P)
slogan
special events
sponsorship
spot advertising
standard advertising unit (SAU)
subheadline
tear sheet
visual merchandising
white space
zoned edition

References

Glamour. (2001). *Advertising rates*. Retrieved July 15, 2001, from http://www.srds.com/cgi-bin/srds/common/srdslisting.cgi?407167961636+LISTING

Horyn, C. (2000, January 25). Before models do their turns, publicists do their spins. *New York Times*. Retrieved January 25, 2000, from http://www.nytimes.com

Horyn, C. (2001, February 6). Front row. *New York Times*, p. B9.

Junior League of San Jose. (2000). *Fashion Show 2000*. Retrieved July 12, 2001, from http://www.jlsj.org/media/fs2000_pr2.html

Kent State University Museum (2001). *Press releases*. Retrieved July 12, 2001, from http://dept.kent.edu/museum/pr/press.html

Lockwood, L. (2000a, June 6). Chanel, Vogue.com plan a trunk show. *Women's Wear Daily*, p. 2, 19.

Lockwood, L. (2000b, September 13). Style to air 7th on Sixth shows. *Women's Wear Daily*, p. 2.

Marin, R. (2001, July 15). A publicist consumed by fires she fanned. *New York Times*. Retrieved July 16, 2001, from http://www.nytimes.com

Marks, P. (2001, February 18). Cable stations turn Fashion Week into fashion telethon. *New York Times*. Retrieved February 20, 2001, from http://www.nytimes.com

New York Times on the Web. (n.d.). *Rates and product specifications*. Retrieved July 15, 2001, from http://www.nytimes.com/adinfo/rates.html

Newsom, D. & Carrell, B. (2000). *Public relations writing: Form and style*. Redmont, CA: Wadsworth.

St. Petersburg Times Advertising Rates. (n.d.). *Advertising rates*. Retrieved July 11, 2001, from http://www.sptimes.com/ratecards/pagetwo.html

Swanson, K. & Everett, J. (2000). *Promotion in the merchandising environment*. New York: Fairchild.

Wilson, E. (2001, May 7). Ralph launches multimedia platform: Runways and trends. *Women's Wear Daily*, p. 1, 5.

THE WORKROOM
AND THE RUNWAY

5

The *raison d'être* for producing fashion shows is to present merchandise. The starting point of the cycle comes from the designer's inspiration, which is a never ending process of presenting collections and going back to the drawing board to start the next season's merchandise selection. A typical 7th on Sixth event in New York features more than 75 men's and women's shows on the official Bryant Park roster plus at least 25 shows in other locations. And, what does that mean? Over 8,000 outfits presented (Horyn, 1999). Michael Kors, with a fatigued voice, summed it up by saying, "I feel like the Dunkin' Donut man. Time to make the fashions" (p. B9).

Alex de Betak, the show producer for Michael Kors, Donna Karan (Fig. 5.1), and John Bartlett, was working very close to the wire. From Donna Karan's multi-million dollar line, he had only seen sketches. She had only designed a handful of looks during the week before the shows were scheduled. John Bartlett was sending faxes from Italy, where he was still working on his collection, which was influenced by the relationship of Alfred Stieglitz and Georgia O'Keefe in New York and the Southwest (Horyn, 1999).

Despite the designer's last minute work on their merchandise collections, the shows must go on. Show producers, such as Mr. de Betak, must develop themes, cast models, and work on music selections based upon the designer's faxes and sketches. Designers and show producers hope that fashion editors for the major publications, such as the *New York Times* or *Women's Wear Daily*, will take notice of the collection and cover it in a review article such as the one about Viktor & Rolf's first men's wear collection highlighted in Box 5.1.

Chapter 5, The Workroom and The Runway, takes us from the designer studios, where the merchandise is created, to the runway, where the latest trends are presented as a theme to the press, retail buyers, and influential consumers. We also look at the merchandise selection and coordination, as well as the fitting process.

Figure 5.1 Donna Karan
works behind the scenes
with merchandise, models,
and a masseuse to ease the
stress the night before her
show. *Courtesy, Fairchild
Publications, Inc.*

Merchandise selection process

Merchandise selection is the designation of apparel, shoes, and accessories for presentation
in a fashion show to the target customer (Fig. 5.2a and b). Several factors must be considered
when selecting merchandise. Because most fashion shows are produced to sell clothing, merchandise selected for a fashion show must make a clear fashion statement to the audience

FLORENCE-After generating their share of headlines in women's fashion for two years with theatrical runway shows and fanciful ready-to-wear, Dutch designers Viktor Horsting and Rolf Snoeren set out to do the same with their first men's wear collection.

The designers had said they were launching men's because they wanted to dress themselves. On Thursday night at Stazione Leopolda here during the men's trade show Pitti Uomo, they took that anchoring idea to the literal extreme in the form of a precisely executed ballet of dressing and undressing.

In almost perfect synchronicity, the designers-stationed at opposite ends of an elevated stage-barely twitched as valets pulled cropped velvet trousers and slim one-button jackets off the rack and slipped them on the designers.

As the piano reached a crescendo and a recorded voice thick in a German accent began chanting "Viktor and Rolf," the audience, some amused, some baffled, knew the designers were injecting their own form of wit and irony into their debut men's runway collection.

Once dressed, Viktor and Rolf walked down the runway toward each other, mostly stone-faced before stopping in the middle to strike a pose-hips popped, fingers meticulously placed on their horn-rimmed glasses. All the while that voice bellowed from the soundtrack: "Viktor and Rolf, VIKtor and Rolf, Viktor and ROLF."

"We rehearsed for a very long time, but we were still very nervous," Horsting said after the show. "It was a different feeling for us to actually be the ones wearing and showing the clothes."

The designers braved the catwalk 10 times, modeling a fitted denim tuxedo with black satin lapel, brushed velvet cargo pants, printed shirts covered in mini black top hats and a sweatshirt with "monsieur" across the chest.

Pitti Uomo organizers invited the designers to launch their men's collection, which is produced by Tuscan-based manufactured Gibó. It's the latest project in a series of measures aimed at expanding their presence. Last year, they linked a deal with L'Oréal to launch their first fragrance.

Although not as elaborate or conceptual as their women's presentations, Viktor & Rolf nonetheless distilled their clever, hyper self-conscious aesthetic into a viable men's line, or as they like to describe it, "the next element in the Viktor & Rolf universe."

Viktor & Rolf show a merry men's line. (2003, January 13). *Women's Wear Daily*, p. 3.

and be seasonally current in order to stimulate sales after the show. The merchandise should be appropriate to the age, sex, income, and lifestyle of the intended audience, and be priced according to what they will spend on fashion. Too many times fashion shows display clothing suitable for the models or show planners, but not the audience. The merchandise must have strong stage appearance to the entire audience regardless of personal characteristics or where an individual is seated.

Figure 5.2a and b The coordination of merchandise and model arrangement must be developed and confirmed in advance of the show (top). Right: Organization of merchandise is crucial to the smooth running of a show. Each model's garments are pulled together. *Courtesy, Christopher C. Everett.*

Trade shows will display certain garments from the current season's collection selected to show the depth and breadth of the current line. While the whole line may be presented, the best-selling trends or garments will be repeated many times during the show. As we learned at the opening of this chapter, these garments may not be selected until hours before the show as the garments are literally finished in the workrooms of the manufacturing facilities just in time for the show.

Consumer shows display merchandise from a specific retailer or group of selected retailers in a geographic area. The fashion show may be sponsored by one store or by a local charitable organization using merchandise from several retailers. Some fashion shows may choose to show merchandise created by local artists or designers who are members of the organization or a designer within the community with merchandise not found in typical department or specialty stores. These shows should be encouraged as the trend for individualized or one-of-a-kind merchandise grows. Consumers are constantly challenging vendors to provide innovative and creative goods. Shows featuring these designers may become a vehicle for artisans/craftspersons to show their creations and can be very successful if produced correctly. Fashion show producers can create the atmosphere of a gallery exhibit with the designer available to the audience following the presentation.

Merchandise categories

Decisions regarding the **merchandise categories**, which are the divisions of general types of merchandise presented in the show, are made during the planning sessions. There should be a rhythm or flow between the groupings. Merchandise within categories must be grouped in a pleasing manner. Pieces within a group may be classified according to color, styling details, sophistication of the designs, popularity of the trend, or some other identifiable theme. The specific categories should have been selected in the planning stage of the fashion show, and confirmed using the ideal chart, which will be discussed later in this chapter. After reviewing merchandise available from merchants, groupings of merchandise should be formed. Common categories for merchandise groupings include: *play/casual clothing, intimate apparel/lingerie, career/business clothing, leisure/active/sport clothing, cocktail/evening clothing,* and *bridal/special occasion clothing.* Variations of these categories based on the show theme are common in many presentations. A show may divide activewear and leisurewear into two categories if enough merchandise is available. Some shows will be based on only one category such as bridalwear or lingerie. A bridal show may classify the merchandise according to styling details such as Victorian, sophisticated, traditional, and attendant dresses. A lingerie show may classify the garments according to fabric type such as silk, jersey, flannel, and terrycloth.

The first sequence must capture the attention of the audience. The last sequence must leave the audience with a positive attitude toward the fashion show and an urgency to try on the fashions viewed.

The merchandise flow must allow for the audience to see how garments not shown together may be worn together. Several mix and match pieces should be shown in succession rather than at the beginning and end of the category. Models may switch jackets on the runway to show the audience how they might mix and match the various pieces shown. It may also be possible to show the audience how to mix pieces they already own with the new pieces in the show. A merchandise planning chart (Fig. 5.3) helps estimate the number of garments needed for the show.

The broad merchandise categories are then translated into the scene themes, which were developed during the early planning stages. If a scene featuring work clothing is included in the show, the merchandise category would include suits, separates, and coordinates that would be appropriate to wear to an office or to other business situations. For instance, the business apparel segment for *Rock the Runway* was given the scene theme, "Suit Suit Riot." All of the women's clothing was borrowed from the local retail outlet of Anne Klein, whereas the men's apparel was selected from a branch of Dillard's Department Store.

Consumer show merchandise may be divided into two groups. The first group should be clothing that the audience can wear and afford. The second group should be show-stopper items—experimental and/or expensive items—which the audience may not be able to afford but will enjoy viewing and possibly experimenting with after the show. Affordable, wearable clothing should make up 75 percent of the collection with show-stopping garments accounting for 25 percent of the collection. Creating this balance will reassure the audience that the producers know who they are while showing them ways to expand their wardrobe. The industry calls this 75 / 25 percent balance "merchandising to your audience."

Figure 5.3 A merchandise planning chart helps the merchandise and model committees assess the number of outfits and models needed for the show.

	NUMBER OF OUTFITS	NUMBER OF MODELS	TIME (minutes)
Small Show	25 – 40	4 – 6	15 – 20
Medium Show	40 – 65	8 – 10	25 – 39
Large Show	66 or more	12 or more	45 – 60

The fashion show director or merchandise coordinator for civic-or school-produced shows should make sure the retail organization selected has enough merchandise of the right types and quantities to match the merchandise categories planned. It is a reflection of poor planning to select a merchandise category and then later realize the retailer carries only limited selections within that category. When retailers agree to lend merchandise for a civic or school show, merchandise categories should be tailored to match the store offerings.

Merchandise should be new to the audience and represent the latest trends to create as much excitement as possible. Merchandise that the audience has already seen in the store will not encourage sales of the goods. Trends may be influenced by past seasons, but it is important to select details that reflect the current season. Commentary, if used, may be used to explain to the audience how long the trend has been around and the variations that have occurred from season to season.

Using merchandise from more than one retailer has both advantages and disadvantages. The advantages include having more items to choose from and having more categories from which to draw for ideas. Small stores, which may carry only limited volumes of merchandise, also have the opportunity to participate because they do not have to worry about providing large quantities of clothing. Using more than one retailer may be considered a disadvantage if favoritism is shown to one store or if an individual store's merchandise is not distinguishable. All retailers should be aware of other participating merchants, and the same policies should be enforced for all retailers.

A civic or school group should not try to use a retailer just because they volunteer clothing. Show coordinators may in their excitement use this merchandise only to realize later that the merchandise does not fit the audience. If a junior store, specializing in sizes 3 to 13 aimed at the teenage and young adult market, volunteers merchandise, but the mature audience attending the fashion show purchases missy apparel, sizes 6 to 16, the fashion show will be of little benefit to the merchants or the audience. Merchandise from all the retailers used should match the theme of the show and the needs of the audience, as we discussed in Chapter 3.

Timing

The merchandise selection process should occur after the show theme has been determined. The first step in selecting merchandise for a fashion show by the merchandise committee is to visit local retailers to review available merchandise to determine what ideas they can incorporate into the show. This should be planned close enough to the show so that the merchandise selected will be available in retail stores for immediate purchase, but with enough time before the show to avoid last-minute time conflicts. The type of show and the audience will determine how long it will take to select the merchandise.

Merchandise should not be reserved at this time. It may be important to visit a store two or three times to investigate new arrivals especially during seasonal transition periods. The merchandise selection committee needs to be familiar with the fashion preferences of the local market so they can know what merchandise to select.

Ideal chart   Merchandise is selected to fit the fashion show theme according to a plan called an **ideal chart**, which lists all categories of merchandise that will be represented in the show. Within each category the important trends or looks are listed so they will not be missed when selecting merchandise. The number of garments per category to be pulled will also be listed. These numbers may be double the amount that will actually be used in the show. Important accessories for the season should also be included on the ideal chart or a separate accessories chart to avoid missing an important trend or idea for the season. These charts should be completed before merchandise is physically pulled from the stores. Figure 5.4 is an example of an ideal chart.

Relationships with merchants

When borrowing merchandise from retailers it is imperative to project a professional image. Merchants may be very reluctant to participate if they feel they have been taken advantage of in the past. A good working relationship with retailers is crucial if the show is to be a success. When approaching merchants to borrow merchandise, have as much information about the show as possible to give credibility to the show.

In most cases all the merchandise used in the show is "on loan" from stores. Show personnel are accountable for any lost or damaged merchandise and will be held accountable when the merchandise is returned. Merchandise loan procedures vary from store to store. Ask the merchant how inventory records should be maintained to account for the borrowed merchandise. It is best to ask each store what they prefer.

If no preference is expressed, provide a **merchandise loan record**, which is a standardized form used to record details of the borrowed merchandise. The loan record should include a description of the garment, manufacturer, color, size, price, date of loan, store authorization, merchandise department, when it will be returned, and who will be responsible for returning the merchandise. A copy should be kept by the store loaning the merchandise and the person responsible for returning the merchandise. Inform the merchant of security measures that will be taken to insure the safety of the garments while they are out of the store. Figure 5.5 is a sample merchandise loan record.

Merchandise Quantity

When planning the merchandise for a show, plan for a minimum of one garment per minute depending on the length of the runway. Many shows plan one outfit every 30 seconds to hold the audience's attention. A 45-minute show presents a minimum of 45 garments with closer to 90 garments for a faster paced show. Most shows do not exceed one hour, 15 minutes for non-fashion portions of the event including refreshments and announcements, and 45 minutes for

Figure 5.4 An ideal chart is a projection of the merchandise to be presented in each fashion show scene. This ideal chart was created for *Rock the Runway*.

IDEAL CHART

Rock the Runway

Scene 1: Oops I Wore it Again — casual wear — 25 pieces

Denim jeans and skirts, khakis, cargo pants, stretch pants

Shirts, baseball T's, sweaters, blouses, denim and leather jackets, and pea coats

Merchandise from Gap, Target, Buckle, and Eddie Bauer

Scene 2: Wild Wild Dress — western wear with an edge — 30 pieces

Leather pants, broomstick skirts, cowboy hats and boots, fringe trim jackets,

blanket coats and jackets

Merchandise from Jones of New York, Gap, Eddie Bauer, and Pleasure Bound

Scene 3: To Glam or Not to Glam — date wear — 30 pieces

Dance dresses and shirts with animal prints and oriental designs

Merchandise from Black Hound Gallery and Thredz

Scene 4: Suit Suit Riot — business suits and outerwear — 25 pieces

Men's and women's suits and dress coats

Merchandise from Anne Klein, Dillard's, and Jones New York

Scene 5: Classical Couture — evening wear and bride's dress — 20 pieces

Special occasion/formal dresses, tuxedos, suits, and a wedding dress

Merchandise from Dillard's and The Bridal Boutique

---

fashion presentation. Some designer shows may show up to 100 outfits per show, sometimes more (Widdows & McGuinness, 1997).

Merchandise pull

A **merchandise pull** is the physical removal of merchandise from the sales floor to an area reserved for storage of fashion show merchandise. Twice as many garments should be pulled as will be shown, avoiding problems at fittings. By pulling extra merchandise last-minute frantic searches for replacements can be prevented.

Ideally, pulling the merchandise should begin two to four weeks before the show date to give ample time for fittings, pressing, and deciding the final lineup of the show merchandise. Unfortunately, that is not always possible. Basic seasonal items may be pulled first, while new looks may not be available until closer to show time. Merchandise for apparel mart shows is often pulled 24 to 48 hours in advance of the show.

Merchandise Lineup

When the grouping of the merchandise is completed, it is necessary to create a show lineup. The **lineup**, a term borrowed from competitive sports, refers to an organized listing of models, the order in which they will appear, and the outfit they will be wearing. A **tentative lineup** that includes the order of the models and the merchandise from the theme groupings is prepared before fittings. The tentative lineup is created using the **model order**-the rotation in which the models will appear throughout the show. The merchandise is in unconfirmed order. If the lineup has to be changed, the coordinator must try to change the order of the merchandise without upsetting the theme or model rotation previously established. Changing the order of the models should be last resort, for this adds confusion during the presentation. Changes in the lineup are made during the fitting and rehearsal sessions. These changes result in a **final lineup**—a complete listing of merchandise and models in order of their appearance—which is prepared and distributed to everyone after the dress rehearsal. Sample tentative lineup and final lineup charts are shown in Figures 5.6 and 5.7.

MERCHANDISE LOAN RECORD

Date _____   Department _____

Store _____

Show _____   Date of Show_____

Issued to _____

Qty	Style #	Size	Color	Description	Price

Received in Stock by _____   Date _____

From _____

Figure 5.5 The Merchandise Loan Record provides documentation about where the merchandise is borrowed from and when it is returned.

TENTATIVE LINEUP		FINAL LINEUP		
Rock the Runway		*Rock the Runway*		

Order of Appearance

Model Order	Outfit	Props/Accessories

Scene 1: Oops I Wore it Again (25 outfits)

			Scene 1: Oops I Wore it Again (25 outfits)		
1	Alexia		1 Alexia	black jeans, yellow sweater	All models carry
1	Mike		1 Mike	black jeans, orange sweater	cell phones
1	Joan		1 Joan	black jeans, red sweater	
1	Tom		1 Tom	black jeans, green sweater	
1	Pam		1 Pam	black jeans, blue sweater	
2	Erica		2 Erica	black stretch pants, red turtleneck	red hat/black scarf
3	Carly		3 Carly	black trousers, pale blue sweater	messenger bag
3	Brett		3 Brett	black pants, pale blue turtleneck	black scarf & hat
4	Sara		4 Marcy	red plaid skirt, black leather jacket	daypack
4	Jake		4 Jessica	black plaid skirt, red sweater	daypack
4	Melissa				
			5 Sara	gray pants, purple baseball shirt	
5	Kenny		5 Jake	navy pants, gray baseball shirt	
			5 Melissa	navy pants, purple baseball shirt	
6	Nacho				
6	Jasmine		6 Kenny	jeans, jean jacket, green plaid shirt	green hat
7	Marcy		7 Nacho	navy cargos, gray sweatshirt	
7	Jessica		7 Jasmine	navy stretch pant, light blue sweatshirt	
8	Dawn		8 Dawn	denim miniskirt, blue mock neck	green hat
8	Dusty		8 Dusty	denim miniskirt, green mock neck	blue hat
8	Mark		8 Mark	jeans, blue/green plaid shirt	green hat
9	Whitney		9 Whitney	khakis, plaid shirt, brown suede jacket	
9	Bart		9 Bart	tan pants, brown sweater	
10	Breezy		10 Breezy	tan skirt, brown leather jacket	tote bag
11	Paige		11 Paige	khaki cargos, brown tweed sweater	
11	Terrance		11 Terrance	khaki plain front pants, brown herringbone sweater	
12	Angel		12 Angel	brown herringbone pants, turtleneck, camel pea coat	

Scene 2: Wild Wild Dress (30 pieces)

			Scene 2: Wild Wild Dress (30 pieces)		
13	Kari		13 Kari	black leather pants, blue cowboy shirt	cowboy hat
13	Dan		13 Dan	black leather pants, white cowboy shirt	cowboy hat
13	Jennifer		13 Jennifer	black leather pants, blue/white cowboy shirt	cowboy hat
14	Lisa		14 Lisa	denim skirt, suede fringe jacket	cowboy boots
14	Susanna		14 Susanna	denim skirt, suede fringe vest	cowboy boots
15	Alexia		15 Alexia	red Hudson Bay blanket coat	cowboy boots
16	Mike		16 Mike	brown pants, Pendleton waist length jacket	
16	Tom		16 Tom	tan pants, Pendleton pea coat	cowboy hat
17	Joan		17 Joan	dark green velvet broomstick skirt, bustier	cowboy boots
18	Pam		17 Pam	burgundy velvet broomstick skirt, vest	cowboy boots

Figure 5.6/Figure 5.7 Figures 5.6 (left) and 5.7 (right) compare the tentative lineup and the final lineup, which is established after model fittings and before the rehearsal.

The final lineup is used for many different purposes throughout the show. Dressing areas are organized according to this lineup, placing each model in a specific area to avoid confusion. The dressers, fitters, backstage manager, and cue personnel use it for an order to follow. Choreographers, music technicians, and lighting technicians can record any cues on their copies of the lineup. Commentary, if used, can be written and organized using the final lineup.

Merchandise fittings

Fittings are planned and executed when the tentative lineup is completed. **Fittings** involve matching the models to the merchandise (Fig. 5.8). Fitting sessions are scheduled to avoid wasting models', coordinators', and merchants' time. If professional models are being used, they are paid for their time at fittings, and this cost must be budgeted. Shows involving only a few models may schedule individual fittings. Shows involving 15 or 20 models should schedule three or four models at a time to avoid mass confusion within the store. Apparel mart or trade shows may use standard size fitting models. When professional models are used to wear clothing in the show, the fitting may be the first time they wear the garments.

Some retailers will reserve a specific area in which show coordinators and models can work so that they will not disturb customers. Other retailers with limited space may ask show staff to work around regular store hours, customers, and dressing rooms. With retailers it is critical to act professionally and not distract the store's clients.

Fitting sheets

A fitting sheet should be prepared for each outfit as the tentative lineup is determined. The **fitting sheet** (Fig. 5.9) is an information sheet coordinated to the merchandise and model. It should include sizing information, the order number in the lineup, and a detailed description of the garment. The description must be so detailed that anyone could locate the item within the store by reading it. During the fittings coordinators and models should list accessories, shoes, and hosiery to be worn with the ensemble during the show. If an accessory must be worn in a certain way, this information is included. The coordinator may choose to put the model's name on the fitting sheet prior to the fittings if the model order will not be altered. If the garment is of such importance that it has to be included regardless of who wears it, a notation should be made. Then the model's name should be added when it is determined who will wear it. Fitting sheets and the tentative lineup are used to prepare the final lineup. One set of fitting sheets should be organized in a notebook to serve as a running checklist as accessories are gathered and alterations are completed.

Fitting supplies

Before beginning the fittings, the merchandise committee should gather materials that may be needed. A fitting supply checklist should be used to avoid forgetting important items. Once the checklist has been designed, it may be used repeatedly for many shows. Fitting supplies should include the following items: fitting sheets, garment tags, pens, pencils, and staplers for record keeping. Straight pins, safety pins, tailor's chalk, scissors, and measuring tapes should be available to assist with alterations. Miscellaneous materials to help protect the merchandise including cellophane tape, masking tape for protecting shoes, garment and accessory bags, hangers, dress shields, and scarfs to protect garments from model's makeup should also be part of fitting supplies. Accessories, shoes, and foundation garments should also be gathered.

Figure 5.8 Making sure the model and the merchandise are complementary takes place at the fittings. The lineup sheet can be finalized after the models try on garments. *Courtesy, Fairchild Publications, Inc.*

Pre-fitting organization

Model sizes must be known, and the merchandise tentatively selected, ordered, and matched to the model before he or she arrives for the fittings (Fig. 5.10). In ideal situations a model should arrive at a prearranged time and find specific ensembles waiting. The garments are fitted to the model, and he or she is able to leave in a timely manner. Store staff should be included when fitting merchandise to models because the retailers know how the merchandise should look.

In the worst-case scenario all the models arrive at the same time to find the merchandise has not been selected or pulled and their sizes were not provided by the show producers. Merchants are disappointed at the lack of professionalism and leadership within the group. Precious time is wasted, tempers flare, and the attitudes of all involved become very negative at a crucial time in the show preparation.

FITTING SHEET

MODEL NAME _____ POSITION NUMBER _____

DRESS SIZE _____

SHOE SIZE _____ HOSIERY SIZE _____

GARMENT DESCRIPTION

ACCESSORIES

OTHER INFORMATION

Figure 5.9 The fitting sheet is used to record the garments and accessories that a model will wear. It is completed during the fittings.

To avoid this scenario, plan fittings ten days to two weeks before the show and be fully prepared. The coordinator for school or civic groups should show organization to the retailer and the models. Use the tentative lineup and know the specific merchandise that each model will wear before they arrive for the fitting. Do not allow personal preferences of the models to interfere with the merchandise order. Garments should only be exchanged among models if size or fit problems occur. If a garment cannot be fit to a specific model, it may be necessary to discard the garment from the lineup and use a substitute rather than find a model who may fit the garment but upset the flow of merchandise. It may be advisable to have each model fit into several extra garments at the fitting so substitutions may be made within the lineup without calling the model for a second fitting.

Merchandise selection is a very involved process, critical to the image of the show. Goods must be identified to attract the specific target market of the fashion show. Considerations of demographic information and lifestyle orientations of the consumer must be reviewed in merchandise selection to ensure merchandise sales. Also, these products must make a strong visual impact and a strong fashion statement. Many people are involved—designers, stylists, fashion show directors, and/or retailers providing the merchandise. The responsibility of

Figure 5.10 Accessories should be bagged and positioned near the merchandise they will be worn with to allow models and dressers smooth changes. *Courtesy, Fairchild Publications, Inc.*

selecting merchandise should not be taken lightly. Only a very professional individual who understands the vastness of the task assigned should coordinate the merchandise for a fashion show.

Key fashion show terms

final lineup	lineup	merchandise selection
fittings	merchandise categories	model order
fitting sheet	merchandise loan record	tentative lineup
ideal chart	merchandise pull	

References

Horyn, C. (1999, February 8). Before the shows, eavesdropping on Seventh Avenue. *New York Times.* p. B9.

Widdows, L., & McGuiness, J. (1997). *Catwalking: Working with models.* London: B.T. Batsford.

THE CATWALK

6

After being named *Vogue* magazine's model of the year in 1999, Brazilian super-model Gisele Bündchen (Fig. 6.1) appeared on the cover of more than 250 magazines, paraded down 1,600 catwalks, and brought international recognition to herself as well as the Brazilian fashion industry (Rich, 2000). With a $7,000 per-hour fee reported by her New York agency (Benoit, 2000), Miss Bündchen has become the envy of young girls who want to become fashion models, from China, Africa, and the rest of the world.

More than 5,000 females between 14 and 22 applied to compete in the Elite Model Look China Contest, which offered the 46 finalists a chance to be the world's next supermodel with a glamorous future. The Elite Model Look contest has been held in 50 countries around the globe, seeking multi-ethnic models. Finalists from the Chinese contest won an all-expense paid trip to Geneva, Switzerland, to compete in the world finals. The winner of that contest received $150,000 and a two-year modeling contract ("Stars," 2000).

In another part of the world, 136 aspiring male and female models took part in the East Africa Model and Talent Convention, organized by a Nairobi, Kenya-based marketing and promotional company, Creative Concepts. Participants heard about career opportunities from successful black American actor and model, Horace Bass, in addition to learning to walk the runway and the basics of being a model. The contestants paid 1,000 Kenyan shillings, about $13, to participate and possibly win one of three $1,400 scholarships for modeling courses and a trip to the United States to take part in the American modeling convention the following year ("Aspiring models," 2001).

Twice each year, long-legged and improbably thin young girls carry their huge modeling portfolios and cell phones along the cobblestone streets of Milan, hoping to be cast in one of the 100 fashion shows listed by the Italian fashion trade group, the Camera Nazionale della Moda Italiana (Trebay, 2000). The famous models don't arrive until just before the shows

Figure 6.1 Gisele Bündchen, one of the highest paid supermodels, walked down the runway for London-based Luella Bartley during the New York shows. *Courtesy, Fairchild Publications, Inc.*

start, since their bookings have already been scheduled. But, the novices, eager to be noticed by designers, editors, and photographers, have traditionally gone to Milan during the weeks before the shows start, trying to get a spot walking the runway. Traditionally, it has been easier to assemble a portfolio, make business contacts, and leave small-town girlhood behind in Milan than in other major fashion markets. Fashion designer Ruffo's freelance stylist interviewed a potential model every three minutes for six hours. Although there was an appointment list with 200 names, there were only 16 openings for the Ruffo show (Trebay, 2000).

With such limited prospects, why do so many girls (and in the modeling business, women are always called girls) and boys submit themselves to such bad odds and potential disappointment? Each year, the lure of money, a glamorous image, and the ability to wear the latest designer fashions have drawn thousands and thousands of young people from around the world to try modeling as a career.

In this chapter, The Catwalk, we discuss the role of the fashion model, including the different model categories, various career opportunities, model resources, training, responsibilities, and the reputation of models and the modeling industry. We also report the role beauty plays to create a specific look on the runway. Hair and makeup professionals are given the responsibility to create and to present an image that supports the designer's clothing on the catwalk. Finally, we look at the role of choreography as it contributes to the overall impact on the catwalk.

The individuals engaged to wear the apparel and accessories for a fashion show are **models**. They must be able to effectively promote the image of the clothing to the audience in a believable manner, and are very important to the image and success of the fashion show. Models may also infer a standard of excellence, something to be emulated. Many people are inspired to wear and accessorize their clothing in a certain manner by watching and imitating fashion models. To other people, models are exploited, too thin, and a symbol of an unhealthy lifestyle.

Models should be attractive, not necessarily "beautiful." The audience should be able to enjoy the model's appearance, but the model's looks should not deter from the merchandise being presented. A flair for fashion, as well as an instinct about how clothing and accessories should be worn, is helpful. Models are often asked to exercise their fashion sense in showing clothing to its best.

A model should be well-groomed and immaculate. Good hair and skin are necessary qualities. The model's figure should be well proportioned and as close to sample sizes as possible. Alterations are expensive and time-consuming (standard sample sizes are discussed later in this chapter).

Whether you are using an amateur or professional model, all models should project a professional attitude. A professional attitude involves being cooperative with the fashion show staff and other models. Although some models have the reputation for being difficult to work with, moodiness and self-indulgence have no place behind the hectic scene of the fashion show.

The backstage pace is chaotic. When the model rushes to change clothes, she jumps out of one outfit and quickly puts on another with her dresser's assistance. Despite the tension of getting into and out of outfits, the model must be able to promptly gain composure before walking out on the runway. The model must also be able to keep her poise when mistakes or unexpected events happen. A prop might be forgotten, a zipper might break, or a shoe strap could slip off—the model must be able to gracefully cover up such incidents.

Demanding schedules prevail during market weeks, when a model may do as many as four or five strenuous shows in one day. The model must maintain a fresh, enthusiastic, and energetic attitude throughout each show. With experience professional models develop an intuition and sense what to do in any circumstance.

Models do not have to like the particular garments they are wearing. They should respect the clothes and be able to communicate the appreciation of the look or theme of the garments to the audience (Fig. 6.2).

Figure 6.2 At the Galeries Lafayette show, male and female models wear clothing from various departments in the Paris store. *Courtesy, Galeries Lafayette.*

Categories of models

The type of show being produced, the targeted audience, and the merchandise selected, will determine the category or type of model to be featured in the show. Models fit into various specialty markets in today's fashion industry. Fashion show production and photographic work may require a variety of different specialties or emphasize just one type. This depends upon the type of show and audience. Categories of models include missy, couture, mature, petite, plus size, child, junior, and male.

Missy models are generally between 17 and 30 years of age. Although missy models do not have to fit into any specific age, they should project a fashionable and youthful image. Models in this group have slim figures and are typically between 5 feet 9 inches and 5 feet 11 inches in height. According to Preston (1998), these classic female models generally weigh between 110 and 140 pounds, and have a bust measurement between 34 and 36 inches, a waist measurement between 24 and 25 inches, and hips that measure 34 to 35 inches. Fitting within these general specifications increases the odds of missy models finding employment.

Couture models are a rare and limited number of women who are internationally known and work the catwalks for the top American and global designers in such fashion centers as Paris, London, Milan, and New York (Fig. 6.3). These high fashion models are typically between 18 and 30 years old, with a minimum height of 5 feet 9 inches tall, but may be 6 feet or taller. To fit into the couture clothing, these women are extremely thin in addition to being tall.

Once considered "over the hill" at 31, a number of the older couture models continue to work beyond historical expectations. At 46, supermodel Iman is still in demand. Linda Evangelista, at 36, was selected to pose for the coveted *Vogue* cover for the September 2001 issue. But, due to the extreme emphasis on youth, some industry insiders suggest that a number of couture supermodels keep their real age a secret in fear of not being able to find work. According to Ann Veltri, president of T Management, one top model has been 24 for roughly 10 years (Trebay, 2001). As baby boomer fashion editors mature, older models started appearing more frequently in print and on the catwalk.

Mature models, such as Lauren Hutton and Christie Brinkley, continued modeling well into their 40s and 50s. The article, "Life After the Catwalk," featured in Box 6.1 discusses how current and former supermodels transition into a second career as their modeling days end.

Although modeling has been dominated by tall and thin women, the increased popularity of special sizes has led to career opportunities for petite and plus size models. **Petite models** are generally between 5 feet 2 inches and 5 feet 7 inches tall. Many designers offer clothing in petite sizes; therefore, most petite models work for specialty fashion shows featuring petite sizes or as photographic models for the beauty industry.

Another model category gaining popularity is the **plus size models**, also known as 10/20 models (Fig. 6.4). These models generally wear from a size 10 to 20 dress. Larger women with perfect skin, even features, long legs, and who are able to move well in front of a camera or down a runway are finding work in this growing market. Most plus size models are 5 feet 8 inches to 5 feet 11 inches tall, with bust measurements between 36 inches and 42 inches, waist measurements between 26 inches and 32 inches, hip measurements between 36 inches and 45 inches, and weight between 140 and 170 pounds (Esch & Walker, 1996).

Carré Otis, one-time cover girl and couture model, started working as a plus size model after she gained weight. Although she was 5 feet 10 inches tall, weighed 155 pounds, and wore a size 12, Ms. Otis was actually smaller than the average American woman who wore size 14 (Wadler, 2001). She chose to stop starving herself to artificially fit the ideal of a high fashion model after visiting an orphanage in Katmandu, where she saw an infant dying from starvation. That incident was a turning point in her life. Ms. Otis said, "I've spent a lifetime being upset with the way I look" (para. 7). She decided a healthy lifestyle was more important than a couture modeling career. After gaining 30 pounds she joined other well known plus size models, Emme and Kate Dillon, working in the plus size category. Ms. Otis did the cover for *Mode* magazine and catalog modeling for plus size retailer Lane Bryant.

Junior models, also known as teen models, are girls and boys between the ages of 12 and 17 years of age. Depending upon how old the model looks and what size he or she wears, a junior model typically is suitable for back-to-school shows and other teen oriented fashion work. The girls generally fit into the sample sizes for junior apparel, which according to Frings (2002) is a size 7 or 9.

Child models are needed to display merchandise for the baby, toddler, children, boys, girls, and preteen markets. Additionally, they are prominently featured during the back-to-school season. Although younger children are used in photographic modeling, professional child

continued on page 142

Figure 6.3 This model represents couture models, a limited number of women in the world who are highly-paid to work for the top international designers in Paris, London, Milan, and New York.

Box 6.1
Life After the Catwalk

Gisele, where's your résumé?

Once upon a time, a model's career generally came and went faster than a speeding limo. A few magazine covers, some runway work and then a quick dive into obscurity.

A few made it in acting, like Andie MacDowell, Lauren Hutton, Cybill Shepherd, Farrah Fawcett or Brooke Shields, or did apparel lines like Cheryl Tiegs and Jaclyn Smith.

But, the recent generation—Cindy Crawford, Christy Turlington, Naomi Campbell, and Elle McPherson, to name a few—are becoming brands in their own right, and the potential for big bucks makes those runway fees look like cigarette money.

Crawford is practically Cindy, Inc., with corporate offices under the name Crawdaddy in New York and Los Angeles that do nothing but deal with her deals. She's got a slew of carefully selected contracts and endorsements that include Kellogg's Special K, Omega Watches, Pepsi, and Revlon; plus she has her own projects, including exercise tapes, a makeup book, and equity stake in Estyle.com, where she writes a regular fashion and advice column. Turlington is behind the Puma-manufactured Nuala yoga line and will have her own area on a new magazine-format Web site, Simplicity.com.

Campbell has a beauty deal with Cosmopolitan Cosmetics, the prestige beauty arm of German beauty giant Wella, and has been touring the world to launch her new signature fragrances. She's also involved with politics in South Africa and has done numerous fundraisers there using her fashion connections. Elle McPherson has a lingerie line and a regular gig on "Friends."

Can a model go from being just a face to a brand that consumers will flock to?

Why not, say their agencies. By the time a model's career is slowing, she's already been around the world a few dozen times and met a few hundred rich and powerful people. That can be parlayed into great job opportunities.

"These girls make incredible connections when they work," said Monique Pillard, president of Elite U.S.A. "They know how to dress, how to speak, how to present themselves. That's very valuable when they decide to go onto the next phase."

"I'm not sure what it says about our culture, but these days, anybody with fame or notoriety is sought after for endorsements," said Crawford in an interview from her Los Angeles office. "If you want to go into business, modeling isn't necessarily the ideal way to start out. But, if you are smart, and lucky, and people start to know your name, you can build on that momentum."

For the majority, the next phase is acting. It works for some in every generation, from Lauren Bacall to Andie MacDowell to Brooke Shields. Most recently Carolyn Murphy played at uptight W.A.S.P. in Barry Levinson's film "Liberty Heights." Shalom Harlow has been going to auditions instead of runway shows for a few seasons, and Amber Valleta has been reading scripts backstage at shows during fashion week.

continued on page 141

Box 6.1 continued from page 140

But, what about other business ventures? Can models work in a boardroom after they've left the showroom?

"As long as what they are doing is appropriate to the fashion field, it makes sense," said Jeff McKay, owner of his own ad agency, Jeff McKay, Inc. "But some projects have zero credibility. For instance, I can't stand it when people in fashion or celebrities try to get political. My feeling is, I don't want a model telling me what to think any more than I want a politician telling me what to wear."

"There are pros and cons," said Ellis Verdi, president of the ad agency DeVito/Verdi. "It works best if the field is related to being a model, like fashion or health. In any case, you are grabbing onto a known quantity and that is a leg up for any new company. Ultimately, any brand can become a super brand. There are people out there who have started with a hell of a lot less and done very nicely."

"Being a model doesn't work against someone anymore," said Michael Flutie, president of Company and Flutie Entertainment. "In the new media, especially with the internet, it enhances the marketability. You can build model's careers now in the same way that you build a celebrity. The whole entertainment industry propels models into a new career."

In some cases, all that time spent in front of a camera can be a help to the business plan.

"You don't have to hire a model for the initial ad campaign, and that's a big help to the bottom line right there," said Verdi. "There are some cost efficiencies there that can be pretty significant for a startup."

But, personality does come into play a lot more once models are doing more than catwalking.

To keep her credibility clean, Crawford said, she goes for projects that build on each other. And, she's got the marketing lingo down pat.

"With any new proposal, I ask myself, do I believe in the product, does it fit with my other projects?" she said. "For example, a cigarette ad wouldn't add value to Revlon."

The silver screen is the top-ranked destination for most models looking to their career futures. But Flutie, who has a division that deals only with models moving into acting careers, said he tries to get his clients to think more broadly about their future-especially if their talent is not exactly Oscar-potential.

"We had a girl who wanted to be an actress," he said. "She was taking lessons and working with a coach. And the coach came to me and said, "This is not going to happen." I had to tell her, because it would have been wrong not to. You have to be delicate, so what I say is, 'Let's keep the acting as a hobby, and develop something else at the same time.' I try to look at the girls' interests. I say, 'What would you be doing if you weren't modeling?'"

But what if the former-model-turned-CEO indulges in stereotypical model behavior-moody, unreliable, and diva-esque?

That doesn't matter as long as it doesn't affect the bottom line, said Verdi.

continued on page 142

Box 6.1 continued from page 141

"The awareness of a famous model as someone who is attractive and healthy and vibrant is far greater than the small awareness of someone as difficult," said Verdi. "Frankly my bigger concern is that you are dealing with someone who is used to going first-class everywhere. What happens if her business manager comes to her and says, 'We can't afford this. You have to fly coach.' To me that is a bigger issue."

Not a problem, said Flutie. Unlike previous generations that took the money and ran, Flutie said the cadets he's seeing know a lot more about their image and long-term market appeal.

"We are going to see a new generation of models driven by the entrepreneurial spirit," he said. "Girls today know about commerce and business."

Adapted from:Ozzard, J. (2000, February 11). Life after the catwalk, *Women's Wear Daily*. p. 22.

continued from page 139

runway models generally start training between the ages of five and ten. Younger girls and boys wear sizes 4 to 6x, and they wear larger children and preteen sizes as they get older.

Children are great audience pleasers during fashion shows, often earning the greatest audience recognition. But, caution must be used to avoid unpleasant scenes with children. It can be very difficult to work with children under the age of five. Young children may appear able to handle modeling during rehearsals, but they can become frightened when they see a large number of strangers staring at them on the runway. Small children may cry or act in poor taste when frightened on stage.

If the show planners decide to use children in the show, the following suggestions may help avoid unpleasant situations. First, try to identify children who act somewhat mature, even if they do not understand the idea of a fashion show. It may be helpful to show them videos of other fashion shows in order to teach them what it is all about. These children should be told that an unknown person will help them change clothes and give them stage directions. Introducing them to their dresser before the rehearsal will help overcome their fears. It will also be helpful to have child models practice on the runway in front of an audience made up of show staff and family members to help them feel more at ease in front of a crowd. Mothers or other adults supervising the children should understand the responsibilities of models. An adult or child sitter must be able to watch over the child during all rehearsals of the show but not interfere with the production of the show.

Although females are dominant in the modeling industry, many men find careers as **male models**. Ever since the 1960s, male models have become important to the production of fashions shows for the male trade market as well as for consumer shows. Male models offer a strong appeal to a consumer-oriented shows featuring women's and men's wear. Male models typically wear a size 34-waist trouser and size 38 regular suit, which are sample sizes in men's wear (Frings, 2002).

Career opportunities for models

Now that we have considered the categories of models, we turn our attention to the various places where models find jobs. Career opportunities are the greatest in large cities, such as New York, Los Angeles, Paris, Milan, and London, with strong fashion industries, both at the trade and retail levels. Modeling work in other cities, such as Phoenix or Minneapolis, may only be part-time, since the demand for models is not as great. Models find work as fit, showroom, runway, catalog, editorial print, advertising, body parts, and television commercial models. Modeling jobs, once very specialized, are now more integrated. A runway model may also find work as a photographic model.

A designer or manufacturer employs a model, with a particular attitude and specific body measurements that meet a manufacturer's ideal standard size, as a **fit model**. Sample garments from the manufacturer's line are adjusted on the fit model. Designers also use their fit models for design inspiration. Designers may use their fit model, a friend or a celebrity as a **muse**, or an inspiration for their ideal customer. Audrey Hepburn served as the inspiration for Givenchy, whereas Yves Saint Laurent used Loulou de la Falaise as his muse for his couture collections for many years.

A showroom model works freelance or as a manufacturer's house model during market weeks. They may work for a few days or a few weeks. Showroom models wear sample garments in an informal manner in the sales area, showing the samples to visiting retail buyers who might be interested in seeing how the garments look on a real person. Because the showroom model wears the season's sample garments, he or she must fit into the company's standard sample size.

Runway models find jobs at trade shows and major fashion centers in addition to working for retail stores. Runway models experience the energy and excitement of a live performance, connecting with the audience and photographers to promote the clothes they are wearing. Models who work the big international fashion shows have style, poise, and confidence to present clothes on the runway (Fig. 6.4). They expect to see their photographs and videos of the runway shows in major newspapers, magazines, and on television broadcasts around the world.

Catalog models are photographed wearing clothing and accessories that will be sold through direct response media such as mail order catalogs, brochures, billing statement inserts, and so forth. It is considered the bread-and-butter job for many models. Catalog bookings may be for a one-hour shoot or several days in an exotic location. This type of modeling requires realistic models who resemble the target audience. Catalog photographs are generally straightforward shots that emphasize the selling features of the garments. Nordstrom gained positive recognition for placing people with disabilities photographed in their wheelchairs as models for some of their catalogs.

Every up and coming model hopes to have her picture on the cover or in the editorial pages of *Vogue, W, Harper's Bazaar,* or *Elle.* Although these **editorial print** modeling jobs do not pay the highest fees, they are considered to be stepping-stones to building a portfolio and other more lucrative modeling jobs. Models use tear sheets from magazine covers and editorial shots, which involve non-advertising magazine pages, to find jobs or contracts for major advertising campaigns.

Figure 6.4 A plus size model wearing garments from Givenchy's special size line.

Editorial modeling involves a cooperative interaction between the model, photographer, and staff, which consists of a photographer's assistant, stylist, hair stylist, and makeup artist, to find a creative image. Several rolls of film are shot to find just the right photograph to capture the look and attract the audience's attention. Once a model has gained some recognition through editorial print work, she may be asked to model for fragrance, cosmetic, or fashion houses for their advertisements.

The purpose of advertising is to promote and sell clothing, fragrances, or other merchandise from the sponsor. **Advertising models** are needed to display and enhance these products for publication in newspapers, magazines, point-of-purchase displays, and other media. Depending upon the clothing or cosmetic line, fashion shots for advertisements may be done in editorial or catalog style. Advertising modeling fees are among the highest in the modeling industry. An exclusive or contract model can receive several million dollars for his or her work. The contract excludes the model from working for the competition. Both Paulina Porizkova and Elizabeth Hurley have been the Estée Lauder "contract" model, whereas Kate Moss has been featured in Burberry ads distributed throughout the world. Miss Porizkova had a $6 million contract with Lauder until Liz Hurley took over in 1995 (Kelly, 2000).

Men and women with attractive hands, legs, feet, and/or hair may find jobs as **body parts models**. This type of modeling is a sub-industry within the modeling industry. Many large modeling agencies have body part models. Hand models are used for hand lotion, nail polish, or jewelry. Hosiery, shoes, and grooming products are shown on models with eye-catching legs. Some celebrities use body part models as doubles for dangerous or revealing scenes in movies.

Because models are confident and composed when photographers take their picture, many models make the transition from fashion modeling into **television commercial** acting. After taking classes in acting and script reading, many models learn how to sound natural for commercials. A great deal of money can be earned from television commercials, especially when the advertisements are nationally distributed. Thousands of dollars in residuals, money paid each time the advertisement is broadcast, are paid to the principal performers featured in commercials. If a model has several commercials running at any given time, his or her income can increase.

As we have learned, there are many different career opportunities for models. From informal modeling for a local retailer to walking the international catwalks as supermodels, a variety of modeling jobs are available. We now turn our attention to the resources that help train, build portfolios, and find jobs for models.

Resources for models

Once an individual decides to become a model, that person has a variety of resources, including modeling schools, agencies, as well as contests and conventions for models, which are available to help prepare and find jobs for the developing model.

Modeling schools

Modeling schools, specializing in training men, women, and children in modeling techniques, are a primary resource for models. These schools exist in every major city. Classes may involve such lessons as runway methods, makeup application for photography or runway, hairstyling, voice, figure control, and new modeling procedures. Many modeling schools provide agency services, booking students or models after they finish their training.

While modeling schools are not an absolute necessity for a beginning model, they can provide the educational background and preparation for a model to get started. A regional modeling school may also have an affiliation with a large international agency, such as Ford or Wilhemina. Once in a while, a promising student may be sent to New York, Paris, or Milan to test with the prominent agency.

Modeling Agencies

As we learned in Chapter 1, modeling agencies began in the 1920s with pioneer John Robert Powers. Since then, a number of highly regarded as well as several disreputable agencies have come on the scene. **Modeling agencies** are companies that represent a variety of fashion models and act as scheduling agents for them. Many modeling agencies are structured similar to Wilhemina, described in the career handbook, *The Wilhemina Guide to Modeling*, by Esch & Walker (1996). Models are placed into divisions, which emphasize the type of work a model does, such as editorial, advertising, or catalog, based upon the model's particular strengths. Each group is managed by its own set of bookers, who are the individuals hired by the agency to promote, coordinate schedules, and negotiate fees for the models. These activities are done from the agency's boards, which are divided into a working board and a high board. As models gain editorial experience and other success, models move from the working board, where employed models are booked into their early assignments, to the high board, where the models with the most demand and highest fees are managed. An agency might also have a test board for beginning models to discover if the business is for them, and the agency can explore if the promising newcomer is marketable.

Most new models contact modeling agencies for possible representation. Many agencies schedule open calls each week, looking for new faces. If the modeling agency representative chooses a model, he or she will be given a trial period on the test board. The new model will be introduced to photographers for test shots so that potential can be assessed and a portfolio created. The **portfolio** is a book of photographs that show the model in the most flattering way. A variety of shots are taken to show the model's versatility. Tear sheets from editorial work are added as the model gains experience. The portfolio is often presented before a model goes to a **casting call**, where many models audition for a slot on the runway or for print work.

The agency will also suggest creating a **composite** or a **headsheet**, which includes the model's name, measurements, and agency contact information with various photographs (Fig. 6.5). These composites are valuable promotional tools that are sent to prospective clients in order to find jobs. Some agencies combine the composites from several new models into a book, which is distributed to potential clients. Electronic promotion using the Internet is the newest way agencies promote their models.

Although most agencies are legitimate, professional, and have the best interest in promoting careers of young and aspiring models, some agencies have the reputation for unethical practices. Agents from disreputable agencies have asked new models for large sums of money for photo sessions, composites, and other promotional tools with no intention of hiring and

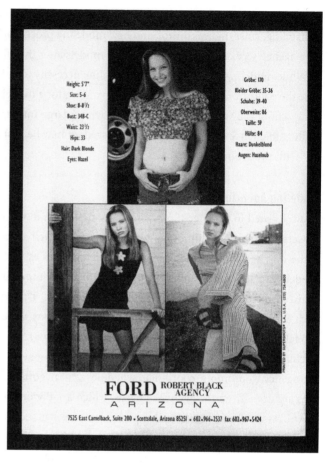

Figure 6.5 Composites, also known as headsheets, are used to promote models from a particular agency to potential clients. *Courtesy, Sara Frain.*

booking models. More information about the negative image of modeling is discussed later in this chapter.

Modeling contests and conventions

Modeling contests, frequently held in conjunction with model conventions, are another way for a model to start a career. As we learned at the beginning of the chapter, modeling contests have taken place all around the world, from Africa to China. Additionally, model Carmen Kass helped judge a modeling contest in her homeland, Estonia, a part of the former Soviet Union. As part owner of Baltic Models, Miss Kass returned to Estonia to encourage other Baltic women to pursue modeling careers. Nearly 6,000 girls entered the contest, with the hopes of achieving a dream career like that of their idol, Miss Kass (Spindler, 2001). Typically, the grand prize for such contests is a modeling contract for a year.

Modeling conventions are held in various cities to look for promising young models, who are not able to travel to New York or other major fashion centers. These conventions have classes in basic modeling techniques in addition to motivational speakers, telling the audience about their experiences in the modeling industry. While many conventions, like modeling agencies, are reputable, some are not and have hurt the image of the modeling industry. Huge registration fees for contests and conventions should also send up a red flag of warning to potential models. Promising to have agents from major agencies in attendance, these convention organizers make enormous profits from anyone willing to pay the fees, regardless of their ability or potential to become a model. An individual interested in a modeling career must realistically assess his or her likelihood of earning money in such a limited market. If an individual is really interested in modeling career, he or she should contact a local agency with a good reputation.

Professional versus amateur models

Figure 6.6 Amateur models come from many sources including schools and civic organizations. They have great enthusiasm to compensate for limited training. *Courtesy, Christopher C. Everett.*

Professional models are trained in modeling techniques and are hired through modeling agencies or schools. **Amateur models** are not trained as professional models and are selected from other resources. Some effective resources for finding amateur models include: a retail store's fashion advisory board, the store's customers and personnel, the members of the organization sponsoring the event, or students from performing arts or fashion schools (Fig. 6.6).

The decision to use professional versus amateur models frequently depends upon the show budget. Professional models must be paid. Shows working with a limited budget may be restricted to using amateur models and offering a gift, discount or gift certificate to the model in lieu of payment. This helps to ensure a positive feeling among all the parties involved. It may also encourage purchases at the store. Many fashion show directors feel that despite the cost of using professional models, they create a smoother, more masterful show. Experienced models can handle last-minute changes and the confusion associated with fashion show production. They have developed an authoritative attitude in presenting clothes properly. This confidence shows as the professional model walks down the runway. Trained models are quick to pick up modeling choreography and routines. Directions and cues are easily learned and remembered. Appointments are responsibly met. Clothing and accessories are taken care of and respected. Any unforeseen problems or emergencies are maneuvered with expert execution.

Professional models (Fig. 6.7) frequently make excellent suggestions about how to wear or accessorize an outfit based on their years of experience and love for clothing. Pros know how to stress the importance of the clothes rather than themselves.

The success or failure of months of fashion show preparation can depend upon the performance of the models. Many amateur models take their role very seriously. Unfortunately, some of the disaster stories regarding fashion shows come from the ranks of unprepared amateur models. Without some training and direction, amateur models have flown down runways with arms flapping like birds, others have frozen with fear on the runway after seeing the audience. Untrained models have damaged clothes by not taking proper care of them. Amateur models demand more time and attention to train due to their lack of experience. The show may require more amateur than professional models since it will take them longer to change garments.

Figure 6.7 Ethnically diverse professional models are popular trendsetters for fashion shows. *Courtesy, Christopher C. Everett.*

When selecting the amateur model, the model coordinator and committee need to be sure that model is willing to make a commitment to participate in fittings, rehearsals, and the show. Being a model is not the glamorous job that many amateurs think it is.

If members of a civic club are selected to model, the model committee must use diplomacy in selecting and training participants. Since these members are not always standard model sizes and often have very strong opinions about what they want to wear, model and merchandise committee members must be ready to handle objections with tact. Inexperienced models may not understand that a fashion show is an important part of doing business for the store or manufacturer providing the clothes. They may resist wearing anything they dislike.

Despite some of the challenges, amateur models have a great drawing power. Audiences love to see their friends and relatives participating in fashion shows. They can certainly add to the audience's enjoyment of the show. Another reason amateur models contribute to a show is the believability factor. When friends and relatives see garments on "real people," they can see themselves wearing the clothes. Professional models often look so sophisticated, customers cannot see themselves in the garments.

Any union rules that may affect the show and the models should be investigated. Shows that are held in television studios, convention halls, or theaters might be influenced by union activities. The specifications may bias the selection of models and their compensation.

Photographic versus runway models

Top name designers such as Ralph Lauren, Donna Karan, or Calvin Klein may insist upon using **photographic models**, known for their print work for their runway shows. Photographic models require higher fees than models who do straight runway modeling. Although there has been a blurring of these two separate careers, some models continue to specialize.

Training amateur models

Walking, timing, posing, and turning are very important aspects of the model's presentation on the runway. Confidence and ease in executing these attributes are instrumental for the professional appearance of the fashion show. The show's model committee or choreographer will need to train amateur models.

The model must walk with a smooth light pace. Body weight should be forward. The body should be straight, but not stiff. Arms are placed down at the side seams of the garment with palms toward the body. They should be kept loose and easy and not swing out from the body. Hands and arms may be used to point out some design element such as a pocket of the costume. Using hands gracefully is important to modeling. Hands should be relaxed. A slight bend to the wrist is more attractive than a perfectly rigid, straight arm. Placing the hand in a ballet position or bend will be more becoming. Shoulders should be down, back, and relaxed. The stomach should be flat and buttocks tucked under. The steps should be just long enough to keep the body erect. Reach with the front foot and push with the back foot for the appearance of walking on air. Feet should follow an imaginary straight line on the floor.

Models and the commentator or stage manager are responsible for the timing of the show. The speed and pace of walking or dancing can accelerate or prolong the show. Models can remain on the runway for longer periods of time, giving other models time to change or get ready, by repeating the basic pattern of walking and turns.

Amateur models frequently walk too fast or want to get off the runway quickly. One technique that helps to keep the pace at a good level is ask the model to stop and pose on the runway. If a photographer is used, the models can be trained to stop at the end of the runway, pose, and wait for a photograph to be taken. This will help to slow down the pace of a fast-moving model.

Expression and personality are often overlooked in the technical aspects of walking, turning, and posing. Although some designers require a different mood or attitude, smiling is a positive expression to show the model likes what she is wearing. The model must be able to communicate a variety of emotions depending upon the type of merchandise or show. The model may be called upon to act in any manner from casual to elegant. If the outfit is fun or casual a smile is very appropriate. On the other hand if the item being presented is sophisticated or serious a smile may seem out of place. It is important for the model to practice various expressions in a mirror.

For the *Rock the Runway* fashion show introduced in earlier chapters, the model committee held model tryouts for amateur models during several open calls in the early part of the academic semester. No prior modeling experience was required. Potential models were asked to fill out an application (Fig. 6.8) and practice some walking routines that were demonstrated by members of the model committee. The model committee observed the candidates walking to music and selected the top applicants, which included 15 females, 10 males, and 2 children.

Figure 6.8 Models who tried out for *Rock the Runway* were asked to complete this application.

MODEL APPLICATION

Rock the Runway

Name_____

Phone_____

Address_____

E-mail_____

Measurements: Women: Men:

Height_____   Bust_____   Chest_____

Weight_____   Dress____   Hat_____

Waist_____

Pant Size_____

Shirt Size_____

Hair Color_____

Eye Color_____

Modeling Experience:

***If you are selected, you will need to be available on Tuesdays at 7:30pm for practices.

***You will need to attend a dress rehearsal on Friday, November 17th during the day and participate in the fashion show that evening. Institutional excuses will be available for those who need them.

Thank you for your willingness to be part of our event. We hope you have fun, as we will try to make this a great event.

Models were given the dates for each practice, the rehearsal, and the show upon their selection. Each model was asked to make a commitment to participate in each of these sessions. The model committee spent the first couple of practices, which took place each week for about a month before the show, teaching models to walk, turn, and pose on a floor outlined with masking tape to the dimensions of the runway that was used for the show. Then, the committee matched models into groupings of two or three that would look good together on the runway. Next, they coordinated model fittings with members of the merchandise committee. Model release forms (Fig. 6.9) were signed to allow show producers to use their images in a video, as well as in other promotional and print media.

Number and rotation of models

There are no hard and fast rules determining the number of models needed for a show. The show organizers need to know how many models will be in a show, and how long each model will need to change between outfits. Adequate time must be arranged for models to change outfits.

Setting up a rotation schedule for models will help the show run smoothly. One way to use models effectively is to arrange a specific order for the models for the first scene prior to the fittings. Then keep the models in approximately the same order throughout the show. For example if 15 models are needed for a show these 15 models are placed in order. In this way model #1 would always be before model #2 and after #15. The audience will not be able to detect that models are always in the same order, but the plan gives models adequate time to change. It also helps models to recognize the established order.

Each model should be made fully aware of the outfits that he or she will be wearing and the order the garments should be worn. The **Individual Model Lineup Sheet** helps to clarify

---

MODEL RELEASE FORM

Rock the Runway

I hereby give the Merchandising Program at Northern Arizona University and/or their designate the absolute and irrevocable right and permission, with respect to the photographs that have been taken of me or in which I may be included with others during the rehearsals and production of *Rock the Runway* fashion show:

(1) To copyright the photographs,

(2) To use, re-use, publish and re-publish the photographs individually or in conjunction with other photographs,

(3) To use my name in connection therewith.

I hereby release and discharge the Merchandising Program of NAU and/or their designate from any and all claims and demands arising out of or in connection with the use of photographs, including any and all claims for libel or invasion of privacy.

_____

Name (print)

_____

Name (Signature)

_____

Date

Figure 6.9 A model release form was created to allow the *Rock the Runway* show producers to use any of the model's photographs for publication and promotional purposes.

the model's order of appearance, outfit, shoes, hosiery, accessories, props, and whether the model is alone or part of a group. Sample blank and completed forms are shown in Figures 6.10 and 6.11.

Depending upon the number of outfits, type of show, facilities, and experience of the models, a 30 to 40 minute show may use as few as five or as many as 20 models. A market show in New York generally lasts about 30 minutes or less. During that time 75 to 100 garments are presented. With that large number of garments to show and to make a visual statement two or three models and sometimes as many as ten models are on the runway at one time. The number of models will increase as the distance between the dressing and stage areas increases. Four or more extra models may be necessary if the dressing area is not on the same floor as the stage area.

When selecting and booking models, the planning staff should have one or two alternative models to prevent the inevitable disappointment and scramble if it is necessary to replace an absent model. Professional models rarely miss a booking unless there are some extenuating circumstances. However, working with amateur models almost always results in at least one "no show." Contingency plans will help to relieve pressures on the show day.

After models have been selected, the model committee should prepare a formal **model list** (Fig. 6.12). A model list will include the model's name, telephone number, email address, gar-

Figure 6.10 The Individual Model Lineup Sheet is used to identify the ensembles worn by a particular model in her order of appearance.

| Name of Model _____ |
| Name of Show _____ |

Order of Appearance	Description of Apparel	Hosiery	Shoes	Accessories Props

ment size, and shoe size. People in charge of working with the models will find this information beneficial.

Model responsibilities

Models have a variety of responsibilities during the fittings, rehearsals, and show production. It is most important that at all times the models associated with a show cooperate with the show personnel. A positive attitude and professionalism are also appreciated by the fitting, rehearsal, production, and clean-up crews. Model expectations are specified in Figure 6.13. See Fig. 6.14 for an example of a model contract.

Responsibilities during fittings

Fittings are generally scheduled at predetermined intervals, and the models need to be on time. If a model is late, it can throw off the entire schedule. The merchandise selection committee or stylist should have a series of garments ready for her when she arrives for fittings. The model should be ready to try on clothing. The model should come to the fitting with makeup and hair appropriately fixed and neatly dressed, including pantyhose.

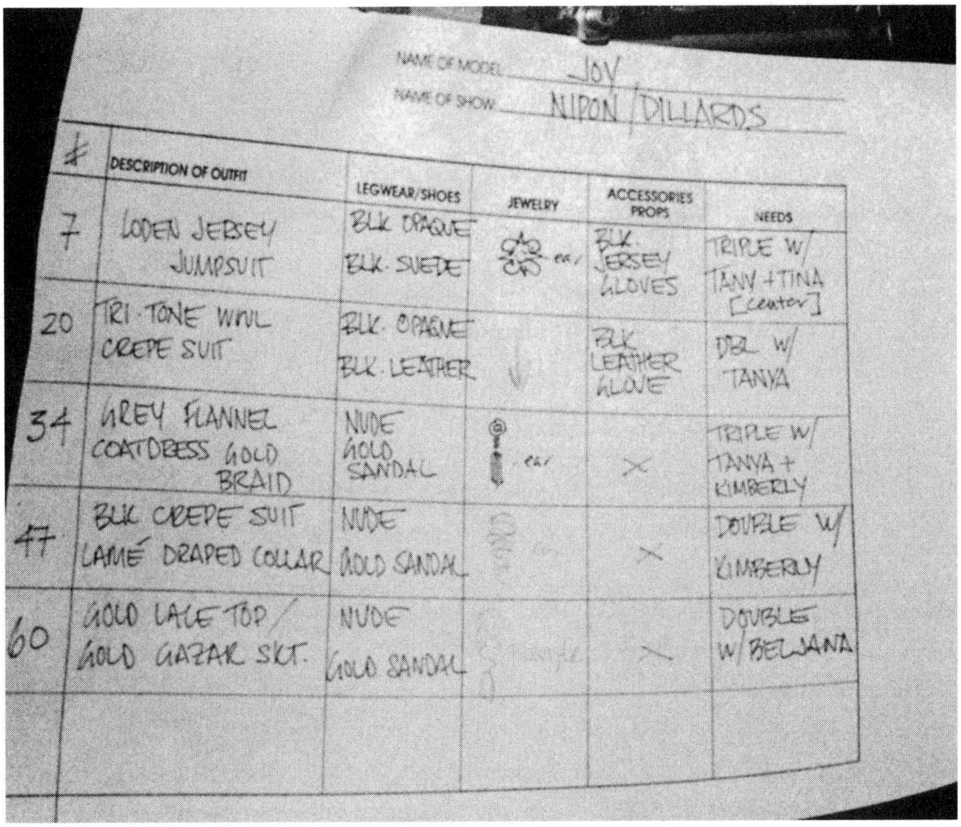

Figure 6.11 This shows how the completed Individual Model Lineup Sheet is placed in the dressing room. *Courtesy, Christopher C. Everett.*

Figure 6.12 After the models are selected for the show, a model list with contact information and sizes is created.

MODEL LIST

Name of Show: _Rock the Runway_   **Date:** _November 17th_

Name	Phone	e-mail	Size Garment	Shoe
Females				
Alexia Thomas	532-7127	A.Thomas@nau.edu	6	8 1/2
Joan Points	523 3226	J.Points@nau.edu	8	9
Pam Hiers	774-1718	Pet67@hotmail.com	8	9 1/2
Erica Warren	523-1562	E.Warren@nau.edu	6	7 1/2
Carly Mercier	779-4568	seacat@aol.com	4	7
Males				
Mike Gibson	526-1287	Mikemouse@aol.com	Large/34	10
Tom Anderson	774-8912	T.Anderson@nau.edu	Medium/30	10
Brett Harwood	525-1025	woody43@hotmail.com	Large/33	11

Cooperation by the show staff as well as the models is very important. The model should never mention if she likes a garment, unless asked. That is not an important factor when most items are selected to make a fashion trend or color statement.

Responsibilities during rehearsals

The rehearsal requires teamwork by all involved. Models should come prepared with a tote bag containing a few supplies: a complete set of makeup, a selection of accessories such as jewelry, gloves, belts, and scarves, and lingerie such as a strapless brassiere or half-slip to use if necessary. An extra pair of sandalfoot pantyhose might be necessary for sandals as well as if hose snag and run. It can destroy the image of the ensemble when hosiery is not perfect. A seasonal basic shoe wardrobe will help the show coordinators see how a complete ensemble will look. Other items to have include: a scarf, a hood covering, to help protect clothing from makeup as it is tried on, pins, a first aid kit, and clear nail polish. Personal hygiene is very important. Dress shields or extra deodorant might be necessary.

Caring for clothing is a joint responsibility of the show personnel and the model. The model should never pull a garment overhead without a scarf or zip-hood covering, worn to protect clothes from makeup. Merchandise tags should not be removed unless specifically told to do so. Shoes should be removed while stepping into or out of a garment. To protect clothing the model should never sit, eat, drink, or smoke while dressed in garments for the show. Clothing should be returned to hangers and properly stored as soon as possible after trying it on and having it approved.

The model should be neat, clean, and pick up personal belongings. The model should not expect the dresser or fitter to be a personal maid. Children and friends should be left at home during fittings and rehearsals. Although children may love to see the process, they would be in the way. Friends may offer helpful suggestions, but they too are in the way.

Model Expectations

Be on time for fittings, rehearsal, and show.

Be cooperative.

Keep merchandise in perfect condition. Clothing and accessories must be ready for sale after the show.

Never sit in an outfit.

Do not eat, smoke, or drink around clothing.

Step in and out of clothing in the area with floor protection.

Use a scarf to protect clothing while pulling clothes over the head.

Keep backstage conversation to a minimum, using a low tone voice or whisper.

Dress and undress quickly.

Line up immediately.

Listen to commentator or cue personnel for instructions.

Do not bring friends or children backstage or in the dressing room before, during, or after the show.

Figure 6.13 A list of model expectations provides guidelines for the behavior and behind-the-scenes activities for amateur models.

Responsibilities during the show

Models should be on time and arrive at least 30 minutes before the start of the show, unless given other instructions. This will be enough time to get ready for the show. Models may need the assistance of hair and makeup personnel on the show day. In any case models should arrive with their tote bags with personal supplies as discussed previously (Fig. 6.15).

Although a dresser is assigned to assist the model, the model should check the clothing and accessories to make sure they are arranged in the order they will be worn for the show. The dresser should prepare the garments by hiding the tags or removing them and putting them in a safe place so they can be re-attached later when garments are returned to the store. The garments should be ready to step into—zippers are unzipped, buttons unbuttoned, and scarfs pre-tied if possible. Shoes and jewelry should be lined up. The model should be aware of the model lineup and where the lineup sheets are posted. This protocol should be followed during all rehearsals using clothing and accessories as well as during the show.

Models should step into and out of clothes only while standing on a covered area of the dressing room. Once the model is dressed, he or she must follow the rule not to sit down. The no smoking rule must also be adhered to. Food and beverages have no place near the merchandise. The merchandise must be kept in immaculate condition and be able to go back into stock for sale immediately after the show.

Models and dressers should keep conversation to a minimum immediately before and during the show. If it is necessary to speak, use a soft voice. Help to keep the backstage area free from excess confusion.

Figure 6.14 *Rock the Runway* models were asked to sign a model contract, after reading the model expectations (Fig. 6.13), to ensure professional behavior and instill a sense of responsibility toward the merchandise.

MODEL CONTRACT

Rock the Runway

As a model in the Northern Arizona University, School of Communication fashion show, *Rock the Runway*, on November 17, 2000, sponsored by the merchandising program and Northern Arizona Merchandising Association, I agree to abide by the following rules:

- I agree to be fully responsible for all the clothing and accessories I will be wearing and be in contact with during the fittings, the dress rehearsal and the final show. I will be asked to pay for any damaged or missing items and will report the items to the Model chairperson immediately.

- I agree to be fully responsible for my actions. The NAU merchandising program is not responsible for any injuries or ailments that may occur during my volunteering with the merchandising students.

- I agree to display a reputable manner of professional conduct while associating myself with the fashion show.

_____

Model's Printed Name

_____

Model's Signature

_____

Date

Models need to be cooperative. They should dress quickly and line up promptly. Listening to the commentator or backstage starter and watching for any special cues will help to make everything look smooth and polished.

Models should be pleasant, discreet, and poised. If the model has an accident or makes a mistake, he or she needs to continue without drawing attention to the situation. Such occurrences as tripping on the steps or stage or dropping a prop or accessory are very common. A professional model will just ignore the circumstances and carry on.

The ugly reputation of modeling

Model: The ugly business of beautiful women, the groundbreaking book by Michael Gross (1995), clearly profiled the seedy side of the modeling industry. With vast sums of money at stake, disreputable people have entered the industry. Some lucky models were never exposed to the corruption and immoral actions by some powerful agents, but many unlucky

Figure 6.15 Models learn makeup techniques from each other and cosmetic specialists backstage.

young girls were lured by the glamorous, yet dangerous, lifestyle each year. Some agency owners were also exposed on the television show *60 Minutes* for allegedly having sex with underage girls. Rumors of drugging and raping young models were brought out into the open.

Milan in the mid-1970s through the early 1980s gained the reputation of being the place for whores and pimps. Models were flown in from various global locations and unexpectedly met at the airport by playboys with a dozen roses in one hand and a big bag of cocaine in the other (Gross, 1995).

Despite attempts to improve the image of the industry, the negative reputation of modeling has been difficult to shake. Vanessa Grigoriadis (2001) profiled some models as bed-hoppers, pill-poppers, and man-swappers for an article in *Talk* magazine. She reported that supermodel Kate Moss spent significant time in rehab, while covergirl Carmen Kass was caught speeding and driving drunk in her home country, Estonia. Carré Otis admitted to her drug addiction, indicating that her modeling agents gave her as much as two grams of cocaine a day to try to keep her weight down (Wadler, 2001).

Top models travel first-class, are pampered with the latest beauty innovations and products, and treated like royalty, just for being attractive on a runway or in a photograph. But, stereotypical model behaviors of being moody divas and unreliable are making models both loved and hated in the 21st century.

Beauty on the runway

Designers cooperate with their fashion show producers to create a story for each of their shows. In addition to using this story for the merchandise, a beauty image is created to further emphasize the vision. From sultry señoritas to rebel chic outlaws, the mood is established for models and merchandise at each fashion show. Now, we look at the show image created by the show staff with assistance from various beauty professionals.

Show image

Many people watch the catwalk shows for hair and makeup trends in addition to discovering the changing clothing styles. Yohji Yamamoto, famous for his fluid clothing that flows with the body, wants a "geisha girl" look for his models. Paris trendsetter, John Galliano characterizes one of his Dior couture collections as "rebel chic," with energy and passion. Jean Paul Gaultier explores "China" with his clothes, stage design, hair, make up, and music, featuring David Bowie's "China Girl" playing in the background.

A backstage pass reveals the beauty trends developed to coordinate with the designer's fashion ideas. Whether the look emphasizes the eyes, cheeks, or mouth, beauty trends emerge from the runway shows.

Beauty professionals

A select group of beauty professionals are hired each season to create beauty images through makeup and hair at the fashion shows. Various makeup artists for the shows use products from Bobbi Brown, MAC, and Sephora, among others.

Bobbi Brown, one of the world's leading makeup artists, developed a line of cosmetics in support of her career as a beauty specialist. Ms. Brown said that makeup worn on runways is not meant to be worn on the streets. "Fashion shows, just like Broadway shows, are about drama and showmanship. I'm not suggesting women ignore beauty trends, but it's a tricky balance to try to be up with the times without looking like a fashion victim" (Brown & Iverson, 1997, p. 133). In her book, *Bobbi Brown Beauty*, she offered suggestions on how to modify runway beauty looks for everyday.

In preparation for the shows, Ms. Brown meets with each designer a few weeks before the clothes are presented. She looks at the fabrics and colors that will be used and starts to create the makeup look for the show, sometimes based upon a phrase the designer used to describe the collection or a significant color being featured. Ms. Brown reviews her plan with the designer, frequently demonstrating it on a design assistant at the designer's showroom. Even though there may be an overriding theme, such as darker eyes or a richer mouth, Ms. Brown tries to come up with a different look for each designer (Brown & Iverson, 1997).

MAC, the extremely popular makeup line, sends makeup artists to the four major fashion show cities to consult with designers prior to show week. Working with such designers as Badgley Mischka in New York, Roland Mouret in London, Allesandro Dell'Acqua in Milan, and Cacharel in Paris, the MAC artists work under a great deal of pressure, often finishing the look just hours before the show is presented. Roland Mouret, meeting with MAC artist Sharon Dowsett, decided he wanted a beauty image that was extreme yet beautiful. He decided on a vivid blue lipstick. But, backstage a week later, Mouret changed his mind and the blue lipstick was replaced with blood red, except on three models who each wore blue, green, or purple lipstick. After the show, Mouret said he was pleased with the ultimate look (Cambridge, 2001).

Hair has been worn long and straight, waved, crimped, short and messy, slicked back with gels, or in pigtails. The variety of hair looks is almost endless. Celebrity hairstylists, such as Orlando Pita at Prada, Sally Hershberger for John Frieda at Diane Von Furstenberg, Odile Gilbert at Pucci, Eugene Souleiman at Louis Vuitton, and Guido Palau at Valentino, create the runway hair images to coordinate with beauty and clothes each season.

Yohji Yamamoto hired Parisian hairstylist Eugene Souleiman to design a fluid hairstyle that complemented his fluid clothing designs. The image was created with a large floppy swoop that bounced as the girls walked down the runway. Slicked down sides with long, straight tresses draped down the back. The makeup was a delicate pale hue, with virtually no eye make-up and part of the lips stained berry. With whitened geisha faces lit up by the spotlights, which were turned on and off, the clothing, hair, and makeup coordinated to achieve the desired movement and effect.

Beauty, as created and emphasized by makeup and hair, is closely associated with presenting fashion worn by beautiful models. In order to fully coordinate the clothes, models and beauty, we next look at the way models walk down the runway by using choreography.

Choreography

Choreography refers to the art of devising movements for dances such as classical or modern ballet or musical show performances. This term is used in the broadcast sense for fashion show production. Fashion show **choreography** includes the plan for the models' walking or dancing runway routines as well as any specific dance numbers. The theme, merchandise, and music selected are elements that reflect the look and feel of the show and the choreography should enhance this image.

Choreography is an important aspect of a fashion show and is often overlooked by inexperienced show planners. Models should not be expected to just enter and walk down the runway at random. All the runway routines for the show should be worked out before models arrive for the rehearsal. Models will either be posed on stage as the curtain opens or enter quickly and assume a position on cue. The travel patterns will ensure the appropriate commentary or music is emphasized on cue. A **choreographer** is responsible for determining the pattern that a model will walk down the runway and the interaction of the models on the runway as they enter and exit the stage area. A large show may use an individual choreographer for these routines. Other shows may rely on the fashion show director or model coordinator to give models their cues.

Choreography need not be expensive. Simple routines that are repeated will keep the costs low. Choreography becomes expensive when more elaborate dance numbers are included, and when it becomes necessary to pay professional dancers to learn, rehearse, and perform production numbers.

Patterns of choreography include:

- Opening the show
- Entering the stage or runway

- Planning paces, pivots and pauses on the stage on runway
- Exiting the stage and/or runway
- Ending the show

Opening the show

Perhaps the most important part of show choreography is the opening. It is critical to the success of the show to get the audience involved right from the beginning. The house lights are dark. A spotlight is focused on one model at the stage entrance. As the general lighting is raised, the model or several models enter the runway. At this point the merchandise, music, lighting, and choreography must all come together. There is a significant difference between the tempo of a fashion show and a theatrical performance. A theatrical performance may open slowly and quietly and build to a climax and conclusion. A fashion show must start and end with emphasis. For example a very effective entrance for a fashion show with an active or casual theme may involve several models wearing similar styles in different colors coming onto the stage to a dance number. Four or five models wearing leotards doing an exercise routine to some upbeat music is bound to grab the attention of the viewer. The choreographer may plan an entrance to give the illusion of going to work on a subway or train and bring out a group of male and female models dressed in business apparel.

Another possible show opening may involve some type of visual effects on the background such as a slide, video, or a light show while the models enter onto the stage. This can also be used to entertain and perhaps educate the audience before the models come on the runway. Each scene of the show may open using a technique similar to the one used in opening the overall presentation.

Pace, pivots, and pauses

The choreographer will give the models specific directions regarding the **pace** or relative tempo. The pace may be fast or slow depending upon the merchandise being presented and music, and where **pivots**, turns, and **pauses**, or a temporary halt to movement, should take place on the runway. Although it is easiest to have each model enter, pivot, pause, and exit in the same manner, the audience would become too bored with the show. There should be some variety in the walking patterns and model routines to interest the audience. The choreographer may chose to control the model's pivots and pauses, and actually determine where they will take place on the runway.

Runway turns should be smooth, graceful, and a continuous motion. The half turn is essential for this movement and accomplished by turning on the balls of the feet. No weight is placed on the heels. Put one foot in front of the other. If the right foot is forward, turn to the left. If the left foot is forward, turn right. With both knees flexed, turn to the opposite direction (180 degrees) smoothly. The body turns halfway, front to back and from the back to the front to reverse directions. Models should practice this until it is performed flawlessly.

The walking pivot combines a number of steps with the half turn. Take three steps. On the fourth step, make it a short one. Make a half turn and turn around. This combination can be used at any point on the runway as directed by the choreographer. Sometimes models are asked to make turns simultaneously with other models. Practicing and perfecting turns with other models makes this look very effective.

Mapping

It is not necessary to create a different route for each model as he or she demonstrates each new outfit. It would be difficult for the models and choreographer to remember each separate walk. A compromise of approximately four to eight walking routes could be mapped in advance, and will allow for some variability. Then as models are given directions, these **mapped routes**, planned paths, can be explained and presented as visual diagrams. This number of variations will not be too confusing for the models or show personnel to remember. The route can be numbered and posted with each model's outfit in the dressing room.

Dancing

Dancing routines can add a great deal of interest to the show. During the 1960s and 1970s dancing took on a new and engaging impact on fashion show production (Fig. 6.16). Professionally trained dancers can easily pick up the routines during the rehearsal. Amateurs may require an additional rehearsal to learn, practice, and become comfortable with the routines.

A dress with fringe may be complemented by doing a simple Charleston on the runway. Evening clothes may be emphasized by a waltz or tango. Large production numbers can be used to emphasize a particular look or theme.

Dance numbers may be used between the various scenes of a show, such as between scenes of workout wear and business attire, to allow models more time to change. At one show a Native American dancer provided entertainment between show segments featuring

Figure 6.16 Dancing models such as this one for Courréges became the norm in the 1960 couture shows. *Courtesy, Bruce Davidson/Magnum Photos.*

southwestern fashions. The dancer emphasized the theme of the show and give models extra changing time.

Model groups

A simple parade of models walking on the runway, one after the other can also be boring. It generally adds more interest and variety when the show is broken up with different patterns and **model groups**. Two models entering the runway wearing the same or complementary outfits creates greater impact and the repetition will help the audience remember the look.

Variations using multiple models are endless. It is common to have two, three, four, or more models on the runway at any given time. The show will be more complex in staging, but it will be more entertaining and effective in showing different colors and designs to the audience. A greater number of models will require more coordination in fittings and rehearsal.

When working with two or more models, the model on the left is considered the lead model. Stage left is considered the left part of the stage from the viewpoint of the audience facing the stage. The other models should keep pace with the lead model. Followers need to practice when to start, turn, and stop in relationship to the lead model.

Two models together (Fig. 6.17) may walk to the center of the runway. At the point where a pause or pivot takes place, these two models may make simultaneous turns and continue or separate, walking in different directions. Planning choreography in advance will ease the transi-

Figure 6.17 A fashion show is more interesting when model groupings or pairs are used in addition to single models. *Courtesy, Christopher C. Everett.*

tions. When three models come on stage together, an effective choreography method is to have all three models pose together center stage. Then the center model moves away and walks to the middle of the runway, called the **pivot point**. As she turns, the other two models walk to the pivot point. They pass the center model, turn at the pivot point, and continue to the end of the runway. The center model may return to the center of the runway, meeting the other models as they return. All three models return to the exit point, leaving the stage one at a time.

Careful coordination during the merchandise selection process and coordination of amateur models into groups will lead to an organized appearance. The models should look good together on the runway. One fashion show featured identical horizontally striped dresses on a petite, curvy figured model and on a tall slender model. The coordinator tried to make the point of featuring the same dress in the complementary colors. Although each individual model looked wonderful in the dress, the desired impact was not achieved.

"The show must go on," is one important point to emphasize with amateur models. Despite elaborate planning and rehearsal, the model may forget the exact route. It is more important to show the garments in a professional manner than to act confused trying to figure out what to do next. If the model who forgets some part of the choreography remembers to smile warmly, the audience is likely to be forgiving.

Exiting the stage

As the model leaves the runway or stage, he or she may stop, turn and pause, enabling the audience to take one last view of the item being presented. The model's personal flair may be revealed with some special pose or exit. It will also give a photographer time to take another photograph.

The plan must include directions for the models who are simultaneously entering and exiting the stage area. It must be determined if the first model will remain on the runway while waiting for the next model to enter or vice-versa.

One fashion show used a unique method to cue models for their exit. Stagelights were dimmed briefly as a signal for the models to leave the runway. A technician who could view both the runway and backstage could see when the next model was ready. This simple yet effective indication allowed for a smooth transition of the models on and off stage without being obvious to the audience.

The finale

The end of every show should be well coordinated and powerful. It should leave the audience satisfied and applauding. The **finale** is the last impression.

Generally the merchandise in the final scene is dramatic in nature. It may be elegant hostess apparel, evening clothes or bridal fashions. The most effortless ending is to bring all of the models, wearing their final outfit, back on stage. By bringing all of the models back on the runway, the audience is able to review the most spectacular clothing shown during the performance. This type of finale benefits from a large number of models, who by their presence on the runway provides dramatic impact. Each model can be positioned along the runway. Models may pivot and leave on cue as individuals or as a group.

Special stage sets may be used to emphasize the finale. A stained glass window can be used as a prop for a wedding scene. A gazebo with distinctive lighting can be used as a tableau. Furniture and background posters may symbolize a room setting.

Even though editors seated in the front row are frequently asked by photographers to tuck in their legs and feet, they quickly did so at Franck Sorbier's couture finale in 2001. A model wearing a wedding gown robe entered the runway on the back of a galloping horse. When the horse reared on its hind legs, some editors gasped in fear ("Fashion Scoops," 2001). No doubt that finale left a long lasting impression.

One basic rule of thumb in planning the show finale is to save the best for last. The garments should have been selected with this in mind. The category or theme of merchandise for the final scene may suggest some creative finale, such as carrying balloons, tossing streamers or confetti for a celebration or holiday theme.

When a show features designs from a celebrity designer, it is customary to have the celebrity join the models on stage during the finale. The show may be a charity event or a retail store promotion where potential customers like to see and meet the creator of the garments. Personal appearances by the designer are very popular events for retail stores. If the show is held during market week, buyers and media personnel will be able to recognize and cheer the achievements of the designer's work as part of the finale.

Models wearing the last outfit go back stage and bring the designer out on the runway. The models applaud the designer; the designer recognizes his or her models, fashion show staff, and audience by clapping for them. The audience is also likely to applaud the show and designer.

Importance of choreography

Properly organized and performed choreography can be used to create focal points for the show. The viewer's attention is drawn to the specific merchandise or trends the show producers want to emphasize (Fig. 6.18). A poorly choreographed show looks amateurish and unprofessional, and does not leave a good impression on the audience.

Choreography should be appropriate for the type of show being produced and the audience. Up-to-the minute dance routines will interest a younger audience. Ballroom dancing would appeal to a mature audience. The type of dancing or walking planned for the choreography can be used to reflect the interests and experience of the audience.

Choreography can be used to reveal certain moods. Elegant and sophisticated merchandise may be accentuated through slow deliberate movements and dramatic pauses. Athletic apparel can be highlighted through spirited and energetic gestures. Children's apparel can be stressed through skipping, running, playing games, and so forth. The viewers should be entertained and satisfied with the show so that they will support the mission of the program, whether it is for charity or profit.

The catwalk is where all of the creative and theatrical elements of the fashion show come together. This chapter discussed the role of the fashion model in helping to create excitement on the runway. In order to achieve the final polished look on the runway models have been trained to project a confident appearance. Beauty professionals, the hair and makeup artists,

Figure 6.18 Variety and emphasis can be achieved by placing models at different locations on the stage and runway. *Courtesy, Christopher C. Everett.*

have worked their magic to transform models into the dramatic creatures who strut along the runway. The choreographer contributed walking routines to emphasize the merchandise and beauty of the models. This chapter has looked at all of the contributors, making the catwalk an exciting place to be.

Key fashion show terms

advertising model	fit model	muse
amateur model	headsheets	pace
body parts model	individual model lineup sheet	pause
catalog model	junior model	petite model
casting call	male model	photographic model
child models	mapped route	pivot
choreographer	mature model	pivot point
choreography	missy model	plus size model
composite	model	portfolio
couture model	model group	professional model
dancing	modeling agencies	runway model
editorial print model	modeling schools	showroom model
finale	model list	television commercial model

References

Aspiring models take to African catwalks. (2001, January 16). *CNN.com*. Retrieved January 17, 2001 from www.cnn.com/200...n/01/16/model.dreams.ap/index.html

Benoit, R. (2000, February 18). Paris models demand extra pay. *Women's Wear Daily*, p. 15.

Brown, B., & Iverson, A. (1997). *Bobbi Brown beauty*. New York: HarperCollins.

Cambridge, C. (2001, April 18). Roland Mouret. *Women's Wear Daily: The Magazine*, 142-144.

Esch, N., & Walker, C.L. (1996). *The Wilhelmina guide to modeling*. New York: Fireside.

Fashion Scoops. (2001, July 12). *Women's Wear Daily*, p. 5.

Frings, G. (2002). *Fashion from concept to consumer* (7th ed.). Upper Saddle River NJ: Prentice-Hall.

Girgoriadis, V. (2001, September). Model mayhem. *Talk*, 132-133.

Gross. M. (1995). *Model the ugly business of beautiful women*. New York: Morrow.

Kelly, V. (2000, December). *Fashion roundtable*. Retrieved July 4, 2001 from www.lookon-line.com/modelsintro.html

Preston, K. (1998). *Modelmania: The working model's manual*. Marina Del Ray, CA: Dog Gone Books.

Rich, J.L. (2000, August 1). On fashion's catwalks; Milan, 7th Ave., Brazil. *New York Times*, Retrieved August 22, 2000 from www.nytimes.com

Trebay, G. (2000, October 3). Milan casting call: Novice models test walks and nerves. *New York Times*. Retrieved October 3, 2000 from www.nytimes.com

Spindler, A. M. (2001, August 19). Home sweet home. *New York Times Magazine*, 157.

Stars in young eyes: Chinese modeling contest offers shot at international stardom. (2000, August 22). *CNN.com*. Retrieved August 22, 2000 from http://www.cnn.com/20.../22/chinese.models.reut/index.html

Wadler, J. (2001, August 12). Turning a corner: A model at size 12. *New York Times*. Retrieved August 19, 2001 from www.nytimes.com

THE SOUND CHECK

7

Rapping, hip-hop dancing and a fashion show featuring Enyce's (pronounced en-ee-chay) Fall 2001 collection all sparked energy at the Southeastern Men's Wear show's *Back to the Old School* party held at the Atlanta Apparel Mart's Fashion Theatre (Lloyd, 2001). Enyce was guest designer for the show and the brand displayed a mix of men's and women's apparel that is cross-directional between urban and more mainstream sportswear (Fig. 7.1). The show also featured New York's deejay Red Alert, local radio personality Ryan Cameron as fashion show moderator, and Big Daddy Kane as the guest performer. Models included the Atlanta Falcons' Ray Buchanan, Cincinnati Bengals' Takeo Spikes and Carlos Emmons, and Rico Wade of the musical group Organized Noise.

In this example, music and the moderator play a vital role in producing an exciting fashion show. This chapter, The Sound Check, introduces the reader to two audio components of fashion show production: music and commentary. The chapter begins with a discussion of music including the music director and music mix. Then the use of sound libraries is discussed followed by talk about the sound system. Next, the chapter focuses on commentary and the individual who delivers the commentary, the commentator or moderator. The content of commentary, what should and should not be included, is discussed next, followed by dialogue on how to develop commentary. The chapter finishes with a description of the different types of commentary used in fashion shows.

Music has always been an essential element in fashion shows. The first retailer to set fashion shows to music was Stanley Marcus, who in the 1920s used the Ted Weems band as background music for his weekly fashion show (Diehl, 1976). Music was as important in the 1920s as it is today in setting ambiance and creating excitement for fashion shows.

In current times, the media is full of examples of celebrity musician attendees at runway shows. Fashion designers are teaming up with musicians for fashion events. Tommy Hilfiger

Figure 7.1 Models at the Enyce's fall show. *Courtesy, Fairchild Publications, Inc. Photographer, Kevin Schaefer.*

teamed up with Atlanta recording artist Jewel in a joint fashion and music venture. The company sponsored her North American Tour and featured her in the national Fall 1999 advertising campaign for the women's sportswear collection. Sean "Puffy" Combs is a further example of the merging of music and fashion. He is a musician, the CEO of Bad Boy Worldwide Entertainment Group (BBWEG) a Hip/Hop recording label, and the designer for his own clothing line called Sean John.

Music can also be used as inspiration for fashions and fashion shows. At the French Fall 2001 collections, John Galliano said his inspiration was the rave culture of kids in England and elsewhere, turned on by music and new forms of style (Horyn, 2001). He interpreted this inspiration in psychedelic prints, fur, and knits and a boom box bag shown in Figure 7.2.

Figure 7.2 This boom box bag was inspired by music of the rave culture in England. *Courtesy, Fairchild Publications, Inc.*

Music

Music is considered the pleasing or harmonious sounds, or combination of sounds, used to heighten the atmosphere of the show for the audience and models. Many fashion show producers believe the right music is essential to the success of a show. The right music can get an audience excited about what they are going to see more rapidly than any other element of preshow ambience. Because some shows, such as trade shows, do not use commentary, music is relied on exclusively to create the mood and emotions of the show.

There are as many different options for music as there are different items of merchandise to choose from for a fashion show. Figure 7.3 is a general listing of musical styles that are available to choose from. Blues, rock, jazz, or any of the other styles listed can be successful in influencing an audience. Just as the clothing shown on catwalks follows trends, so does catwalk music. Classic rock was the dominant music of the Fall 2001 runways (Trebay, 2001). The Beatles, Bryan Ferry of *Roxy Music*, U2, and Michael Jackson were heard at Ralph Lauren, Michael Kors, and Helmut Lang, among others. The key to choosing the right music is to match the music style with the demographics of the desired audience. Young audiences are influenced by teenage music idols such as Britney Spears or Christina Aguilera; older audiences may be influenced by music of their past (such as classic rock) or contemporary music.

Models, too, depend on music to set the pace of the show. They listen to the music to move easily and rhythmically on the stage and down the runway. If the music has a fast beat, models will walk faster which may require more outfits to fill the show time properly. Pace of the music should be considered when selecting music and merchandise.

Music director

The **music director** (Fig. 7.4) is the person responsible for researching and selecting the appropriate music, obtaining permissions to use copyrighted music, mixing the music at the show, and preparing the sound system at the show venue. The use of music may be limited to the show itself, or played as background as the audience enters and leaves the show site. Silence in a room can frequently make people feel uncomfortable talking or moving around

Musical Styles

Modern Rock
    Alternative Rock
    Grunge
    New Wave

Rock
    Classic Rock
    Hard Rock

Heavy Metal

Electronica

Jazz
    Cool Jazz
    Big Band
    Vocal Jazz

Blues
    Chicago Blues
    Country Blues

Pop
    Dance Pop
    Easy Listening
    Soft Rock
    Teen Pop

Hip Hop

R&B
    Funk
    Gospel
    Soul

Reggae

World
    African
    Asian

Figure 7.3 A sample listing of musical styles.

before the show begins. Background music will make an audience feel more comfortable and at ease.

Music directors or technicians are hired to prepare and play music during the show. The music director may be a professional affiliated with the fashion show site or a freelance technician. Local theaters and auditoriums often have their own technical staff who know the specifics of the equipment at the location. Although these technicians are provided by the facility, the fashion show producer is responsible for their wages for working the show. A **music technician**, an expert in musical styles and sound systems, is more aware of problems that can occur with the sound system and can make any needed corrections. Technicians should attend all rehearsals in which music is needed to note cues from the commentator, starter, and models.

Music mix

Music mix is the combination of different musical styles to create a specific mood. The music should match the merchandise, starting with a strong musical selection to capture the attention of the audience and finishing with a finale they will remember. The middle segments of the show should have music that flows so easily the audience is unaware they are listening to anything. When commentary is used, it should flow smoothly with the selected musical styles.

Figure 7.4 Music directors and fashion designers work very closely in planning music for the show.

A variety of music should be used. Music may become monotonous if there is not enough variety in the selections. Ideally, each scene should have music specifically mixed for its merchandise selection. Sportswear requires fast tempo, upbeat music, while evening wear requires slower, sophisticated, subtle music. Youth shows require music the audience will identify with and immediately recognize. When planning music for the show, many more songs will be reviewed than will be used to match the merchandise grouping.

Rock the Runway, a fashion show featured throughout this text, was entirely themed around music and dance. The show had five segments, each focused on a specific musical style. Merchandise was selected to portray each musical style. A dance performance in the musical style of the segment was used to introduce each segment and a deejay who was located at back center stage spun music for the show. Additionally, two moderators used minimal commentary to introduce each fashion theme after the dance. The commentary was brief and concise presenting a strong statement at the beginning of each scene to set the mood.

The opening segment adapted a Britney Spears song as its title, "Oops...I Wore It Again." Dance pop was the featured musical style, and the models wore casual clothing for men and women from retailers such as Buckle, Eddie Bauer, Gap, and Target.

"Wild Wild Dress" was the second segment of the show. As the name implies, western music and clothing were highlighted in this segment. A square dance was used to move the audience from the pop style of the first segment to the country style of this segment. Music by Dwight Yoakum, Shania Twain, and Alan Jackson filled the room as models featured leather pants, fringed coats, and bustiers straight from the old west.

In the next segment, "To Glam or Not to Glam," the audience was transformed from the wild west to big city glamour using the rock music style of Madonna and Lenny Kravitz to set the mood. Trends of the moment including animal prints and wrap dresses, along with lingerie, were featured merchandise in this scene.

Swing was the featured musical style of the next segment and a swing dance performance prepared the audience for "Suit Suit Riot." The segment name was a take off on the song "Zoot Suit Riot" by the Cherry Poppin' Daddies. Featured merchandise included suits and career wear for both men and women.

The show's final segment was titled "Classical Couture" and featured evening wear, tuxedos, and the traditional wedding dress finale. The segment was introduced by a ballet performance, and classical music from Beethoven, Bach, Chopin, and Mozart was used as background music to highlight the fashions.

Music play list　All of the music selections to be used for the show are listed on the **music play list** (Fig. 7.5). The title of the song, recording artist, and length of the song are included. The initial list will have more selections than will be actually used. Music edited for the final show will be slightly longer than the length of the show.

Live or taped music　Music may be performed live or taped for a show. Each form has benefits and drawbacks, which should be evaluated before a style is chosen.

Live music is music performed by musicians during the show. Live music can provide excitement and adds personal touch over taped music, however it requires a budget large enough to pay professional musicians for their time, both during the show and at rehearsals.

Musicians can be limited to a soloist or a small group to minimize expenses, while still providing diversity within the musical style. Although live music may be expensive, the musicians are able to adapt to the show's pace by viewing the actions on the stage. John Galliano hired the entire string orchestra from the National Opera of Paris to play live in the background at a Christian Dior haute couture show (Limnander, 2001).

MUSIC PLAY LIST

Rock the Runway

Song	Artist
Scene 1: Oops I Wore it Again	
Dance: *Oops I Wore It Again*	Britney Spears
• *Bye Bye Bye*	'N Sync
• *Come On Over*	Christina Aguilera
• *When the Lights Go Out*	Five
• *I Think I'm in Love With You*	Jessica Simpson
• *Dancing Queen*	A Teens
Scene 2: Wild Wild Dress	
Dance: *Turkey in the Straw*	John Renfro Davis
• *Crazy Little Thing Called Love*	Dwight Yokam
• *Man, I Feel Like a Woman*	Shania Twain
• *I Should Have Been a Cowboy*	Toby Keith
• *Way Down Yonder On the Chatakoochie*	Alan Jackson
Scene 3: To Glam or Not to Glam	
Dance: *Waste*	Chemical X
• *Music*	Madonna
• *Blue Monday*	Orgy
• *Fly*	Lenny Kravitz
• *Atomic Dog*	George Clinton
Scene 4: Suit Suit Riot	
Dance: *Swing Lover*	Frank Sinatra
• *Zoot Suit Riot*	Cherry Poppin' Daddies
• *Swing, Swing, Swing*	Brian Setzer Orchestra
• *Jump, Jive and Wail*	Cherry Poppin' Daddies
Scene 5: Classical Couture	
Dance: *Concerto Grosso in G minor, Op. 6 No. 8*	Corelli
• *Canon in D*	Pachelbel
• *Spring from The Four Seasons*	Vivaldi
• *Concerto Grosso in B minor*	Handel
• *Brandenburg Concerto No. 2*	Bach

Figure 7.5 Music play list for *Rock the Runway.*

Live mixed music is an alternative to live music. A deejay uses playback equipment to play music live during show segments. A deejay may be less expensive than hiring musicians, and timing problems associated with prerecorded music are eliminated.

Taped music is pre-recorded music from cassettes or compact disks (CDs) copied to play during the show. This music type is more popular for fashion shows because of its convenience. Costs involve fees to mix the tape professionally or privately by a knowledgeable committee member. Costs for preparing a tape may range from several hundred dollars to five thousand dollars for sound operation during the show. It is more cost effective than live music because it has a one-time cost, regardless of the number of rehearsals needed. Taped music allows for the most trendy and familiar songs of the moment to be used, adding to audience excitement. Using taped music may add more musical categories, which live musicians may not be able to recreate. Music for each scene may be completely different to provide added theme emphasis.

In order to have smooth transitions between scenes, two systems can be set up to play tapes or CDs during the show. Music for each scene should be alternately taped on two tapes or CDs so the music may be faded in and out at the proper time. The music for the first, third, fifth, and so forth scenes should be recorded onto tape A while the second, fourth, sixth, and so forth scenes should be placed on tape B (Fig. 7.6).

At the beginning of a scene the music should fade in, starting very softly and gradually accelerating to the volume to be used throughout the scene. Fading out the music is used at the end of a scene to reverse the process, gradually lowering the volume of the music until it is inaudible. Unless a dramatic effect is desired, music should not start out loud as this may startle the audience. Just as variety is required in musical selections, volume of the music should also be varied to avoid monotony. Fading in and out allows for longer or shorter scene transitions as needed by the models or behind the scene staff without making the audience aware of any problems.

Vocal Music   There is a fine line whether to use vocal music or instrumental music to accompany a fashion show. It was thought in the past to never use vocals because the audience could be distracted by the lyrics. Today, music with vocals is so popular that it is hard to ignore this music when planning a fashion show.

Vocals can have a positive or negative influence on a show. If the vocals are popular with the audience they can add familiarity to the show. Caution should be taken not to make the vocals too loud if commentary is used or the audience will tune out the commentary and listen only to the music.

Sound library

Music from a sound library should be used when possible because it eliminates the need for copyright permission. A **sound library** is a collection of records, cassettes, and CDs to be used by the public. **Copyright permission** is authorization from the owner of the copyright to use copyrighted materials. Permissions from a sound library have already been obtained for use by the general public. In some instances, a tape which will only be used for the fashion show and then destroyed, may not require copyright permission. However, it is best to check with the sound library for necessary permissions.

Figure 7.6 Music should be recorded on alternate tapes or CDs for smooth transitions between segments.

Copyrighted music If a commercial CD or album is used, copyright permission must be obtained. To acquire permission it is necessary to determine who owns the copyright. Usually the record producer or the artist holds the copyright. A letter to the recording company should be sent asking for specific permission to use selected cuts from the album. Permissions may be easier to obtain if the show will not be making a profit for the show producer. It is advisable to allow enough lead time to obtain the necessary permissions before the materials are needed. Ask for permissions as far in advance of the show as possible to guarantee the music chosen can be used at show time. If you do not receive a response to your request for permission, you cannot assume you have been granted the necessary permission. Two other organizations which may provide information about the use of recordings are the *American Society of Composers, Authors, and Publishers*, www.ascap.com 1 Lincoln Plaza, New York, New York 10023 and *Broadcast Music Incorporated*, 40 West 57th Street, New York, New York 10019.

Sound System

In addition to preparing music for the fashion show, the music coordinator must arrange to have a sound system and public address system available for the commentator or moderator. The **public address system** consists of the microphone, amplifiers, and speakers. The **sound system** is the equipment needed to play the music, and may include a turntable, cassette player, or CD player; speakers, equalizer, and necessary wiring to allow the sound to be heard at the location (Fig. 7.7). Certain locations will have sound systems available for use. If a sound system is not provided at the site, the components may be rented from local rental companies. The rental fee must be included in the budget.

It is important to test the sound system with the music system before rehearsing with the models. Often a technical run-through with lights and sound is necessary to learn cues. If the music or commentary is inaudible the audience will loose interest in the show. Annoying hums or shrill whistles of microphones will also detract from the fashions of the show.

Commentary

This chapter opened with a description of an Enyce fashion show. In addition to music, a local radio personality, Ryan Cameron, served as fashion show moderator. When the Metro Channel broadcast *Full Frontal Fashion*, wall-to-wall coverage of Fashion Week, André Leon Talley, editor-at-large of *Vogue*, served as moderator, adding dialogue about the designs, designers, and models (Marks, 2001). The comments delivered to the audience by Cameron and Talley served as commentary.

Commentary is the oral delivery of descriptive details of garments and accessories presented in a fashion show. It is used to entertain the audience and make clear fashion statements to help sell the merchandise. Good commentary tells the audience something about the merchandise they may not see by viewing the garments. Commentary may also focus on

Figure 7.7 Sound technicians work the board at an outdoor fashion show. *Courtesy, Christopher C. Everett.*

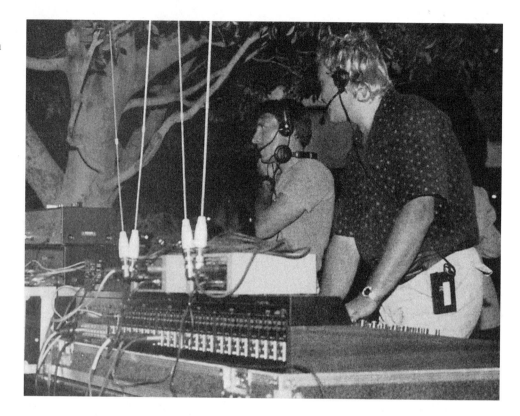

the designer, telling the audience of his or her inspiration, use of fabrication, or some other detail to excite and inform the audience. With effective commentary, the audience does not realize their attention is moving back and forth from commentary to fashions. Enjoyable commentary puts the audience and models at ease and creates a welcoming environment.

While music is essential to fashion shows, commentary is an optional element of fashion show production. Historically, most fashion shows had a commentator who narrated descriptions to the audience as they viewed the fashions. In contemporary society, audiences are so attuned to interpreting images visually, and music has grown so important as a communication and entertainment device, that oral narrative is not as important. This is not to say commentary is not important. Metro Channel employed André Leon Talley to educate and entertain a viewing audience that expected to learn additional information beyond what they could visually see. Commentary serves an important function in fashion show production and a critical understanding of the audience will allow it to be most effective.

Some show types, such as trade shows, haute couture shows, and designer shows, do not use commentary. Instead, these shows create ambiance with music, and models may carry style numbers referenced in a buying guide. Buyers are looking for trends and are interested in the visual images they are seeing rather than listening to specific details that they can refer to later when placing an order. Necessary information such as style descriptions, price, and minimum ordering requirements are printed in the buying guide where buyers take notes as they view the fashions on a runway.

Production shows incorporate commentary into a script, treating the show as a theatrical performance and using the commentator as actor performing specifically scripted commentary. Informal shows use minimal commentary.

Consumer-oriented shows are more likely to use commentary than trade shows are. These audience members want information about the fashions. The commentary is informative giving details to the consumer, pointing out seasonal selling features to encourage the audience to purchase the fashions after the show. Many clients use fashion shows to identify new looks and commentary can be used to more easily identify the trends for the audience. Commentary is used to emphasize important fashion ideas for the season.

Commentators and moderators

The **commentator** (Fig. 7.8) or **moderator** is a member of the show staff with the responsibility of preparing and delivering the commentary during the show. Commentator is the traditional title, but recently moderator has been used to describe this function. This person should be very knowledgeable about fashion trends and be able to share this knowledge with an audience.

In some instances, a well-known celebrity may be used as a commentator or moderator to add newsworthiness to the show, draw a larger audience and increase enthusiasm. If a celebrity is used, he or she must be thoroughly prepared and rehearsed in speaking about the fashion trends. Their knowledge of the fashions must surpass their star status. If they are not prepared, their use as a spokesperson may backfire and leave a bad impression with the audience.

The best commentators are comfortable speaking in front of an audience and have a good working knowledge of current fashion. Other qualities of a good commentator are illustrated in Figure 7.9. The commentator must understand the purpose of the show and use commentary to support the purpose, selling merchandise and entertaining the audience. Like models, commentators should at all times act in a professional manner, spotlighting the fashions, not themselves. Egos are checked at the door.

A commentator should prepare by knowing current fashion looks, terminology, colors for the season, fibers, and accessories. Current fashion publications, such as *Women's Wear Daily* and *Vogue*, can provide necessary fashion knowledge of latest trends. Additionally, commen-

Figure 7.8 Fashion show commentators may be fashion experts, such as this editor from *W. Courtesy, Fairchild Publications, Inc.*

Figure 7.9 Qualities of a good commentator.

Quality of a Good Commentator
Comfortable as a public speaker
Good knowledge of current fashion terminology
Ability to make the audience feel at ease
Professional in actions and appearance
Not place oneself above the designs being shown
Illustrate the store philosophy in dress and appearance
Complement the theme of the show
Not be flamboyant or overstated in appearance
Neat in makeup, nails, and grooming

tators should use a fashion dictionary such as *Fairchild's Dictionary of Fashion* to define the looks and terminology they will use in the commentary. Identifying current trends and brushing up on fashion terminology can begin as soon as the commentator has been selected.

The commentator and production personnel often use commentary to set the pace of the fashion show. Incorporating additional commentary, dramatic pauses or fashion information can slow a show that is proceeding too fast. Certain shows are staged with continuous commentary regardless of model entrances and exits. Other shows recite specific commentary choreographed with the models. It is the responsibility of the commentator not to bring mistakes of the models to the attention of the audience. If an obvious mistake that cannot be overlooked does occur, the commentator must be gracious to the model and be poised throughout the situation allowing the audience to be at ease.

Starters and models must have knowledge of the commentary. Models, commentators, and starters must know commentary signals for entrances called **cues** to send models out. Models must know on-stage commentary cues to highlight details of the fashions, such as linings, pockets, or other finer points of construction.

The dress and appearance of the commentator must express his or her fashion expertise without being flamboyant. The dress of the commentator should complement the theme of the show if appropriate. If the commentator is representing a retail store, the store's philosophy must be evident to the audience. If the theme of the show does not lend itself to be used by the commentator, the individual should dress in classic, understated clothing not drawing attention away from the fashions on stage. Hair, makeup, and nails should be appropriate without upstaging the models. Current accessories should be worn as long as they do not interfere with the microphone.

Shows may choose to use one or two commentators (Fig. 7.10). Working in pairs, commentators often put each other at ease to overcome their nerves and stage fright. Another variation to a commentator may be to use an emcee or announcer as a master of ceremonies, making the audience feel comfortable during intermissions. Using an emcee and a commentator allows the audience to experience variations in speaking styles.

It is important that the commentator understand the sophistication of the audience when preparing commentary. More sophisticated audiences require less commentary to interpret

Figure 7.10 Commentators review their notes before a show. *Courtesy, Christopher C. Everett.*

fashion statements. Audiences with less fashion knowledge welcome commentary and the detail provided to understand the current fashion statements. Further demographics of the audience, such as age, gender or nationality, may also dictate commentary.

Commentary content

The show's theme and fashions tie together using commentary. The narration allows for easy transition from one segment to the next without confusing the audience. Commentary is also used to hold the audience's attention. It can keep an audience interested in the fashion show by creatively analyzing what they are viewing. Buttons have new importance when narrated as part of a current trend as in the following example:

You would think the age of corporate casual would have spelled doom for the suit, and it has for the Power Suit of past decades. But this season's takes are not just for business hours, there's something for everyone. Louis Vuitton has traded Reagan-era brass buttons for fanciful mink pom poms on a contemporary suit jacket.

Commentary can set the mood for the show and create excitement in the audience. The right introduction will have the audience primed for what they will be viewing and have them excited about adapting the fashions into their wardrobes. Commentary throughout the show can maintain the excitement by leading the audience to a climax, tying into the exciting finale of evening wear or bridal wear.

Commentary should be written to establish a fashion feeling or mood of the clothing. The point of commentary is to distinguish the current season's clothing from the past season to encourage the audience to update their wardrobes. It should describe the clothing using the most current fashion terminology. Correct terms for sleeves, closures, decorative details, and other construction components should be used to communicate the seasonal trends. Commentary should include the season's silhouettes, proportions, colors, fabrics, accessories, and distinguishable details. Audiences react to color more readily than other elements of design, and it is often a starting point when delivering commentary. The commentary should also incorporate the lifestyle of the consumer. Commentary fails when the audience presumes the garments are not necessary or appropriate for their lifestyles. Wording should inform the audience of what the garment can do for them as well as what it looks like.

Commentary should go from general information about the garment or trends to specific information about a detail. It should allow the audience to travel with the trends from item to item showing congruity between outfits. Notice the transition from conventional dressing to contemporary dressing in the following example:

Suiting up for spring may include a traditional gray, checked ensemble, but throw in a twist of color with a polka-dot pocket square. A big trend of dots, large and small, is here to stay for spring.

Customers are often equally concerned for function and fashion. Fabric details may be examples of function as in the following example:

Have you ever wondered why a Terrycloth robe feels soooo... good after a shower? It's because it has loops! The looped structure of Terrycloth makes it one of the most absorbent fabrics available on the market. This "pretty in pink" robe will definitely keep you warm and dry after that long, hot shower.

Commentary should not be so detailed that it bores the audience. The audience should not be made to seem unintelligent by delivering commentary that states every detail of the garment. An example of unacceptable commentary follows:

The ease of wearability of polyester makes these next ensembles especially good for traveling. The jacket has a three-button front closure and a back slit. The pleated pants have a front zipper, front pleat and side elastic. The skirt is a flattering A-line style shaped with darts and side elastic, a back zipper, and a back slit. The dress allows the sleeves to be rolled up or down. The models are showing this set in red, tan, and black.

Overly opinionated words and superlative words are also undesirable in commentary. Descriptive words such as *ravishing* that mean nothing should be avoided. The audience should be able to make up their own minds without editorial comments from the commentator. Overusing terms or icons from popular culture can also detract from the commentary. Another example of *unacceptable* commentary follows:

Our next spectacular model looks fabulous in this traveling suit. The alluring jacket sets the model apart from the crowd and just look at the precious shoes that make the outfit!

Good commentary can be developed from the unacceptable examples. Keeping in mind that commentary provides information about the trends of the season, new details, and the current color palette, an acceptable commentary describing this outfit follows:

At home or away, these clothes make every day a pleasure trip. These wrinkle-resistant travel separates unpack with hardly a wrinkle. The jacket is featured in the new longer length for this season, updated with three buttons. Both the skirt and pants have side elastic to make them fit just right at the waist. We're showing great fall colors that can be mixed and matched in clay, khaki, and black. All pieces are by Spencer Jeremy and available at Nordstrom.

Two other factors should be considered when writing commentary—the use of price and the use of the model's name. The type of fashion show and the audience will determine whether or not to include price of apparel or accessories in the written commentary. Many individuals feel the amount of money they spend on clothing is personal and do not want the prices of items they look at disclosed publicly. However, if the price will be perceived as a particularly good value, it may be an asset to include price in the commentary. Prices can be overused in commentary making the commentary monotonous. Price may be mentioned for the shock value, and may be essential information if the show's primary purpose is to sell goods the consumer is unfamiliar with such as wearable art.

The type of show and the audience also determines if the models' names will be used. Shows using professional models do not generally include the model's name in the commentary. However, in school productions and civic shows, using models' names can bring recognition to amateur models who have invited many friends or relatives to watch their performance at the show. In these cases, using the model's name allows the model to be more at ease and more connected with the audience, and recognized for their efforts. If models' names are used, they should be used for all models.

Developing Commentary

Fashion show commentary is developed from two sources. First, information about current trends and fashion vocabulary is gathered from fashion magazines and reference books. This information is general, used by the commentator to become familiar with the images and looks of the season. The commentator should have this research completed before fittings.

A second, more specific source used to develop commentary is viewing the merchandise and accessories at fittings. The information is gathered on fitting sheets (see Chapter 5) and commentary cards are created. **Commentary cards** are full descriptions of the garments and accessories used in the show. Commentary cards are prepared on index cards to be read as narration during the show. These cards are easiest to read and keep in order during the presentation. If the order of the models is disrupted after the start of the show, the commentator can effortlessly adjust the cards to match models as they make their entrance. Sheets of paper, on the other hand, often rustle and cause noise that can be heard over the sound system. It is also impossible to reorganize the information if the models get out of their planned order.

Commentary cards should include the model's name, the position in the lineup (segment and number at the top of the card for easy reference), a description of the ensemble and accessories, and special selling features. Only one garment or ensemble should be included on each commentary card. Commentary cards should be filled out at the time of fittings so the commentator can see subtleties of the fit that might not be noticed on a hanger. Selling features of the garment should also be included on the commentary cards. For example, Tencil® Lyocell has recently gained popularity in the marketplace. Consumers may not be aware of the ease of care and lightweight nature of this new fiber. Sharing this information may entice the audience to purchase garments made from this fiber after the show.

Types of commentary

The commentary may include a total description (full commentary) of the garments, a partial description of the garments, or have no description of the garments allowing the commentator to ad lib the commentary. There are four types of commentary:

1. Full commentary (script commentary)
2. Partial commentary
3. Impromptu commentary
4. Filler commentary

Each may be used according to the type of show, the expertise, and the preference of the commentator.

Full commentary **Full commentary** involves writing every word of commentary on cards or in script form prior to the show. It is important that the commentator deliver full commentary in a natural manner, to avoid demonstrating that it was prepared in its entirety before the show. This type of commentary does not allow for last-minute changes in the lineup. A pre-written script follows strict fashion statements, which may be lost with any last-minute changes in the lineup. The commentator may also not have proper filler information available in case of any changes or delays.

Production shows may use an adaptation of full commentary, known as **script commentary**. Commentary in script form is full commentary written out word for word for the commentator to read and speak like that of a broadcast with staging and other elements noted. Script commentary is used because it has all cues listed for the commentator. Scripts are written on pages with two columns. The left-hand column denotes scene, music, lighting, and model cues while the right-hand column cites the actual commentary with planned pauses (Fig. 7.11).

Partial commentary Some commentators are more comfortable using commentary that is less than complete as they stand at the podium—**partial commentary** is only a portion of the commentary. The major details of the garments may be listed in outline form or written in partial script with very little detail on a card. More detailed description of the fashions and accessories are stated by the commentator as needed. This may be less time-consuming to prepare prior to the show but is more difficult to use during the actual show (Fig. 7.12).

Impromptu commentary **Impromptu commentary** is commentary created spontaneously during the show using only brief cue cards for assistance. This type of commentary may sound misleadingly simple as if it requires no preparation, but indeed it does require advanced readiness. The commentator must accumulate fashion phrases on cards to use as a lead off to the scene or to describe each garment. It is important that the commentator have one and one half the number of phrases for the number of garments being used. This may sound like an extreme, but it is important that the commentator have enough buffer commentary to be flexible in case of last-minute changes in the lineup during the show. The cards also provide the commentator with added confidence in describing fashion trends. Impromptu commentary will also be delivered more naturally putting both the commentator and the audience at ease.

Highly experienced commentators, such as retail fashion directors who work with current fashions and fashion terminology on a regular basis, may choose not to have any prepared commentary. Instead they may review the garments prior to the show and then speak about the garments as they appear on the stage or runway, eliminating time demands prior to the show. This type of commentary allows for the most changes in the model lineup because the commentator is not influenced by the order when speaking. Often the commentator will have a conversational style when speaking and be very spontaneous about the fashions. Designer shows may use the impromptu approach if the designer serves as the show commentator. Only the most experienced commentators can do this with the style needed to influence the audience.

Filler commentary Commentary problems may sometimes occur during the show. First, the commentator may become nervous in front of an audience, and deliver the commentary much faster than intended. Second, many commentators believe they will be able to think creatively on their feet and decide to use partial commentary. However, only during the show do

Figure 7.11 Script commentary example

Script Commentary

Page 2 of 6

MUSIC: OOPS I WORE IT AGAIN

DANCE ENSEMBLE PERFORMS DANCE (3:05)

TEAM EXITS STAGE LEFT

MUSIC FADES

LIGHTS TO SPOT

ADAM		The secret is out. This season's hottest fashion trend is denim. From the streets of Paris to Flagstaff, denim is everywhere.
	CRYSTAL	And black is the color of the moment. Whether it is loose-fit, relaxed fit, or classic-fit, there is a jean to fit every guy or gal.
ADAM		Alexia, Joan and Pam are wearing Fair Isle cardigans in linen/cotton blends, specifically dyed to give each sweater incredible color and a unique texture.
	CRYSTAL	Mike and Tom are wearing cobble cloth pullover sweaters. The cobble cloth is an update to traditional pique knits seen in both men's and women's knitwear.
ADAM		These sweaters and jeans are available at Sage Brush Trading Company.

they realize they cannot think of enough different information to relay to the audience. Also, if they have decided to use impromptu commentary, commentators assume they have prepared enough commentary. Not until show time do they realize how fast they have used the prepared commentary.

To avoid these problems and not be caught off guard, prepare far more commentary than will be used or prepare filler commentary, which can be used at any time during the show to fill in unexpected pauses that may occur. **Filler commentary** may include fashion and beauty tips, credits to hair and makeup technicians, store services and facilities if produced by a retail store, or other facts of interest to the audience. Each category of filler commentary such as fashion tips or credits should be separated into piles before the show so a variety of comments can be easily accessed during the show (Fig. 7.13).

Figure 7.12 Partial commentary example

Partial Commentary

Alexia   Oops I Wore It Again   #1
Mike
Joan
Tom
Pam

GARMENT DESCRIPTIONS: loose-fit, relaxed-fit and classic-fit black jeans, Fair Isle
cardigans of linen/cotton blend and cotton cobble cloth pullover sweaters

ACCESSORIES: Italian leather belts with silver tone buckles

PROVIDED BY: Sage Brush Trading Company

We began this chapter with a description from an Enyce fashion show and we end this chapter with a description from a Lady Enyce fashion show. Box 7.1 documents a fashion show from beginning to end, letting the reader absorb the ambiance of the show and recognize the influence of music on the show.

This chapter has described the use of music and commentary in preparing a fashion show. The use of commentary must be carefully considered when producing a fashion show.

continued on page 187

Figure 7.13 Filler commentary example

Filler Commentary

Fair Isle Sweaters – both pullovers and cardigans, imported from Fair Isle off the coast of

Scotland. They are characterized by soft heather yarns, and bright-colored knits in traditional

patterns. They were popularized in the 1920's by the Duke of Windsor as a short-waisted

sweater with a V-neck, worn instead of a vest.

Box 7.1
Fashion and Fantasy at Lady Enyce's Spring 2001 Collection

The Call
"Everything's set. All you have to do is show up and tell them who you are. You'll be on the list."

"Really?" I ask, in awe.

"Have fun."

continued on page 185

Box 7.1 continued from page 184

The backstory

Four years ago, Seattlites Tony Shellman and Lando Felix founded the Enyce Clothing Company (pronounced en-ee-chay) with Evan Davis, who hails from New York. By 1998 Enyce, a wholly owned subsidiary of Fila sportswear, had pulled down $12 million in revenue. Presently, Enyce serves 500 retail accounts nationwide. They also handle 100 international accounts out of offices in Frankfurt and Tokyo and own a manufacturing plant in Hong Kong. Oh, and I shouldn't forget, they're tight with 'N Sync.

Last year, the trio launched Lady Enyce, which on August 16 unveiled the Spring 2001 Glam Rock Collection, its latest line of sports fashion wear for the modern women, at a gala event attended by the cream of New York's in-crowd, and myself.

Anticipation

Exterior. The Metropolitan Pavillion. Night. Glass front doors look onto the polished hardwood floors of a vast, gallery-like space. Weird. I expected a glitzy hotel. The place is deserted but for a small, styling group of buppies who sport white tops and khaki bottoms like a fashionable uniform. Three young women who are skinny enough to be models sit on the floor, lounging. It must not be time yet. When I ask, an attractive, darkly suited man confirms my observation. "We're not starting until 8:30," he says.

One and a half hours and two glasses of wine later, I return to find a scene straight out of a hip hop concert. The street is packed with young black folks crying, "I'm on the list! Let me in! My girlfriend is the stylist!" I start shouting, too. "I'm a journalist!" I'm press! I'm on the list!" Two burly brothers who can barely contain the surging crowd man the glass doors, now locked. "Just step back from the doors," they shout in vain. "Please! Just step back. You're all gonna get in!"

We don't believe them. We keep pushing.

An eternity later, my companion and I are finally seated two rows back from the runway. Heads swivel this way and that, checking out who's who and who's wearing what, trying to guess if the person next to us, across the way, or the person who just stepped through the doors, is "somebody." As a matter of fact, I'm dying to know who the athletic-looking, chocolate brother is (Biceps bulging as he holds a sleepy toddler) and why everybody is snapping his picture and shoving microphones in his face.

The lights blink on and off, signaling that the show is about to start. Ten minutes later, it actually does.

The show

It all happens so fast. The lights go down, and a high-energy, MTV-inspired montage is projected onto the back wall of the stage, showcasing crowd after crowd of young rock enthusiasts. Cool, I think. I'm in. then the lights come up, the video disappears, "I Love Rock 'n' Roll" blasts, and the models start to walk.

continued on page 186

Box 7.1 continued from page 185

This is what I remember:

Big Hair. <u>Hair</u> teased within an inch of its life snaps the audience back to the '80s with a quickness. If that didn't do it, then the show's rock soundtrack, which includes tracks like "Eye of a Tiger," "Girls, Girls, Girls," and "Walk This Way," puts in the rest of the work. The music is at once jolting and energizing. It takes awhile to get over the expectation of a hip hop beat, but once you do, you start to enjoy the rock music's relentless kineticism.

The model walk. Leading with their navels, the models' straight-legged gait is curious. I remember days past when models walked as if their hips could kill, carving out the space ahead of them, daring you to touch the untouchable. I'm not quite sure what this new body language is saying…

Desire. There is so much I want: A pair of wine-colored leather pants, a short denim jacket, low-slung, yet form-fitting pants, baby doll tee, and especially the sleek, gray track suit. Then there are the clothes that only Naughty Me of my fantasies would wear: the glittery halter top, denim jeans with rhinestones, the Daisy Dukes, and the last bikini that cruises down the runway (which brings to mind Harley Davidson or S/M depending on your frame of reference).

Lady Enyce's Spring collection is cool. The designs are provocative, the fabrics are hip, and above all, the concept is unique. Two types of people can get away with these fashions: the bold and the beautiful. The beautiful trick of this show is that the designers were willing to boldly take their "urban" (read: black or extrapolated from black culture) Gen-X audience where none of us dared to go-back to the '80s glam rock era.

The dreadlocked guy. The last thing I remember is the sweet-faced, deadlocked guy who rode a bike down the runway at the end of the show, pumping his fist in the air.

The MacZone

When the lights come up, everybody heads over to the massive room next door where a D.J. spins rock, funk, hip, hop and R&B. Alcohol and finger foods are on the house and the feeling is high.

"Their stuff is incredible," exclaims Christen Elmore, one of the models in the show. "There's nothing like it out there." When asked if she would wear the styles out on the street, she doesn't hesitate, Yeah!"

Monique Santos, another model who frequently works with Lady Enyce, agrees that the company's unique styles keep her coming back for more. "I'd always work for them. The clothes are fresh. They're cool."

Damani Higgins who works for FUBU, an Enyce competitor, found the show compelling. "It was really well put together," he said. "Not too long and not too short. They kept you wanting to see more." For the clothes themselves, Higgins showed nothing but admiration. "I liked their flamboyance. The outfits are very sexy, but there's sophistication behind the sexy. I can see where it's going."

continued on page 187

Box 7.1 continued from page 186

While praise for the collection is as ubiquitous as air, not everyone was in sync with the program. One financial consultant who chose to withhold his name enjoyed the party, but not the show. "I didn't like the '80s music. As a black man, I felt like they could have done something else." While his first response to the clothing was standoffish ("I wouldn't personally go out and buy any of this stuff"), when pressed he concedes that a few pieces of the collection caught his eye. "I did like the sweats and the t-shirts."

Tony Shellman, the dreadlocked guy, is cloud dancing. "I'm really happy, it was a wonderful show," he enthuses with a tight hug and a kiss. Recounting his inspiration for the show, Shellman explains, "All of us are big '80s rock kids. I had a Jheri curl. Lisa's (Lady Enyce's designer) hair was feathered. What can I say?" As his boys sweep him away, he promises to talk to me later. I'm not surprised when it doesn't happen.

It's his night. And it's a success.

Coral A. (2000, August 30). *Fashion and fantasy at Lady Enyce's spring 2001 collection.* Retrieved June 5, 2001 from http://www.africana.com/Daily/Articles/index_20000830.html

continued from page 184

Used ineffectively, commentary can loose an audience immediately while effective commentary can leave the audience wanting more. While commentary is optional, music is not. The response and enthusiasm to a fashion show can be impacted by music more than any other theatrical element. Music creates the mood to further emphasize the fashion statements. Music is a universal language pulling the audience and fashion show participants together.

Key fashion show terms

commentary	impromptu commentary	music technician
commentary cards	live mixed music	partial commentary
commentator	live music	public address system
copyright permission	moderator	script commentary
cues	music	sound library
filler commentary	music director	sound system
full commentary	music mix	taped music
	music play list	

References

Diehl, M. (1976). *How to produce a fashion show.* NY: Fairchild.

Horyn, C. (2001, March 15). Galliano plucks life from London streets. *New York Times*, p. A22.

Limnander, A. (2001, July 7). *STYLE.COM: Fall 2001 Haute Couture—Christian Dior*. Retrieved August 14, 2001 from http://www.style.com/styleapps/MSD/top.run?p=style& event=F2001CTR_CDIOR

Lloyd, B. (2001, May 31). Enyce's quick tempo, *Women's Wear Daily*, [Section II] p.2.

Marks, P. (2001, February 18). Cable stations turn Fashion Week into fashion telethon. *New York Times*. Retrieved February 20, 2001 from http://www.nytimes.com

Trebay, G. (2001, February 16). Where the old songs go, on the runway and off. *New York Times*. Retrieved February 20, 2001 from http://www.nytimes.com

THE FRAMEWORK

8

I n 1999, Viktor & Rolf introduced their first haute couture line using minimal staging to thrill their trendy fans. The show was presented in a salon of the Plaza Athenée. At center stage was Maggie Rizer, the solitary model for the show, who stood on a revolving pedestal (CNN.com, 1999a). The theme: a ten-act performance in which the two designers dress their living doll in layers of beige, lace, and sparkle—to the point of superimposing nine outfits. The total weight on Rizer was 150 pounds of jute and crystal (Fig. 8.1).

Unique staging was also the focus for the Givenchy haute couture show during the same season. Alexander McQueen, head designer at Givenchy, showed medieval-inspired designs on transparent mannequins, creating the feel of a museum exhibition rather than a catwalk show (CNN.com, 1999b). The mannequins were lit from the inside and were lifted up through trap doors on the stage, twirled around, and descended back into the darkness (Fig. 8.2). Their appearance on the stage was choreographed to give a feeling of movement during the presentation (Davis, 2001).

Setting the atmosphere for the presentation comes together in the staging framework—the layout of the physical facilities. In this chapter, The Framework, we focus on the staging necessary to produce a fashion show. Staging can be elaborate as illustrated by Alexander McQueen or minimal as illustrated by Viktor & Rolf. In both instances, the staging was effective in highlighting the merchandise, always the spotlight of any show.

The chapter begins with a discussion of the stage and runway areas. These areas are visible to the audience. Then the discussion moves to the dressing area hidden from the audience. In addition to the stage and runway, backgrounds and props are often used to set the mood. These topics are the subjects of the next section. Effective audience seating is critical to a successful show. We will discuss the different options for audience seating in the following

Figure 8.1 Model Maggie Rizer stands on a revolving pedestal dressed in jute and crystal for Viktor & Rolf. *Courtesy, Fairchild Publications, Inc.*

section. Along with staging and music, lighting is a mood-setting device. The chapter will conclude with a section on lighting.

General architectural limitations for the show staging and background depend on the show type and location. Informal modeling on a sales floor or at a restaurant generally does not

Figure 8.2 Alexander McQueen uses transparent mannequins in place of live models to show designs. *Courtesy, Fairchild Publications, Inc.*

require staging or background considerations. Attention to props may be sufficient. However, a large production show with several scene changes may require a great deal of planning for staging and background. Showrooms, galleries, theaters, apparel mart halls, and many other locations present creative opportunities and limitations based on the physical layout of the space. Staging configurations are numerous, limited only by the creativity of the stage manager, show director, and staff.

The haute couture shows of Paris and London are particularly known for their theatrical staging. Viktor & Rolf and Alexander McQueen represent two examples of haute couture staging. Some additional examples follow:

- Hussein Chalayan constructed a stark white geometric backdrop with streaks of inset lights, set the show to a live orchestra, and started it with a beautiful but perplexing computer-animated short film.
- Stephan Schneider had his models play a game of musical chairs. The runway was set with two rows of chairs back to back. When the music stopped each model found a chair. The model remaining standing took his turn walking down the runway and then exited off stage.
- Ungaro converted a former slaughterhouse north of Paris into a Oriental paradise complete with a waterfall, grass covered islands, pink sands, bubbling marshes, and a palette of pink, chartreuse, fuchsia, orange, violet, and turquoise to show his haute couture collection.
- Always focusing on the luxury of fashion, Valentino presented his collection on a golden runway, with audience members dressed in diamonds and fur.

Staging

Staging is the process or manner of putting on a performance on a stage. In fashion show production this involves developing a stage and/or runway, creating a background, and setting the lights. As was discussed in Chapter 3, a stage manager performs these tasks with direction from the show director.

The **stage** is a raised floor or platform on which theatrical productions are presented. This is a common area for models to enter and exit. In most facilities, stages are permanent fixtures that cannot be moved. The **runway**, or **catwalk**, is an extension of the stage or a free-standing unit that generally projects into the audience.

The stage and runway take on various forms according to the needs of the show and the physical facilities. Some fashion shows may only have a stage; others may only have a runway; and many shows incorporate both features based on the physical arrangements of the room where the show will be produced.

The **layout** is a schematic plan or arrangement of the area. The layout is often drawn as a sketch or a floor plan of the area (Fig. 8.3). It is used to give show personnel a general idea of the physical dimensions of the stage and runway, distance from the dressing area to the stage, model route, audience seating, and other details of the layout. This information will assist the model and merchandise committees in planning the timing of the show. For inexperienced show planners a layout may be helpful in visualizing the area and planning model entrance and exits.

The distance from the dressing area to the runway should be considered when developing the layout. The dressing areas and runway should be in close physical proximity to accommodate rapid clothing changes. In ideal settings, the dressing area and stage are adjacent to one another. A greater distance between dressing area and stage means an increased number of models to compensate for travel time between the two areas.

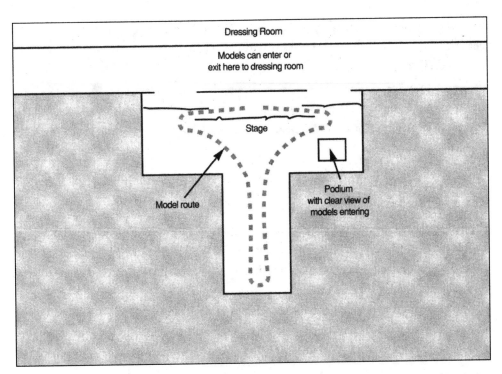

Figure 8.3 Floor plan layout

Auditoriums often have dressing rooms to the side of the stage. Hotel meeting rooms frequently have suites located adjacent to the meeting room that can be used as a dressing area. Public restrooms can work, but some commercial locations will not allow their use. If suitable rooms are not available for dressing areas, temporary dressing areas can be created in the corner of a larger room with the use of screens, tables, and rolling racks.

When planning the layout, audience visibility is crucial. Every seat in the house must have an unobstructed view of the stage and the models. Attention to pillars, curtains, or other architectural obstructions must be noted on the layout.

Runway dimensions

Runways vary in height, size, and shape based on the physical layout of the room and the audience visibility. Some locations have permanent runways available for use. Other locations depend on the retailer or organization to provide a runway. Runways can be rented from local rental companies or built from plywood. Rental units have legs that lock into position for use. When renting runways, the word *stage* or *riser* is often more familiar to the rental agent. The typical size for a runway unit is 4 feet by 8 feet wide by one foot high. Runways are frequently multiples of these measurements (Fig. 8.4). Various height increments may also be available—18 inches, 24 inches, 36 inches, and so on. Smaller rental agencies may only carry one-foot high units.

A show in a small space, such as an art gallery may use 1 or 2 units for a short runway of 8 or 16 feet. Typical trade show runways are 32 to 40 feet (4 or 5 units) in length. This provides adequate space for models to exhibit the fashions and also allows the audience enough time to review the line and make notes.

The length of the runway should accommodate the walking route and traffic flow of models on stage. Models should be on the runway long enough for the audience to adequately see the merchandise being show. The transition area between the stage and the runway often serves as the first position where models stop and pivot. Shorter runways not attached to a

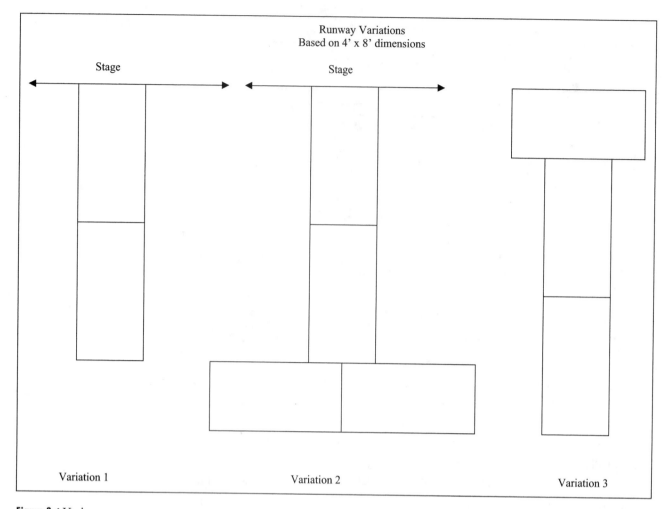

Figure 8.4 Various runway configurations based on four foot by eight-foot units.

stage generally have one primary focal point, at the end of the runway. Longer runways may accommodate several viewing points midway between the stage and the end of the runway (Fig. 8.5).

The width of the runway will determine the number of models who may appear side by side at any given time. If the runway is four feet wide, only two models should walk together. Putting two sections side-by-side doubles the width of the runway. When the runway is eight feet or wider, three or four models can be comfortable walking together, adding visual impact.

The height of the runway often depends on the height of the stage and the ability of the entire audience to see the fashions. Runways are often constructed at the same height as the stage. However, if a stage is very high, one or two steps leading down may be incorporated into the layout to accommodate a lower runway. The runway must be high enough for the entire audience to see the fashions, but low enough so it is not a safety hazard to the models. Typically, the larger the room, the higher the runway must be in order for viewers at the back of the room to see. Ideal heights are between 18 and 36 inches.

Typically, most shows use one runway. However, in a creative alternative to using one runway, Karl Lagerfeld chose to use two raised parallel runways to present the Chanel haute couture line. Models alternately walked down each runway, paused at the end, and then returned to the staging area by way of an aisle at floor level between the two runways.

Figure 8.5 In this creative stage layout, models have multiple viewing points from which to pose. *Courtesy, Fairchild Publications, Inc.*

Runway shapes

The actual runway may be built in a variety of shapes, but the most common configurations include the T, I, X, H, Y, U, or Z (Fig. 8.6). The primary limitation to runway design is the size of the location. There are advantages and disadvantages to each runway pattern.

One of the most frequently used runway shapes is the T shape, which is a combination of a stage and an extended runway. Models enter and exit from the stage and walk down the

Figure 8.6 Examples of runway shapes

straight platform to exhibit the clothes. It is the most simple runway shape and perhaps the least exciting.

A variation of the basic T shape is the I formation. This runway shape adds a platform extension to the extended runway, parallel to the stage. This extension allows models to spend more time on the runway and closer to the audience to feature the garments in a more interesting manner.

The X or cross shape runway is a unique and fascinating formation consisting of two platforms placed at 90 degree angles, generally used without a stage. Models enter and exit from doors in the room or auditorium, bringing them closer to the audience. The models generally use two or four sets of stairs set alongside the runway to ascend and descend the runway.

The H shape runway combines two straight runways with a connecting strip. The advantage of this type of formation is in showing several models at the same time, and may be effective in creating interest and variety. It is also useful in holding the audience's attention, particularly with large shows. Two successful examples of the use of the H shape runway involve French ready-to-wear designer, Sonia Rykiel, and the late American designer Rudi Gernreich. Since the H shape runway can handle many models at the same time, Rykiel brought out 12 models identically dressed to focus attention on her simple houndstooth suits. The Fashion Group of Los Angeles used an H-shaped runway to stage a Rudi Gernreich retrospective show. The runway was so large that it incorporated three separate focal points. The models entered undetected from a secret pathway underneath the stage onto a raised platform, placed in the center of the large stage.

The Y and U patterns are very similar to each other. The Y shape has two angled projections from the basic runway. The U shape has a curved extension, which brings the models out into the audience using a philosophy similar to the "theater in the round." These formations can also be very engaging and add diversity to a show.

The Z or zigzag configuration is a simple yet complex shape conducive to a collection of different routines and movements. The models can turn and change direction to effectively show different views of the garment.

The surface of the runway is another important consideration for the show planner. A carpeted or non-slip surface will help to protect models and shoes. The outside of the runway may be finished with construction materials or covered with fabric tucked or pleated and tacked into place. Another type of covering is a vinyl fabric, which can be used on top of the runway and on the sides. An attractive runway can enhance the theme as well as the image of the location.

The dressing area

The **dressing area** is a room or area designated for changing clothes, applying makeup, and styling hair. Figure 8.7 is a dressing room floor plan for approximately 20 models and 80 outfits. The dressing area should be large enough to accommodate clothing racks, accessories tables, chairs, full-length mirrors, models, and necessary support personnel. Clothing on racks needs to be evenly spaced to prevent wrinkling, and to allow easy access by the dressers. One mirror should be placed near the stage entrance so models can get a last-minute check before leaving the dressing area. If the location does not have mirrors, the fashion show producers should have them at the site. The dressing room must be clean and free of unnecessary clutter. All unnecessary chairs and props should be removed to allow people to move around freely.

Figure 8.7 Dressing area floor plan

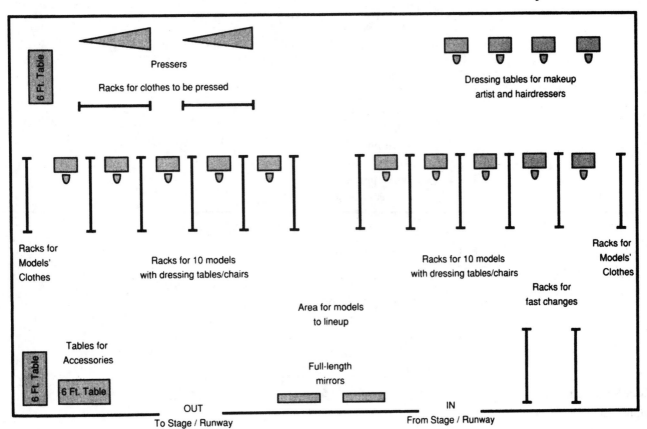

The show director and merchandise coordinator should plan the organization of the dressing area. The type of show, the number of models and dressers, and the size of the room will determine this organization. Each model should have an assigned space in the dressing area. The spaces should be assigned according to the models' order in the show; however, models who appear consecutively or together in the show should not dress next to each other. Models' clothing and accessories should be placed in this area. If a model has several changes, clothing and accessories should be in order to help changes move more smoothly. If there is only one table for accessories, it should be placed next to the dressing room exit so the accessories will be the last items a model puts on. Space should be reserved for models to apply makeup or style their hair, or for makeup artists and hair stylists to set up equipment. The dressing area should have a clearly defined entrance and exit to prevent awkward movements that may be seen by the audience. A list of necessary dressing room supplies is shown in Figure 8.8.

SUPPLIES NEEDED

Office Supplies
_____ Tape
_____ Stapler
_____ Pens/Pencils
_____ Paper
_____ Garment tags

Alterations Supplies
_____ Needles
_____ Safety pins/Straight pins
_____ Thread
_____ Scissors

Beauty Supplies
_____ Anti-perspirant
_____ Dress shields
_____ Hair pins/hair elastics
_____ Brushes/combs
_____ Hair spray/mousse
_____ Makeup: eyeshadows, blush, lipstick
_____ Nail polish

Equipment
_____ Extension cords
_____ Mirrors
_____ Table / racks / chairs
_____ Iron / ironing board / steamer

Miscellaneous Supplies
_____ Stockings
_____ Floor coverings
_____ Hangers
_____ First-aid kit

Figure 8.8 Dressing room supply list

Backgrounds

The purpose of the background is to enhance the products shown, either with stark settings emphasizing the garments or dramatic backdrops emphasizing the theme or merchandise being presented. It may be decorated with a designer's, retailer's, or manufacturer's logo or some type of scenic theme. Staff for the YSL show at 7th on Sixth review the staging and background in Figure 8.9.

Currently the trend in fashion shows is to use simple backgrounds, such as a frame or doorway. The frame may be designed using a gazebo, trellis, or column structure that will also serve as an entry for the models. Large potted plants or architectural boxes or pillars can also frame an entrance and serve this purpose. Dolce & Gabbana used foliage, a scooter, and plants to create a spring theme in Figure 8.10.

Another popular type of entryway consists of a plain white panel or screen, normally 7 to 8 feet high and 10 to 12 feet wide. Slides can be projected onto this screen to emphasize a particular theme or information. Interesting accents can also be developed with video walls. The screen may be used as a background for dramatic lighting and shadow effects created for the beginning or ending of a show segment. The show planners may have the option to use permanent or temporary movable backdrops called **flats**.

Figure 8.9 Staging and background for the YSL show at 7th on Sixth. *Courtesy, Fairchild Publications, Inc. Photographer, Gauthier Gallet.*

Figure 8.10 Background and props at a Dolce & Gabbana show. *Courtesy, Fairchild Publications, Inc. Photographer, Gauthier Gallet, Giovanni Giannoni, Davit Maestre, and Mauricion Miranda.*

Deborah Hampton (who worked as a designer for Michael Kors before designing her own line) introduced her first-ever sportswear line during the spring 2001 New York Fashion Week in a gallery called TriBeCa. Hampton used an interesting background, displaying her clothes on a garment rack and also on a wide video screen with models digitally imposed against background pictures of the Arizona desert taken by her husband, photographer Paul Moore (Bellafante, 2000a).

Scenery, just like a theatrical stage backdrop, may be painted to represent a room setting or an outdoor scene with natural elements. A series of doors or panels through which the models enter the stage and runway area can also be designed.

The extent of the backdrop and scenery are dependent upon the type of show and the budget planned. A single backdrop can be used for the entire show, or different and elaborate backdrops can be built for each scene of the show. A revolving stage may be used to change the scene for each show segment. With a more elaborate stage setting the expense is greater. The staging should never overshadow the clothes-it should be used to flatter the merchandise being displayed. Box 8.1 highlights alternative venues for young designers who cannot afford the tents at Bryant Park. Creative staging and layout provide for interesting shows.

continued on page 203

Box 8.1
Seventh on Fifth? Young Designers Go East

NEW YORK-Chalk one up for the kids. Putting on a fashion show just got a little easier. Brothers Mauricio and Roger Padilha, 33 and 30, respectively, owners of MAO Public Relations, are unveiling a new show venue for Fashion Week called MAO Space. Pitched as the young designer's alternative to Bryant Park, MS offers a treasure trove of advantages to Seventh Avenue's fledgling talents: a cheaper space with loads of amenities just down the street from the tents.

First, the price is right. At $7,500, MS is almost half the price of Bryant Park's least expensive venue, the Atelier, which is $14,000. To offset their costs, the Padilhas have signed up several sponsors, including Ian Schrager Hotels, Red Bull, Physique Hair, Creative Nails and MAC Cosmetics. The latter two are also offering use of their manicure and makeup teams free of charge.

But equally important to the success of MAO Space is location. At 260 Fifth Avenue, at 29th Street, it's a 13-block walk from the tents, avoiding the problems posed by the far-flung venues that designers at this level usually use. The Padilhas will provide a bus to transport editors from the tents, and the M2, 3, and 5 run straight from the New York Public Library to the door of MAO Space.

"We wanted to centralize all these young designers," says Mauricio. "It's easier for everyone to come here than some basement in TriBeCa."

The space boasts a ground floor plate-glass front that will feature a display of monitors running live feeds of shows in progress and earlier footage at other times, a straight 60-foot runway, and seating for 350.

Hair and makeup stations, as well as a lounge area, will be set up in the 6,550-square-foot basement. The extra space allows for more backstage coverage. "In the past, we've had to limit how many journalists could be back there," Mauricio says. "Now, we won't have to turn people away."

At present, 13 of the 15 available slots are filled-seven by MAO showroom denizens Arkadius, Gary Graham, Liz Collins, Zaldy, Michael & Hushi, Tracy 8 Kinney and ChanPaul, and the other six by David Rodriguez, Vasseur-Esquivel, Esteban Cortazar, House of Field, Peter Som and Tawfik Mounayer. While some firms are employing the Padilhas in varying capacities, they are also free to bring in their own production and press teams.

Rand M. Productions president Rand Burrus, who collaborated with 7th on Sixth on spring 2002's alternative venues at the Puck Building, is positive about MAO's effort. "In my opinion, there is a big hole," Burrus says. "Younger designers just don't have a place to show."

Twenty-three designers, including Wink, Custo Barcelona and David Rodriguez, showed at the three spaces in the Puck Building, which ranged in price from $11,000 to $17,000. Although Burrus considers the venue a success, he still contends that its lack of proximity to the tents proved problematic.

continued on page 202

Box 8.1 continued from page 201

Fern Mallis, executive director of Mercedes-Benz Fashion Week, is also supportive. "We think that when more people can get their collections seen in New York, it makes the whole week more important," she says. "We would look forward in future seasons to working with MAO to connect everything to the bigger picture."

And designers themselves are excited about the venture. "It's affordable, which is important since times are hard all around," says Bryan Fuentes, p.r. director of House of Field, which usually shows at Bryant Park. "But we also really like supporting a space that is about young designers. There's a great energy there."

The Padilhas' plan for the future is to eventually have a few spaces around the city that operate on the same principle-a space for young designers to show, underwritten by sponsors, that smooths the way for the talents of the future.

It's no fluke that the brothers came to this point. Their collective industry experience, since they began as Parsons students interning for Marc Jacobs at Perry Ellis, has taught them a thing or two about helping young designers. They did more than their homework on what it takes to begin in this business-they found out firsthand.

In 1993, after he graduated, Roger formed the now-defunct label Spooky with his partner Jennifer Gross. Although Mauricio was working as public relations director of Gemma Khang at the time, he doubled up by doing the same for his brother's label. When editors came to see Khang's collection, Mauricio would shuttle them afterwards across the street to see Spooky-an arrangement that Khang, to her credit, didn't mind.

"Everyone was so supportive of us," says Mauricio. "There weren't that many young designers back then."

Mauricio soon left Khang to work for Spooky full-time, and the Padilhas began to create their DIY methods of working. These included everything from asking top models to paint their own nails before a show to writing an earnest letter to Ellen Von Unwerth requesting that she shoot a picture for their invite gratis. Charmed by their combination of naïveté and talent, she said yes.

"We didn't really understand that Ellen probably made $20,000 a day on advertising," says Roger. "But it was a good lesson that if you want something-and you have something good to back it up with-you should just ask people."

Despite editorial attention in magazines like W and ID, and sales to such stores as Barneys New York and Louis, Boston, they closed Spooky in 1997 because they found it difficult to make ends meet without a backer. During the company's last season, Mauricio and one of their interns decided to produce several other shows in order to finance their own. The birth of MAO was a result of that venture. The firm quickly established a client base, consisting mostly of raw, young talent, mixed with the odd major company, such as Searle and Coogi Australia, that was looking to tweak its image.

Since they had started a new label themselves, the Padilhas easily relate to their clients' trials. "I always tell them stories to make them feel better," says Roger. "Like the time I had my dress on the cover of ID, but I had to choose between buying the magazine and a pack

continued on page 203

Box 8.1 continued from page 202

of cigarettes because I only had $3.75." While the decision was difficult, the cigarettes won out.

The brothers do everything from helping their clients to secure a loan to providing a shoulder to cry on.

"We hold their hands through everything," says Mauricio. "But we've always believed that young New York designers shouldn't be limited to an alternative audience, but exposed to the fashion industry at large.

"And we really love what we do," he adds.

Mistry, M. (2003, February 4). Seventh on Fifth? Young Designers Go East. *Women's Wear Daily*, p. 4.

continued from page 200

Props

Props are supports used to highlight the garments being exhibited. The trend for using props is cyclical. Sometimes it is popular to use props and at other times show planners want the clothes to speak for themselves.

Props may be mobile or stationary. Carrying a tennis racquet or golf club with the appropriate apparel are examples of movable props. There are a wide variety of such types of props including: jump ropes and hand weights with activewear, briefcases and newspapers with career apparel, beach balls and towels with swimwear, or a notebook or apple with back-to-school fashions. For his 2003 Spring line, Karl Lagerfeld had lead models carry surfboards to highlight his swimwear line. Merchandise available for sale such as briefcases or school backpacks or handbags (Fig. 8.11) may be used as props.

Stationary props are generally immobile items. They are placed as part of the scenery. These items might include furniture for a room setting, one or two beach umbrellas for a swimwear segment, a motorcycle or car for a teen or men's wear show, or a gazebo for a bridal show. Although these props are typically heavy and bulky, they can be changed with scene changes.

For a fall couture collection, Jean Paul Gaultier used Chinese references as the theme for the couture designs and the show (Horyn, 2001). Mandarin collars, swishes of black braids, and intricate lace cuffs were evident on the merchandise. The models looked like Oriental dolls complete with red lips and painted-on eyebrows, and carried black lacquered umbrellas as props.

Rei Kawakubo for Comme des Garçons made a statement with the use of props for a spring collection show. She had models come down the runway with strips of Scotch tape on their faces or wearing mountainous crowns of bubble plastic, saran wrap, or tinfoil (Bellafante, 2000b). The intent of this presentation was not a gimmick—Ms. Kawakubo was making a statement that women are often sent out into the world as packages to be looked over or overlooked and she was literally executing the idea forcefully in fashion.

Figure 8.11 Handbags are common props. *Courtesy, Fairchild Publications, Inc. Photographer, Stephane Feugere and Giovanni Gionnoni.*

Seating Patterns

There are two styles of seating arrangements to accommodate the audience. They may be seated in a theater pattern or at tables.

Theater seating

Theater seating involves placing chairs side by side and next to the stage and runway and is best used for fashion shows without meal service. The audience may have assigned or open seating on a first come first served basis. Programs, gifts, or promotional materials may be placed on the seats before the patrons arrive. Theater seating generally provides the best view of the show pieces since all the members of the audience are seated facing the runway.

Table seating

A **table seating** arrangement is used at a show when meal service is provided (Fig. 8.12). A buffet or sit down meal may be served prior to or after the fashion show. There are some visibility problems with this type of seating. Often a round table is set, holding as many as eight to ten people. Some people will not be able to see the stage or runway. Chairs will have to be turned in order to fully view the presentation and some members of the audience may find this kind of seating awkward.

Combination seating

Depending upon the location, available space, and budget, a group may combine both seating styles. The lunch or dinner can be served in one banquet room using table seating. After the meal, the audience can move to another location where the stage, runway, and theater seating are set up.

Lighting

Lighting is the method and/or equipment used to provide illumination (Fig. 8.13). Good lighting is necessary to show clothing to its best advantage, set the mood of the show, and

Figure 8.12 Tables are placed surrounding the runway. *Courtesy, Galeries Lafayette.*

Figure 8.13 Technicians make adjustments to lighting equipment. *Courtesy, Christopher C. Everett.*

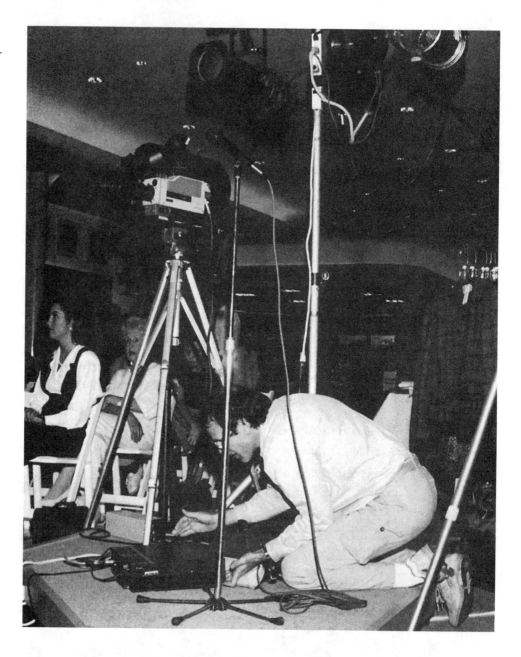

accentuate the theme of the show. Raising and lowering the house lights adds to the theatrical nature of fashion shows. Spotlights or track lighting placed above the runway can be used to highlight models while they are on the runway. Spotlights in a darkened room can be used to introduce, emphasize or close a segment. Spotlights should be located as high as possible. They should not "blind" the audience.

There may be limited lighting in the area where the garments are shown. One fashion show held in the carriage house of a historical site had virtually no lights over the area where the runway was placed. Photographers' spotlights were used to illuminate the runway.

Strobe lights were popular effects used to create a mechanical look during the 1960s. In the 1970s and 1980s, such theatrical productions as *Phantom of the Opera, Cats,* and *Starlight Express* designed by Andrew Lloyd Weber influenced others to create dramatic lighting and staging effects. These influences can be seen in some of the more complex and expensive fashion shows held during this period. Strings of small, white Christmas tree lights are another popular and effective way to light runways. Stringing lights the entire perimeter of the stage and runway creates a glamorous appearance for the audience. When the house lights are darkened, this type of lighting also allows models to see the edge of the stage so their safety on stage is increased.

John Galliano used unique lighting for his couture collection. The show was held under lantern-shrouded chandeliers in an old Paris mansion (Horyn, 2001). Karl Lagerfeld used lighting as the focus of his ready-to-wear line. The show for Chanel, called *Walking on Light*, was literally switched on. Models wore platform sandals with a clear plastic sole that beamed neon light at each step (Horyn, 2000). The entire runway was descending steps outlined in neon lights (Fig. 8.14).

Figure 8.14 Neon lights illuminate the runway for Karl Lagerfeld. *Courtesy, Fairchild Publications, Inc.*

Many designers incorporate colored lights into their shows. Colored gels have been used to accentuate a particular look. A recent fashion presentation by Enrico Coveri used pink runways and, to further enhance this look, pink-gelled lamps. Along with his colorful and youthful collection, the presentation popped!

Care and practice with lighting should take place before the show to prevent any potential lighting problems. Lighting cues should be practiced during rehearsals.

The atmosphere of the show is largely determined through the appropriate use of the physical facilities and effective use of the staging framework. The stage or runway, background, props, seating, and lighting must be planned and coordinated for the most striking and successful presentation to excite the audience and generate sales.

Key fashion show terms

catwalk	lighting	staging
dressing area	props	table seating
flats	runway	theater seating
layout	stage	

References

Bellafante, G. (2000a, September 20). For Chalayan, the past is no crutch. *New York Times.* Retrieved September 22, 2000, from http://www.nytimes.com

Bellafante, G. (2000b, October 10). Paris query: Just what is a woman? *New York Times.* Retrieved October 10, 2000, from http://www.nytimes.com

CNN.com. (1999a, July 29). *Viktor & Rolf's theatrical couture.* Retrieved August 2, 1999, from http://www.cnn.com/STYLE/ELLE/9907/29

CNN.com. (1999b, August 2). *The clothes make the mannequin.* Retrieved August 2, 1999, from http://www.cnn.com/STYLE/ELLE/9908/02

Davis, B. (2001, July 2). *Alexander McQueen, fashion designer.* Retrieved July 2, 2001, from http://www.fashionwindows.com/fashion_designers/alexander_mcqueen.asp

Horyn, C. (2000, October 13). Lagerfeld in neon, seeking to amuse. *New York Times.* Retrieved October 16, 2000, from http://www.nytimes.com

Horyn, C. (2001, July 10). Nostalgia tripping to the mysterious east and psychedelic. *New York Times.* Retrieved July 10, 2001, from http://www.nytimes.com

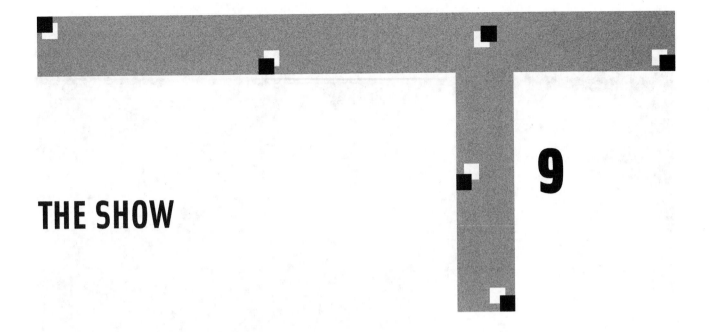

THE SHOW

9

"**Y**ou've been in Palm Beach. Now you're back in New York, the Upper East Side. You eat caviar, drink champagne, and always have a limo waiting! You are sleek, intriguing, and Sexy…Intense, Seductive, and Self-Confident. Be elegant and energetic. Rock their world!! We Love You!" (Kerwin, 2000, p. 82). These words of encouragement were emphasized on a sign backstage at the Michael Kors show. Meanwhile, 20 blasting hairdryers turned the makeshift dressing room at the Bryant Park tent into a sauna. To pass time, the designer posed for photographs with his models backstage and gave an impromptu birthday party for Erin O'Connor, which gave the scene a feel of a cocktail party at the Ritz (Fig. 9.1). Backstage at several of the shows, models were served champagne with straws placed in miniature bottles, adding to the festive mood.

Models, designers, celebrities who will sit in the front row, stylists, hair and makeup artists, boyfriends, girlfriends, beauty editors, tailors, dressers, and the staff from publicity and production are all backstage with the clothes before the show starts. It is organized chaos—or just chaos—behind the scene on the show day. Box 9.1 reveals the chaotic mood on the night before the New York Fashion Week openings.

This chapter, The Show, profiles the days leading up to and presenting the show. This is the time when all of the planning, promotion, merchandise design or selection, model preparation, and theatrical elements come together. First, we consider the importance of a rehearsal to give all of the participants, from dressers and starters to models and technical crew, an opportunity to see how the show will look and how long it will last. Then, we discuss setting up the dressing room, presenting and closing the show, and taking down the stage. Clothing and accessories need to be returned to the showroom or sales floor. Professionalism is necessary to keep all aspects of the event moving smoothly. In a few rare instances, a show might be cancelled. Our final topic in this chapter is a look at why a show might have to be canceled and how to call it off.

Figure 9.1 Michael Kors encourages his models backstage before the show begins. *Courtesy, Fairchild Publications, Inc.*

Rehearsing

The **rehearsal** is a practice performance, held in private, in preparation for a public performance (Fig. 9.2a, b, and c). The fashion show director takes this opportunity to solve any problems prior to the public presentation of the show to the audience. The rehearsal may be a simple run-through or a full dress rehearsal. The **run-through** is a rehearsal of the show sequences and involves showing models the choreography. At this stage, the models are not required to wear their garments designated for the show. A **dress rehearsal** consists of a walk-through with complete garment changes. A **full dress rehearsal** is held to check all theatrical aspects of the show including timing, music, and all other technical aspects.

The need for a rehearsal is dependent upon the type of show being produced and whether professional or amateur models are being used. When to hold the rehearsal is also dependent on the type of show, availability of the venue, and the number of staff people involved. A rehearsal may take place one week prior to the show, the day before the show, or the day of the show. An elaborate production show may need a rehearsal far ahead of time. A show set in a retail department may be rehearsed immediately prior to show time. Unfortunately, during trade or market week shows, models are often booked for several shows each day. In this case, there is only time to give simple verbal directions prior to the start of the show.

A full dress rehearsal is ideal to check lighting, music, and overall fashion show coordination. The dress rehearsal will show the most efficient traffic flow from the dressing area to the stage. Another important reason to hold a dress rehearsal is to determine length of the show. The fashion show director should record the actual time of the full dress rehearsal. Knowing

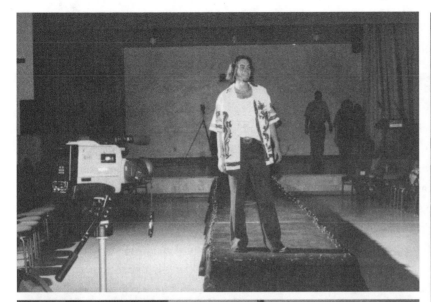

Figure 9.2a, b, and c The rehearsal is an opportunity for models and production staff to polish lineup and choreography, in addition to checking the timing of the show with the music and lighting. *Courtesy, Christopher C. Everett.*

how long the dress rehearsal takes will help coordinators set pace and assist models to understand cues.

If the show uses commentary, the tentative lineup will help the show commentator prepare the pace of the show. The commentator will have a good feel for how long models need to be on the runway. With a full dress rehearsal, he or she will also be able to identify segments where model changes are taking longer than expected. The commentator has an excellent opportunity to plan how to use the ad-lib comments and filler commentary about current fashion trends relating to the fashion story being presented.

After the rehearsal, any problems are ironed out and the final lineup is established. Copies of the final lineup should be available in the dressing room for the dressers and starters, for the emcee or the commentator and the models, for the music and lighting technicians, the stage manager, and the show director. The posted lineup will facilitate the changes for all the fashion show personnel. Everyone needs to know what is expected and when.

continued on page 214

Box 9.1
'Twas the Night Before . . .

What could possibly hinder a procession of pretty girls wearing pretty clothes and walking to and fro? They stroll; they change; they repeat. But as those familiar with the behind-the-scenes circus of New York's show week know, seamless is never as simple as it seems. Six month's work is distilled into a 12-to-15-minute sequence responsible for simultaneously disseminating a creative vision, showcasing a brand and entertaining the world via live broadcast. For designers, who serve as the week's directors, producers, costume designers and stars, the night before the show can be simply harrowing.

"The night before there are just all these little things that you didn't notice," says Daryl Kerrigan. "It's so terrible when a mistake goes down the runway and you say, 'Oh, why didn't I notice that?' You have to make sure that every little thing is under your control. Of course, things do happen, but you can at least try so you don't have to kick yourself for sitting around and laughing it up."

It's unlikely any designer spends the night giggling, let alone laughing, but stress aside, some do thrive on the pre-show electricity. "The night before there are the three Cs," says Donna Karan, "calm, crisis, and creativity." She's not kidding. In her studio, models and seamstresses come and go, while the evening, she says, "bleeds into the morning."

"I'm sure in some companies they plan to do a press release on Tuesday night and fittings on Wednesday," says Patti Cohen, Karan's executive vice president of global communications, "but we do a press release while we're doing the music and 10 other things." That's why there's always a masseuse on hand to tend to Karan's crew.

Some on Seventh Avenue, Oscar de la Renta for example, bring in a chef for the evening. Michael Kors's studio, on the other hand, is full of pizza, candy, and chips. "I rearrange Polaroids for the 90th time, do a full music check, and get lint-obsessed," he says. "I try to eat healthy, but I always end up eating junk food." According to other tenants of 550 Seventh Avenue, however, nothing beats the spread at Ralph Lauren, where lobster tails rise from a grand buffet—although a Lauren spokeswoman claims that the real preshow highlight is the homemade profiteroles that a retired employee brings to the design staff each season.

It's not the time to stick to your diet, says Alice Roi. As they work through the night, the designer, her friends and her design staff break for a big family style dinner. It calms her nerves. "We pig out," she says, laughing. "I feel so nervous the night before the show that I just want to eat steak and creamed spinach until I can't move. I like to divert with food."

This season Nian Fish, creative director for the show production company KCD, will participate in not just one night-before frenzy, but 11, while producing shows on both sides of the Atlantic. She counts on Emergenc-C crystallized vitamin C and a little peace of mind to carry her through. "I go into the bathroom and lock the door and meditate," she says. "I focus all my energy on having a good show."

continued on page 213

Box 9.1 continued from page 212

But, that's only one measure Fish takes in her crusade to prevent errors. "The season when Calvin Klein introduced the 'New Length,' we called every girl back the night before and saw 24 girls between midnight and 5 a.m. so we could recheck the length on each one," she says. "Calvin is all about precision, and we wanted it to be exact."

Alex de Betak, of the show production company Bureau Betak, also promises his clients precision, including real pyrotechnics for the recent Dior couture show. "I quit smoking 10 months ago, so I eat these little mints from France and I make sure my pockets are padded with them," he says. "You can start a rehearsal at eight and be done in 30 minutes and go to your favorite restaurant for dinner, but sometimes it's 4 a.m. and you're still there trying to get the lighting you want."

It all goes to show why Betsey Johnson refuses to participate in any preshow hype or hysteria. "We don't do craziness anymore," she says. "The night before, we bag the show. We very quietly whisper, 'belt, G-string, stockings.' When the last garment bag is zipped up, we bring in the champagne. I insist that everyone is gone by midnight, and I go home and go to bed. I don't believe in the craziness. It's not facing reality."

Though he probably won't leave for home by midnight, Narcisco Rodriguez will reap the benefits of sleeping in his own bed this season, after showing in Milan for seven seasons. "In one sense, it'll be more difficult to be back in New York. I'll be obsessing a lot more," he says. "But what's fantastic is that my masseuse is here, my apartment is here, and I don't have to stay in some strange hotel."

Diane Von Furstenberg, for her part, needn't ever leave the comforts of home. Not only does she own the cavernous West Village space she shows in, but she sleeps next door on the top floor above her studio. "It's easy for me," she says. "It's always homey here, but let's just say that the night before it gets a little homier."

Wynn Smith has no such luxury, but when he flies in from San Francisco to show his Wink collection each season, he does bring a little piece of home along. "Usually I'm really stressed out because there's always some model who can't make it at the last minute, and somehow we never have enough shoes," he says. "I bring my portable rocking chair there with me, and it relaxes me. I rock so I can think and try to picture things and prepare myself mentally. It's therapeutic."

But a quick massage, a plate full of comfort food, or even a good rock aren't the only ways to ease preshow pressure. Though it's certainly not for everyone, sometimes the situation calls for a visit from the folks. "My parents always come down from Detroit the day before the show," Anna Sui says. "They go down to Chinatown to get my favorite things to eat, and my goal is always to get home early enough to eat it."

"One time just when I was leaving for the show," she continues, "my mother said, 'You are going to wear high heels aren't you? You know you're very short.' You spend months getting your way and having them there keeps things real. It just puts everything into perspective."

Adapted from: Kerwin, J. (2001, February 12). 'Twas the Night Before . . . *Women's Wear Daily*, p. 4.

continued from page 211

Rehearsal preparation

There are many considerations that must take place prior to the dress rehearsal. First, all the spaces, including dressing areas, storage areas, and restrooms, must be reserved, in addition to stage and runway set-up. Often there is a cost for reserving the venue and these costs were included in the budget. Since there are many costs involved with holding a rehearsal, it is necessary to keep the rehearsals as short as possible.

Time must be allocated before the rehearsal to set up and after the show to strike it. The show director should inform all personnel of the designated rehearsal time and what time they should arrive. Music technicians, stage personnel, and lighting personnel may need to arrive earlier to have the stage set and ready when the models arrive.

Clothing and accessories should be organized and labeled in the dressing room before models arrive. All the elements of each outfit, including accessories, should be pulled together for each model and placed on clothing racks in the order they will be worn by each model. Models and dressers can refer to the final lineup to verify the order and placement in the lineup.

Models also may need to arrive early to examine the merchandise selection to determine the time they will need to change. Professional models are paid for their participation in rehearsals, therefore planning is necessary to maximize the use of their time.

The first walk-through involves the models wearing their street clothes. The choreographer gives the models directions regarding entrances, groupings, turns, and exits. If the show involves amateur models, the choreographer may also give some modeling tips and techniques. This first walk-through is done without the benefit of commentary, music, or lighting. A second walk-through adds these elements. The full dress rehearsal combines all of the elements into a "pre-show" shakedown.

Dressers

The **dressers** are the individuals who help the models change in the dressing room. They play an extremely important behind the scenes role, avoiding a chaotic scene in the dressing room. Dressers for professional shows are often fashion students looking for experience in fashion show production or modeling agency staff. No matter how big or small the show, dressers make the show run smoothly (Fig. 9.3).

Ideally, each model should have a separate dressing area and a personal dresser. A good dresser can handle more than one model if the changes are not at the same time and the models are spaced far enough apart in the dressing room.

The dresser must be completely familiar with the lineup. Both the dresser and the model must know the order of the garment presentation—exactly what outfit comes first, second, third, and so forth. In order to confirm the order, the model and dresser can refer to the Final Lineup, created cooperatively by merchandise and model committee members after the model's final fittings (see Chapter 5).

The model's responsibility for her outfits was previously stated, but the dresser is also responsible for getting the clothes ready to be worn. Zippers are unzipped, buttons are unbuttoned, and tags are hidden. Speed in dressing is essential and wasted motions should be

Figure 9.3 A dresser works with an individual model or models to assure smooth changes. *Courtesy, Christopher C. Everett.*

avoided. The dresser may wish to make special notes for accessories and/or props to be carried. A sash, scarf, or pin may need to be worn in a certain manner. Simple written directions help to keep the appearance just as it was planned by the fashion director.

Since most clothing used in fashion shows will later be sold, protecting garments is essential. Horror stories about entire racks of clothes stained by food or beverages circulate around fashion offices. While catastrophes of this sort are rare, the dressers need to be concerned with protecting the clothes. Placing a sheet on the floor where the model changes and hanging garments up immediately after they are worn will help to keep the clothes fresh and in good condition (Fig. 9.4). Using a scarf over the model's face will protect clothes from being stained by makeup.

Starters

The **starter** is responsible for cueing the models onto the stage in the correct order at the right time using the Final Lineup (Figs. 9.5 and 9.6). The starter should work closely with the fashion show director at the dress rehearsal and the show. Cues, such as a deejay starting a specific song, a moderator making an announcement, or a lighting specialist lowering the lights, are established to let the starter know when to send models onto the runway. During the rehearsal, the starter will make necessary written notes that they will refer to during the show. The starter will be out of sight of the audience, but will be able to signal the commentator if a model misses a cue in the lineup. The starter will know in advance how fast the models' changes are and have the authority to replace a model if he or she is not ready. The starter is also responsible for the final inspection of the models as they go on stage. Tags should be out of sight, hair smooth, and undergarments concealed.

At minimum, one starter can be used. Depending on the distance between the dressing area and the stage, two or three assistants should be used, at the stage, at the dressing area, and any area in between where sight and timing are necessary. Communication between the stage and the dressing area is vital. The starter will need to know if a model cannot get changed in time or if an accessory will not be worn with an outfit and alert the commentator. Most fashion shows' starters will have headsets to communicate between all necessary backstage personnel. If there is no coordination at the dress rehearsal, the show will not move at the anticipated pace nor will other elements such as music or garment changes be properly anticipated.

The rehearsal often appears very rough. While participants may feel discouraged at this point, the rehearsal points out problems that even the most experienced staff may not have anticipated. The staff should take this opportunity to rearrange the sequence of models, replace merchandise, perfect timing, or solve any other problems that might appear during the rehearsal. The presentation of the show is dependent on the rehearsal, and show personnel always are more confident after the rehearsal.

Figure 9.4 A floor covering such as this white sheet protects the clothing as models make changes. *Courtesy, Fairchild Publications, Inc.*

Preparing backstage

First, the dressing rooms need to be set up if they were taken down after the rehearsal. Mirrors should be available. Racks of clothing should arrive in the dressing area at least two hours

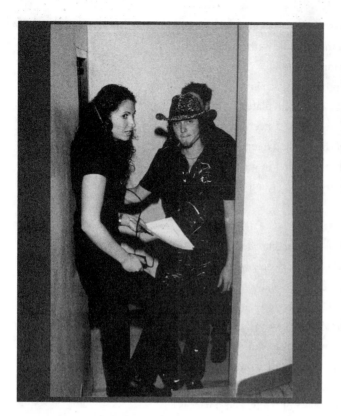

Figures 9.5 and 9.6 Figure 9.5 (left) and Figure 9.6 (right) illustrate the backstage starters who communicate with the show director, located in the back of the audience, and signal the models when to enter the stage. *Courtesy, Christopher C. Everett (9.5) and Fairchild Publications, Inc. (9.6).*

prior to the show. The people moving the clothing should be given specific directions as to the delivery location. Although this may seem obvious, there are stories of clothing being delivered to the wrong location.

Final lineup sheets should be placed in strategic locations with the dressing room being the number one priority. Lineup sheets should also be available for the fashion show director starter, commentator, and lighting, prop, and music personnel.

Following the steps outlined during the rehearsals, dressers organize and prepare clothing and assemble accessories for each model in the order they are to be worn. A final preparation of the garments should include pressing, making sure tags are well hidden, and taping soles of shoes (Figs. 9.7a & b and 9.8). The models should arrive at least 30 minutes to an hour before the start of the show to have makeup applied and hair styled before putting on their first outfit. Figures 9.9-9.12a, b, and c show models getting ready and other behind-the-scenes preparations.

The commentator should be ready, checking any last minute substitutions in clothing or models at least fifteen to thirty minutes before the show. Commentary cards or opening remarks are placed at the speaker's podium for the announcer.

The floor plan should be consulted to be sure the stage and runway are ready. Skirting or trim on the runway should be examined. Stage set or props should be in place. Cues should be reviewed with the starter. Lighting should also be tested and lighting cues should be reexamined. The sound system should be tested for volume and potential feedback noises before the audience starts to arrive. The microphone should be tested at the same time music and sound are checked.

A

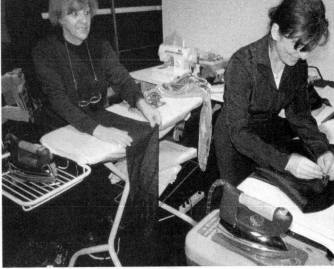

B

Programs are placed on the chairs or tables, or left with the ushers. If hostesses or ushers are going to be used, they are given instructions. They should be ready at least 30 minutes before guests arrive. Large charity shows may require elaborate seating charts, developed in the planning stages, rather than "at large" seating.

Any door prizes or giveaways should be prepared. If a drawing for a gift is going to take place, the procedure for tickets should be ready and in place. A designated person should be responsible for following through with this activity.

Special introductions or oral acknowledgments should be written in advance and rehearsed prior to the audience arrival. The show director or charity chair may wish to have everyone who took part in the show stand for applause at the end of the show. Show staff should know about this in advance.

If refreshments and food service are to be included as hospitality, they should be placed away from the stage or runway. The audience should not be confused by the food service. They should be made aware of when refreshments are to be served, prior to or after the show.

After all of the hours of preparation the show is ready to present to the audience. However, prior to the arrival of the audience, last-minute details are attended to. These checks will help to ensure a smooth, less chaotic presentation.

Figure 9.7a & b When preparing the merchandise backstage, tags should be removed or hidden. Some garments may require pressing or steaming. *Courtesy, Christopher C. Everett (a). Fairchild Publications, Inc. (b).*

Presenting the show

The opening moments of the show are critical. First impressions will influence the show's success or failure. All of the advance preparation pays off with a show, featuring beautiful clothes on attractive models, that is well paced with appropriate stage settings, lighting, and music.

It is important to be ready to start the show on time. A five-minute delay is not disastrous, but too many shows, both professional and amateur, start as much as 30 or more minutes late.

Figure 9.8 The bottom of shoes should be taped to avoid being scratched and marred as they are worn by models during the show. *Courtesy, Fairchild Publications, Inc.*

Figure 9.9 Organized chaos is often a better term for backstage. *Courtesy, Fairchild Publications, Inc.*

If the moderator comes onto stage at the appointed time and says the show will start in fifteen minutes, the organization looks disorganized and unprofessional and the audience may become restless.

Communication between the fashion show director and technical assistants has been planned either by eye contact, headsets, or hand signals. There should be visible contact between the commentator, starter, music personnel, and lighting personnel.

Signals to the technical staff are necessary if there are any problems. If music is too loud or soft, a signal to change volume is sent. The spotlights may be blinding the models or someone in the audience. Even though these points were considered during rehearsal, some con-

Figure 9.10 A final touch of hairspray is added to the model as she leaves the dressing area. *Courtesy, Christopher C. Everett.*

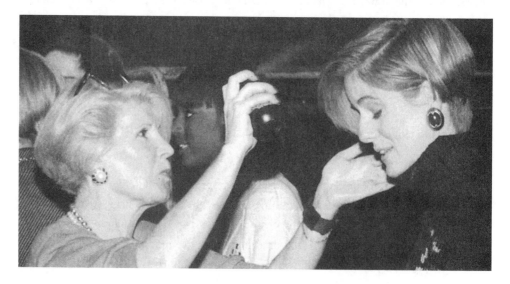

ditions may not have been obvious and need to be corrected when the show is underway. A more sophisticated communication system may be required for a fashion show using complex music, lighting, and staging. In this case the headset must be used to link dressing room personnel with the technical staff.

The show producers need to be aware of audience reaction throughout the show's production. Audience reaction will reveal technical problems in lighting, sound, and music, not detected by show staff. Adjustments in volume of music, public address systems, or lighting may be corrected to make the audience more comfortable. Flexibility is important. Everyone must be able to adjust to changing conditions.

Figure 9.11 Photographs assist models and dressers with merchandise order and outfit completion.

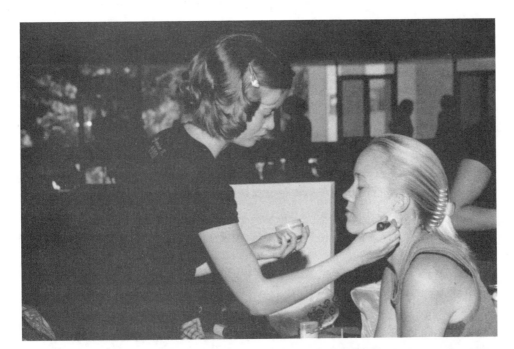

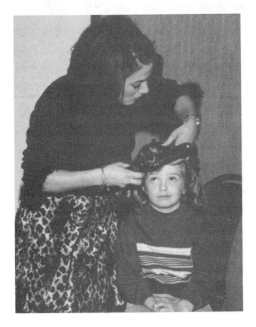

Figure 9.12a, b, and c Some shows use professional makeup artists and hairstylists, while other shows will rely on models to apply their own makeup and do their own hair. *Courtesy, Christopher C. Everett.*

Closing the show

The finale should provide a visual closing to the show. Music and lighting combined with the most dramatic clothing should signal the end of a well-produced fashion show as illustrated by the Giorgio Armani finale in Figure 9.13. The end of the show may include closing remarks by the director or introduction of the designer for recognition. A charity show may close with acknowledgments. The show director or moderator may draw the winning tickets for door prizes while the audience watches—all this creates excitement at the end of the show. If refreshments are planned, the audience will be invited to share food or be served.

Striking the show

A misconception by many people involved in fashion shows is that when the curtain goes down, the show is finished and their responsibilities have been fulfilled. People with this delusion have not yet realized that clean-up and stage strike must occur. **Stage strike**, a term taken from the theater, refers to striking, or physically disassembling, the set. Strike takes place at the close of all fashion shows (Fig. 9.14).

In-store strike includes taking down the stage, replacing all props and equipment in the appropriate locations, and leaving the location as it was found. In addition to these activities, a remote show will require transporting the garments and accessories back to the selling location.

Retail shows

Shows within a retail department should be disassembled immediately after the show. Runways should be returned to storage. Backdrops must come down to be stored or disposed of, and chairs and tables should be removed from the selling floor. Retailers frequently have a prop room where visual display equipment including props and runways can be stored. Sales areas should be returned to the normal arrangement to accommodate customers anxious to try on the garments they have just seen. Crowded sales racks must be spaced properly to allow customers to review the merchandise. Safety is also a concern within a retail department. With customers wanting to enter the sales area soon after the show it is important to remove props and electrical footage (cords, plugs, and equipment used for the sound system and lights) and secure the area against hazards as quickly as possible after the show.

Auditorium shows

If the show is executed at any location other than a retail department, certain arrangements should have been made with the location personnel and the stage manager prior to the show. The use of sound equipment and public address systems, and the return of these items,p should have been discussed at the time of location rental. Further, stacking and returning chairs used for audience seating, hostess tables, and skirting for the tables and stage should have been negotiated.

Figure 9.13 Armani celebrates the conclusion of the show with his models. *Courtesy, Fairchild Publications, Inc.*

Fashion shows presented in auditoriums, or other locations with permanent stages, have different requirements during stage strike. Mobile stages, orchestra pit covers, curtains, podiums, lights, and all permanent props of the stage area must be replaced in the position where they were situated when show personnel arrived on the site. Sound barriers, often used in auditoriums to bring the action on stage closer to the audience, must be returned to the proper location off stage. Sound barriers are fragile and expensive and should always be moved by stagehands familiar with them. Curtains and orchestra pit covers also require special help from knowledgeable stage crew to replace them after the show.

If technical assistance is required to dismantle the sound or lighting systems, the professional technicians used during the show should be responsible for the task. This responsibility should have been discussed with these individuals at the onset of employment and compensation budgeted with all parties in agreement. Rented equipment should be returned as soon as possible after the show to avoid added expenses.

The location of the show should be thoroughly cleaned and left in the order in which it was found unless custodial services were contracted in advance. Dressing areas, restrooms, or offices should be left in their original state. Programs or giveaways not taken by the audience should be gathered. Pins, tape, tags, and so forth should be collected by show personnel and not left for venue personnel to clean up. All trash should be thrown away. The show staff is responsible and must remain at the location until all equipment and garments have been removed. A final check should be completed to make sure no item was left behind.

Figure 9.14 Stage hands dis-
assemble the set after a
show. *Courtesy,
Christopher C. Everett.*

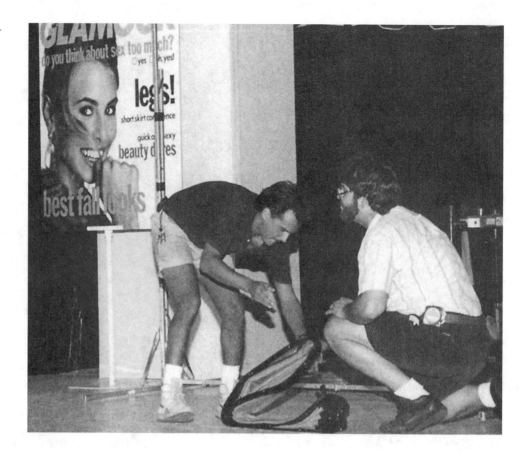

Personnel

Stage strike should include as many people as possible to make the task easier for everyone.
Models and others who are paid hourly rates may be excused to avoid added costs, but all volunteer staff should help. Often in the frenzy of a successful show, many individuals leave the
show to review merchandise or celebrate, leaving the show director to strike alone. It should
be stressed from the planning stages of the show that all individuals will participate in stage
strike. Good show directors turn the task into a fun atmosphere by providing refreshments to
an exhausted staff to entice the volunteer crew to follow through.

A professional stage crew may be hired to set up and take down the stage. A production
crew may be hired to perform all or some of the following services: set design, stage and runway construction, and lighting design, in addition to clean-up services. These crews may be
available by consulting telephone directories under "Theatrical Equipment and Supplies" or
"Theatrical Managers and Producers."

Merchandise return

If an on-site sales area is not required, garments and accessories should be moved from the
show location and returned to the retailers as quickly as possible after the show. The retailers
need time to prepare the merchandise for customers who want to try on the garments displayed in the show. If the show is preformed during the daytime, clothing and accessories may
be returned before the business day is over (Fig. 9.15a and b). If the show is a night perform-

ance, the clothing and accessories may have to be stored at a secure location until the following morning when they can be returned.

Garments should be returned to the retailers in the condition they were borrowed, ready for sale. They should be pressed or steamed, examined for soil or damage, and hangtags should be replaced. Arrangements for soiled or damaged garments and accessories should have been pre-arranged with the merchandise coordinator and the retailer in advance of the show.

Garments, upon arrival back to the retail store, should be inventoried by both the retailer and the merchandise coordinator so both parties are aware of soiled or damaged merchandise. The inventory should be completed and the merchandise loan record signed off by the store representative and the show representative. In situations where cleaning is required, the merchandise coordinator should request from the retailer the name of the preferred dry cleaner. If repairs are needed the same policy should be implemented with the retailer's choice of an alterations' service. It is the responsibility of the fashion show personnel to compensate the retailer for any cleaning or repairing that may need to be performed. These expenses should have been included in the budget.

Accessories should also be returned in saleable condition. Accessories including bracelets, necklaces, pins, hair accessories, and scarfs should be replaced in the packaging the way they

Figure 9.15a and b
Merchandise is immediately returned to the sales area after the show. Shoes and garments must be returned to the department in the condition they were borrowed, ready for sale. *Courtesy, Christopher C. Everett.*

223

were borrowed: cards, boxes, bags, tissue, or other packaging. Some states have health regulations prohibiting the sale of earrings that have been worn. For this reason models may provide their own earrings. The tape applied to shoes should be removed before they are returned. The use of other accessories, such as stockings or lingerie, which cannot be sold after the show should have been negotiated with the retailer and merchandise coordinator prior to borrowing the merchandise.

Following up

Thank you notes should be written as soon as possible after the show. It should be determined during the planning stages of the show who is responsible for writing the thank you notes. Retailers who loaned merchandise or accessories should be thanked along with other businesses or individuals who provided services or time to the show production. Celebrities or personalities who helped promote the show should also be thanked in writing. Amateur models, professional models, and technicians will not expect a thank you note. If the show used volunteers or was an exceptional success, a written message of appreciation is a nice gesture on the part of the show staff. Figure 9.16 shows a sample thank you note.

Being professional

Professionalism is acting in a manner accepted by the occupation. Simply acting in a manner that respects other people's feelings and respects the merchandise being presented is acting in a professional manner. Planning and executing a fashion show is often done on a tight schedule. Murphy's Law, "whatever can go wrong will go wrong," seems appropriate. Tempers often flare up and personality conflicts often magnify during this stressful time. All participants must keep in mind the goal—a coordinated, well-executed, entertaining fashion show.

The director of the fashion show must be able to diplomatically resolve problems during the planning process and during production. One important attribute of the fashion show director is tact—the ability to do or say the right thing while not offending anyone.

Flexibility, the ability to adjust to change, is also necessary for a successful fashion show. Last minute changes in the merchandise, models forgetting an accessory or prop, garments being soiled or damaged, and misplaced music are all a part of fashion show production. Flexibility and a sense of humor help the crew to get through all of the little problems.

Positive working relationships between people involved in fashion show production must be maintained. In a small town, many student and civil groups compete with each other to borrow merchandise from local retailers. If the merchandise is not kept in a clean ready to sell condition or not returned in a timely manner, retailers are not likely to continue to allow outside groups to use their merchandise.

NORTHERN ARIZONA MERCHANDISING ASSOCIATION
P.O. Box 5619
Flagstaff, Arizona 86011-5619
(928) 282-3621
NAMA@flagstaff.net

December 20, 2000

Suzanne Williams
Community Events Director
Dillard's Department Store
West Highway 89, Suite 100
Flagstaff, AZ 86004

Dear Suzanne:

The Northern Arizona Merchandising Association Fashion Show executive committee and I wanted to extend our sincere appreciation for your participation in our *Rock the Runway* fashion show this year! Your support by serving as our commentator gave an added enthusiasm to the event. Your optimistic attitude and extensive fashion knowledge certainly promoted the fashions from the local merchants who lent clothing to the event. We were also very pleased to feature merchandise from Dillard's Department Store in the grand finale of the fashion show.

Thank you so much for helping us raise funds for our activities this year. We hope you will join us for a small celebration to view the videotape of the show on January 10th at the Cline Library Hall at 8:00 p.m. There is no need to R.S.V.P. We hope to see you there.

Sincerely,

Jessica McClain

Jessica McClain
Fashion Show Director

Figure 9.16 A thank you note should be sent quickly after the conclusion of the fashion show.

Canceling a show

It is extremely rare to cancel a fashion show, but certain situations call for this action. Severe weather conditions making travel for the audience and staff hazardous is the most likely reason to cancel a show. Announcements should be made through local broadcast media.

Show planners may be hesitant to cancel a program after they have completed so much work putting the show together. The safety and well being of the audience and staff must be a consideration regardless of the effort. An alternative date may be arranged if a show must be canceled. If this is not possible, refunds should be given to ticket holders, and somehow expenses must be covered by other means.

After 7th on Sixth moved its schedule to earlier calendar dates in 2001, some firms had trouble getting their lines ready in time. One such company, Tuleh, decided to show its collection 40 days after the New York event was over. Designers Josh Patner and Bryan Bradley needed extra time to fill orders from the previous season and put together looks for the upcoming season. Although the firm broke from its Fashion Week time slot, private customers including Aerin and Jane Lauder, as well as corporate customers, including Joan Kaner, senior vice president and fashion director at Neiman Marcus, showed up at the Harry Winston boutique to look at and buy from the collection ("Star Power," 2001). Not every design firm could expect such support, but Tuleh had drawn an enthusiastic crowd from its start.

In an unprecedented move, Mercedes-Benz Fashion Week Spring 2002 fashion shows were cancelled in September 2001. Immediately after the horrific destruction of the World Trade Center, normal activities in New York City came to a halt (Fig. 9.17). The impact of this unbelievable incident and cancellation of Fashion Week led to informal presentations by designers such as Calvin Klein, Michael Kors, and Narciso Rodriguez in show rooms which were attended by retailers and members of the press. The British Fashion Council in London, the Chambre Syndicale in Paris, and the Camera Nazionale della Moda in Milan decided to proceed as normal, despite a decidedly somber international mood (Horyn, 2001).

A fashion show is just like any theatrical or musical presentation. The audience should not be aware of behind the scenes operations. Backstage should be quiet and efficient in its operation. Members of the audience are likely to enjoy the show, buy merchandise, and return to future shows if the quality of the production is at a professional level.

In this chapter we have discussed the rehearsal and presentation of the show. Some show producers are able to schedule the rehearsal on the day of the show, making the merchandise order, announcements, music, cues, and choreography fresh in the minds of all of the participants. Other shows require more time and practice to get ready for the event, requiring a re-

Figure 9.17 On September 11, 2001, the 7th on Sixth fashion shows were abruptly cancelled after the World Trade Center was attacked. The American flag was quickly hoisted in front of the tents, as it was everywhere in New York and throughout the rest of the country. *Courtesy, Fairchild Publications, Inc.*

hearsal a few days before the show. On the show day, all of the planning, preparation, and excitement come together for the live performance in front of an audience. In a rare instance, a fashion show may be cancelled. We discussed some of these unusual circumstances at the end of the chapter.

Key fashion show terms

dresser	professionalism	stage strike
dress rehearsal	rehearsal	starter
full dress rehearsal	run-through	

References

Horyn, C. (2001, September 16). Fashion week cancelled, designers plan small showings. *New York Times*. Retrieved September 16, 2001 from www.nytimes.com

Kerwin, J. (2000, March). All the world's backstage: Sometimes the best seats aren't in the front row, but behind the scenes with the models, the makeup, the madness. *Women's Wear Daily The Magazine*, pp. 80-86.

Star power. (2001, April 3). *Women's Wear Daily*, p. 8.

THE WRAP UP

10

Throughout this text we have highlighted a student produced show from Northern Arizona University, *Rock the Runway*. Students enrolled in a fashion show production class produced the show with assistance from the merchandising student organization. Additional students from the photography, visual communication, and electronic media disciplines aided in video production and promotion. Local retailers provided merchandise for the show and purchased program advertising. Students, university administrators, local businesses, parents, and friends attended the show and created an exciting atmosphere surrounding the event.

The cooperation among students from various disciplines, student organizations, and local businesses contributed to an integrated learning experience beneficial to all involved. In appraising the show after the performance, retailers, show personnel, and the audience believed the show to be highly successful. The audience came away jazzed about the fashions, retailers generated sales based on the show, and the student producers accomplished their goal to generate income for a merchandising scholarship fund.

However, the most rewarding evaluation of the show came six months after the production. The student producers were awarded a university Service Learning Award. The university recognized *Rock the Runway* as a meaningful and important project that extended students' academic preparation through meaningful community service activities. The student merchandising organization received a plaque and a cash award.

This final chapter, The Wrap Up, introduces the reader to an important but often overlooked aspect of show production—evaluation. The chapter will begin with a discussion of the evaluation process. As part of evaluation, each element of the show production process must be reviewed. These elements will be examined in the next section. Show elements to be evaluated include participants, theme and title, location, audience, budget, publicity and advertising, merchandise, models, music, staging, and commentary. The chapter concludes with dialogue on measuring success.

The evaluation process

The fashion show is not complete until personnel involved in the production come together one last time to evaluate the performance. **Evaluation** is an appraisal of the performance, people, places, and processes. While evaluation should be considered an ongoing process throughout the entire development of the show, it is given special emphasis at the conclusion of the show. Evaluation may seem anticlimactic after the excitement of the show but it can provide critical information for procedures and strategies of future shows.

Evaluation takes place at several levels. On one level, the reaction of the audience must be evaluated (Fig. 10.1). On another level, contributing vendors—retailers, manufacturers, suppliers—must evaluate the show based on sales or services generated. And on yet another level, show personnel must evaluate the show as a successfully coordinated special event. Additionally, the amount of press a show generates from fashion journalists is a form of evaluation. Finally, market analysts will evaluate fashions and shows. The evaluation investors make of a fashion stock is based in part on what has previously been seen at a fashion show.

Figure 10.1 The audience evaluates designs as they are presented on the runway. *Courtesy, Fairchild Publications, Inc. Photographer, Dan Lecca.*

The press is an important evaluator of fashion shows. Journalists evaluate shows using **tone**, the manner of expression in speech or writing. If the journalist likes the show, the tone in the article will be positive and upbeat. If the journalist is not pleased with the show, the tone of the evaluation will be negative and critical. Or worse, a journalist may evaluate a designer show as boring, or ignore the show all together.

As a fashion editor for the *International Herald Tribune*, Suzy Menkes believes that fashion needs a dose of reality. In her evaluation of runway shows, she gets irked when designers show fashions that have nothing to do with real lives ("Memo Pad," 2001). According to Menkes, when a bad review is given, the editor gets a phone call to come and see the line in the showroom to see what is selling. That split between runway and reality is a bad aspect of fashion. In her opinion "fashion doesn't live unless it is worn" (p. 12). To her point, a major element of evaluation for any fashion show is the ability of the fashions to be worn by the audience.

Journalistic evaluation also takes place through the length of the article and placement of a designer within an article. The text in Figure 10.2 illustrates this. Hussein Chalayan gets top placement in the article and the only other noted designer in the first paragraph is Alexander McQueen. For the past several seasons, *Women's Wear Daily The Magazine* has printed a feature called Critical Juncture (Table 10.1) in which letter grades are given to all the designers by five top newspapers that publish fashion including: *New York Times, Washington Post, LA Times, International Herald Tribune,* and *Women's Wear Daily*. The scorecard is an evaluation, whether designers, retailers, and/or consumers choose to listen or not.

Fashion journalists evaluate fashion constantly, but does Wall Street care about clothes? You bet—according to Vicki Young, a reporter for *Women's Wear Daily*. To quote Young, "You thought fashion editors were the ones with a license to kill. Ever watch the trajectory of an apparel stock after a securities analyst lets fly with a negative opinion?" (2000, p. 132).

But Young (2000) affirms that while Wall Street's stocks-and-frocks crowd (as fashion is called on Wall Street) knows that numbers tell the story; make no mistake, these folks are scanning runways and store aisles factoring in color, silhouette, edginess, and image into their

---

FASHION REVIEW

In London, Ho-Hum Ends in Smash Finale

By CATHY HORYN

LONDON, Sept. 28—It was close to midnight on Wednesday in the old Gainesborough film studios when the last of the reporters and camera crews elbowed their way into the grim little corner where Hussein Chalayan waited. Mr. Chalayan is famously aloof, and at times his comments add up to mumbo jumbo, but there is nothing vague about his talent. It punches you in the nose with its audacity, and makes you feel grateful for the blow. Without Mr. Chalayan and Alexander McQueen here to deliver such jolts, the British spring 2001 collections would be as inconsequential as a baby's burp.

Figure 10.2 Fashion review from the *New York Times* online. *Courtesy,* The New York Times ©. *Reprinted with permission.*

Table 10.1 Critical juncture feature from *Women's Wear Daily The Magazine*

They loved it; they hated it. Or, even worse, it was a bore. What venom or praise did the critics dish out this season? The following is a letter-grade breakdown based on what five prominent publications (including this one) had to say about some of the major fall collections. Grades were assigned by *WWD*—and not by the individual critics—and were determined by each review's tone, length, and placement within a given article.

	New York Times	Washington Post	LA Times	International Herald Tribune	WWD
NEW YORK					
Anna Sui	A	A−	A	B+	B+
Badgley Mischka	B+	NR	B	B−	C
Calvin Klein	C	C	B−	A	B−
Carolina Herrera	B	B	NR	B+	B
Daryl K	A	NR	NR	NR	A
DKNY	D	B+	C−	D	D
Donna Karan	B	A−	A	C	A
Geoffrey Beene	B	NR	A	B	A−
Helmut Lang	B	A	D	C	B
John Bartlett	A−	A−	B−	B	C
Marc Jacobs	A−	F	B−	C	B
Michael Kors	D	A−	A	C	B−
Miguel Adrover	A+	NR	NR	A+	A+
Nova USA by Tony Melillo	B−	NR	NR	NR	B
Oscar de la Renta	A	B	A	A	A−
Ralph Lauren	C	B	B	C	A−
Richard Tyler	B−	NR	B+	B	B−
Sean John	B+	B+	A−	A−	B+
Tommy Hilfiger	D	C	B−	D	B+
Victor Alfaro	B	B	B	C	B−
LONDON					
Alexander McQueen	B−	NR	NR	B+	A−
Burberry Prorsum	B	NR	NR	C+	B
Hussein Chalayan	A	NR	NR	A−	A
MILAN					
Dolce & Gabbana	C	C−	D	F	D
Fendi	A	B	B	A	A
Gianfranco Ferré	NR	A−	NR	A−	B+

Note. Adapted from: *Women's Wear Daily The Magazine*, March 2000, p. 126.

analyses. Young highlighted some of the characteristics that securities analysts use to evaluate fashion:

- Flawless execution from store layout to helpful salespeople
- Balanced product assortment
- Appropriateness of runway items for the mass market

- Consideration of what touches the consumer, what they are wearing, and what they are buying
- Knowledge of the difference between what you like and what will sell.

The financial results always tell one thing, the markdowns in stores can tell something else.

When to evaluate

The best time to complete the evaluation process is immediately following the show, when successes and problems are fresh in everyone's mind. The fashion office of a retail store may pull staff together the following day. A community group may set a meeting within a week of the production, and students generally evaluate the show at the next class meeting.

Everyone who participated in the show production should do an evaluation. The process should be headed by the show director and all committee coordinators, models, technicians, suppliers, retailers, and anyone else involved should be asked for input in the evaluation process. Additionally, employees who viewed the show from the audience or the sidelines should be invited to the evaluation process. An outside observer can provide a perspective that may not have been touched on by personnel closely involved in the production. If the show was sponsored by a charitable or community organization, members of the group should be asked for their input as well. In rare cases, an outside firm may be hired to evaluate a show. Using an outside firm to evaluate a show is costly. However, it reduces the workload burden on staff and removes prejudices that might affect the process.

Evaluation form

An **evaluation form** is a document with blanks for the insertion of details or information. An evaluation form should be developed and used to summarize the evaluation process. Figure 10.3 provides an example of a simple evaluation form that lists all components of the show on one form for a general summary. Another approach may be to develop a more detailed evaluation form for a specific show component such as models (Fig. 10.4).

After the evaluation of the show has been completed, the forms should be filed with other documentation regarding the planning and presentation of the show—show budget and actual expenses, planning, fitting and model lineup sheets, correspondence—and kept on file for reference.

Evaluation based on goals

Evaluation should begin with a review of the goals of the show. In Chapter 1, we outlined the various reasons to produce a fashion show. These included to sell merchandise, present fashion information, introduce new lines, build store traffic, establish fashion authority, offer goodwill to the community, or provide training. Frequently, the success of a fashion show is tied directly to generated sales. How much of the merchandise presented was actually sold within a specific period of time? Sales may be encouraged in general themes or categories of merchandise. Customers may also be stimulated by color trends or new classifications of goods similar to ones introduced in the show.

Figure 10.3 General evaluation form

```
                        EVALUATION FORM

        Type of Show


        Participants


        Theme / Title


        Audience


        Show Budget (attach Final Budget)


        Summary of Publicity and Advertising


        Merchandise


        Models


        Commentary & Commentator


        Notes for Improvement
```

For a majority of fashion shows the goal is to sell merchandise. The success of New York Fashion Week is ultimately determined by retailer purchase orders. But what happens when retailers don't evaluate a line favorably? As highlighted in Box 10.1, it takes negotiation between retailer and designer to keep both happy.

The presentation of fashion information or trends is also an important goal of fashion show production. In the evaluation, processing audience reaction is a way to identify if the audience successfully recognized the new trends. Did they clap or offer other appropriate feedback? More importantly, did they buy the intended trend-setting pieces? Retailers look for immediate sales, but they also will follow sales trends after the show. With Universal

Figure 10.4 Detailed model evaluation form

Model Evaluation Form

Name:

Show:

Date:

Model Type:

Measurements and physical characteristics:

Contact Information:

Attended fittings: _____ on time _____ late _____ no show

Attended rehearsal: _____ on time _____ late _____ no show

Attended show: _____ on time _____ late _____ no show

Prepared at fittings: _____ yes _____ no

Prepared at rehearsal: _____ yes _____ no

Prepared at show: _____ yes _____ no

Professional attitude: _____ yes _____ no

Would use this model again: _____ yes _____ no

Comments:

Product Code (UPC) and scanner technology, retailers can accurately determine styles and colors that are rapid sellers, as well as those trends that are slow to take off with the public.

Evaluation based on strengths and weaknesses

Based on show goals, event personnel should determine what the strengths of the show were and how problems or weaknesses of the show should be corrected or replaced for the next time. Look for strengths of the event. Even if the team is very satisfied with the fashion show, look for ways to make the show stronger in the future. Build on show elements that were popular with the audience. Did they like the music mix? Was the seating arrangement comfortable? Did the merchandise match the audience?

continued on page 237

> ## Box 10.1
> ## When It's a Bomb
>
> After all the post-show air kisses, back-patting and euphemistic complements ("It was so relevant" was this season's favorite), editors can basically forget about a runway show. But for retailers, the work has just begun-particularly if the show they just saw was, in a word, a disaster.
>
> A stellar show that gets rave reviews and great buzz is a cakewalk. Rearrange some ad budgets, shift around some in-store shops, book a trunk show and *voilà!* Bestsellers.
>
> A bomb, however, has to be handled more discreetly. In that case, there's showroom wheeling and dealing and delicate ego negotiations. After all, if it's a major vendor or an emerging star, stores aren't going to just drop a line because a few misbegotten ideas strayed onto the runway one season.
>
> Retailers also hang onto a name because of runway roulette-a designer who struck out one season can score big next time around, à la Jeremy Scott. Several seasons ago, his gold lamé-and-mink collection was the season's howler; he bounced back within two seasons with witty takes on preppy looks and got more raves the next season. And in retail, nothing stings like seeing your biggest competitor pick up your former exclusive.
>
> You can't walk out. It's a partnership, and you have to talk it through," says Judy Collinson, executive vice president and general merchandise manager of women's at Barneys New York. "The worst thing you can do is walk out of a show and say, 'This is terrible.' If you think something is difficult, you have to express it in a constructive way."
>
> If a major collection gets a panning we don't drop it, although we might scale back," says Kal Ruttenstein, senior vice president of fashion direction at Bloomingdale's. "We don't drop it after one season, not even after two seasons. Three strikes however, and you're out."
>
> "Scale back" generally means focusing on safe looks like jackets or the saviour category, knitwear. And retailers point out that what makes an editor yawn can often be your bestseller.
>
> Designers might privately fume when the stores pass over the runway darlings. But more and more, they have an arena for revenge-the freestanding store. Didn't like the show closer? Think the styling is too weird? Tough. The buyers' rejects can get pride of place in a designer's own shop.
>
> "It's really infuriating when one of your favorite looks doesn't sell enough to make a cutting," says Nicole Miller. "In a past season, I made a printed felt skirt because I thought felt was going to be important, but no one else did. So I made it for my own stores and it sold out pretty close to a piece."

Adapted from: When It's a Bomb, (2000, March). *Women's Wear Daily The Magazine*, p. 106.

continued from page 235

Similarly, look for the show weaknesses. Do not dwell on the negative aspect of show weaknesses, but rather brainstorm to turn the weaknesses into opportunities for improvement next time. For example, was the lighting too dark to adequately see the fashions? Was communication between team members as good as it could have been? Review of weaknesses is difficult but necessary for adequate evaluation and improvement in the future.

Statistics

In evaluating the success of a fashion show, show personnel should secure available statistics about the show. Statistics may include cash intake from ticket sales, audience counts, media coverage, sales generated from the show, or other numeric measures. Statistics provide objective measures. For example, if the goal was to bring in 100 people to a before store hours show of new seasonal fashions, and 110 people turned out, the show staff exceeded their goal.

Audience count is the number of attendees. It is an easy statistic to calculate. In controlled situations, audience count can be determined by the established seating capacities or number of tickets presented at the door. In non-controlled situations, hosts, ushers, security, or personnel involved in crowd control may be able to make reliable estimates.

Media coverage, or the number of exposures generated in the media, can also be quantified. Count the number of press releases distributed and the number of media impressions that resulted from the press releases. Multiply this by the circulation or number of viewers and listeners to determine total media impressions.

Any time a numeric measure can be compared against the same numeric measure from a previous show a non-subjective assessment can be made. For example, a civic show that generated $2000 towards Breast Cancer Research in a past year may have generated $2500 in the current year. The $500 increase in contributions is an objective numeric measure.

Specific elements to evaluate

As we stated earlier, evaluation may take the form of general summary or detailed analysis. Regardless of the depth of the evaluation, the following questions and considerations should be reviewed. There will always be a future show and providing as much detail about the present show can only help to make the future show better.

Participants

Community clubs and novice fashion show production staffs find it helpful to maintain lists of all people who participated and their responsibilities—including names, addresses, telephone numbers, and e-mail addresses of technicians and other outside fashion show production staff. Having a framework of what needs to be done, when, and by whom assists in running a future production smoothly. A retailer or manufacturer may not need to keep such a detailed record of participants and their responsibilities because it is part of their job and day-to-day activities.

Theme and title

Also, as part of the evaluation, the theme and title of the show should be reviewed. Were any special strategies used to capture the mood of the merchandise? Was coordination of the theme and merchandise using music, lighting, props, or any other devices evident? Ask the following questions:

- How did the scenes coordinate with the overall theme?
- Was the theme chosen to correlate with the merchandise?
- Was merchandise readily available to develop the theme and scenes?
- How could the theme be improved?

Location

The location where the fashion show is produced should be thoroughly described. The description should include not only the physical address, but also features such as the proximity of the dressing rooms to the show area, seating, accessibility of runway, helpfulness and cooperation of the restaurant or hotel employees, parking, and any special ambience or amenities. Typical questions relating to the physical location are as follows:

- Was the facility adequate for the show production staff and the audience?
- Were there any problems getting models from the dressing area to the stage and runway?
- Were the commentator and starter able to see each other?
- Were there plenty of restrooms for the audience and show participants?

Audience

The audience reaction is an important aspect to be evaluated. First the staff should consider the size of the audience.

- Was the audience an appropriate size for the location?
- Was the audience large enough to cover expenses?
- Was the audience small enough so that every one had a good view?

A tool commonly used to gauge audience reaction is a survey. A **survey** is a questionnaire distributed to ask people their opinions or reactions. Show planners might ask the audience members to comment on demographic information and their attitudes toward show elements such as merchandise selection, lighting, music, and the stage set. Additionally, they might be asked how they learned about the fashion show.

The following guidelines should be considered when developing a survey. First, make sure the instructions are easy to understand. It is best to keep survey questions short and easy to answer. As questions are formulated, establish an easy way to tabulate the answers to quantify the answers. Avoid asking questions that lead the respondent to an answer. Ask about only one item in each question and pretest the questionnaire to make sure it works (Bovée & Thill, 2000). Figure 10.5 is an example of an audience reaction survey.

It is important to consider the appropriateness of the audience to the merchandise and the type of show produced:

```
                    AUDIENCE REACTION

Age:                                 Sex:
        24 or under      ❑           Male      ❑
        25-44            ❑           Female    ❑
        45-64            ❑
        65+              ❑

Family Income:
        $18,999 or under    ❑
        $19,000-35,999      ❑
        $36,000-50,999      ❑
        $51,000-65,999      ❑
        $66,000 or more     ❑

Rate the Following:
              Like                        Dislike
Clothing       ❑        ❑        ❑        ❑        ❑
Stage Set      ❑        ❑        ❑        ❑        ❑
Music:
        Style  ❑        ❑        ❑        ❑        ❑
      Loudness ❑        ❑        ❑        ❑        ❑
Lighting       ❑        ❑        ❑        ❑        ❑

How did you find out about the show?
        Newspaper advertisement      ❑
        Radio advertisement          ❑
        Poster                       ❑
        Personal Contact             ❑
        Other_____

        _____
        _____

Additional Comments:


```

Figure 10.5 Audience reaction survey

- Was the desired audience attracted? If not, describe the audience that did attend.
- Was the advertising and promotion campaign targeted to the right group?
- Did the merchandise and theme match the type of audience desired?

Audience reaction is also important. Consider the following:

- Was the audience enthusiastic?
- Did they appear to be interested and entertained by the production?
- Did members of the audience ask where to find the merchandise?

Budget

Despite careful planning, the actual expenses may differ from the figures projected in the budget. The actual expenditures should be recorded and compared to the budget. This is important for community groups trying to raise funds for some altruistic or operational project. Ask the following:

- Was the budget realistic?
- What were the unforeseen expenses?
- Were there profits?
- Did ticket sales and donations exceed costs?

Publicity and advertising

A recap of the activities relating to advertising and publicity should be included in the show evaluation. Copies of advertising, publicity releases, names of media personnel contacted, and other relevant information can be included in this section. Samples of news articles, advertisements, radio or television spots, programs, or flyers can serve as illustrations for the future.

Merchandise

A description of the quantity and types of merchandise presented should be included. It may be helpful to include the length of time required to show the number of outfits presented to serve as a guideline for future timing.

Fitting sheets and final lineup charts enhance this basic information. The relationship of the merchandise to the scene theme and fashion show theme should also be discussed:

- Was the merchandise appropriate to the theme, audience and company image?
- What departments participated in a retail show?
- Were any departments that should have been included overlooked?

Models

Any organization utilizing models on a regular basis should set up evaluation criteria. Models that do not receive a favorable evaluation should be eliminated from further consideration. The fashion office should create a file that includes all contact information on the models featured in the show. Information should include the name, address, telephone and fax numbers, e-mail addresses, and relative statistics for each model regularly employed. Measure of performance should be recorded after each show to help show personnel in selecting models for future shows.

Figure 10.4, featured earlier in this chapter, illustrates a model evaluation. For evaluation purposes, models should be on time for fittings, rehearsals, and the show. They should be cooperative, provide their personal supplies, take care of merchandise, and dress quickly. A model should expect to do his or her own makeup and hair unless otherwise stated. The models should be well groomed and polished, providing the ideal image to exhibit the clothing and accessories.

Music

As stated earlier, music has become extremely important as an element of fashion show production. Therefore, is should also be critiqued:

- Did the music mix match the audience?
- Were the sound levels of the music appropriate? Too loud? Too soft?
- Was the equipment coordinated properly?
- Were the technicians easy or difficult to work with?

Staging

The staging is intended to enhance the fashions without overpowering them. The staging also sets a background for theme emphasis. Consider the following:

- Was the staging appropriate for the fashions presented?
- Were there any difficult elements of the staging that tripped up the models, such as platform height or stairs?
- Did the background and the stage blend together in a coordinated look?
- Was the model entrance and exit convenient for the models?
- Was the entrance and exit hidden from the audience?
- Could starters see the stage adequately?
- Were the lighting levels appropriate?

Commentary and commentator

Copies of the commentary should be included in the fashion show evaluation. The commentator or moderator's performance should also be assessed:

- Was it interesting?
- Did the commentary avoid being too descriptive of the garments?
- Did the commentary flatter and strengthen the theme of the show?
- Was the commentator effective in his or her delivery?

Evaluate other shows

As part of evaluation, show personnel should evaluate shows that others produce. Note what others do differently and effectively. It is always good to change some show elements to keep the event fresh and growing (Jackson & Schmader, 1990). Identify strategies that work well. Keep these techniques fresh for the future.

Measuring success

A fashion show is not truly over until the staff completes an evaluation to measure the success of the show. It is difficult to measure the success of any particular show. Some people gauge the achievement by the dollar volume of the sales; others assess the accomplishment by the reaction of the audience and participants. No matter how the success is defined, producing a fashion show can be an exciting and rewarding experience and reviewing the successes and problems will help ease some of the stress when the staff produces the next show.

Key fashion show terms

audience count	evaluation form	survey
evaluation	media coverage	tone

Additional readings

Bovée, C. & Thill, J. (2000). *Business communication today.* Upper Saddle River, NJ: Prentice Hall.

Jackson, R. & Schmader, S. (1990). *Special events: Inside & out.* Champaign, IL: Sagamore.

Memo Pad. (2001, April 27). *Women's Wear Daily*, p. 12.

Young, V. (2000, March). Analyze this. *WWD The Magazine*, p. 132.

GLOSSARY OF FASHION SHOW TERMS

7th on Sixth Nonprofit organization created by the Council of Fashion Designers (CFDA) to centralize the American runway shows.

A

advertising Information paid for and controlled by the sponsoring organization.

advertising content Paid announcements run in the media.

advertising models Individuals who are needed to display and enhance products for publication in newspapers, magazines, point-of-purchase displays, and other media.

amateur models Models not trained as professional models.

amplification Follows the lead in a press release with additional information.

apparel marts Wholesale centers located in major cities throughout the United States leasing space to manufacturers.

art Illustrations or photography of the advertisement.

audience count Number of attendees.

B

banner ads See online advertising.

basic fact sheet Page in a media kit to explain newsworthy details.

biographical information Page in a media kit to explain the principal contributors.

board Place where a model's career, including scheduling assignments and negotiating fees, is managed by a booker.

body Important details of the advertisement or news article.

body parts models Men and women with attractive hands, legs, feet, and/or hair may find jobs highlighting these strengths, as a sub-industry within the modeling industry.

booker Individual who is hired by the modeling agency to promote, coordinate schedules, and negotiate fees for models.

bridge Less expensive alternative to designer fashions.

British Fashion Council Organizers of London Fashion Week.

budget An estimate of the revenues and expenses necessary to produce the fashion show.

C

Camera Nazionale della Alta Moda Italia Governing body of the Italian couture overseeing the activities of couture designers, ready-to-wear, shoe, and accessory manufacturers.

caption A written description that explains a photograph.

casting call The place where various models audition for a slot on the runway or for print work.

catalog models Individuals who are photographed wearing clothing and accessories that will be sold through direct response media such as mail-order catalogs, brochures, billing statement inserts and so forth.

catwalk Another word for runway.

Chambre Syndicale de la Couture Parisienne Governing body of the French haute couture.

child models Youngsters engaged for presenting clothing and accessories for the toddler to preteen markets in addition to the important back-to-school season.

choreographer Individual in charge of planning runway and dance routines.

choreography All of the planning and execution of the model's runway routine as well as any specific dance numbers used in a fashion show.

clip art Prefabricated illustrations generated on a computer or purchased in clip art books.

closing date Date when ad copy must be received by magazine.

commentary Oral delivery of descriptive details of fashion show garments and accessories.

commentary cards Fragments of information prepared to read as narration during the show, usually on a file card.

commentary coordinator Individual who is responsible for all of the show oratory, written commentary, and selection of announcers and/or commentators.

commentator Member of the show staff with the designated responsibility of preparing and/or delivering the commentary during the show.

composite A printed promotional card that includes the model's name, measurements, and agency contact information with various photographs. Also called a headsheet.

consumer show Show presented to the consumer.

contemporary Fasion forward apparel category at a price-point between bridge and budget.

cooperative fashion show Retailer and manufacturer show in which both parties share expenses.

copy Written material in a press release or advertisement.

copyright permission Authorization from the owner of the copyright to use copyrighted material.

couture models Limited number of women who are internationally known and work the catwalks for the top American and global designers in such fashion centers as Paris, London, Milan, and New York.

created audience Individuals who will attend a fashion show as a result of publicity and advertising.

cue Signal on or off the stage for an entrance.

D

dancing Routines or rhythmic movements to music that can add a great deal of interest to the show.

Defiles des createurs Paris designer runway shows.

design piracy Stealing designs and creating "knockoffs."

designer Creator of original apparep designs and the ready-to-wear apparel category with the highest price-points.

diary Written record of all plans and evaluations for the show.

direct mail Advertising sent through the mail.

direct marketing Marketing process by which organizations communicate directly with target customers to generate a response or transaction.

direct response Distribution method requiring a direct reply.

direct response online media Advertising communications done via a computer.

direct response print media Printed materials that require direct reply.

directrice/directuer French term referring to the male or female head of the couture salon.

documentary video Video that focuses on the designer or behind-the-scenes activities of the manufacturer.

dress rehearsal A walk-through with garment changes.

dresser Individual responsible for helping models change.

dressing area Room or area designated for changing clothes, applying makeup, or styling hair.

E

editorial content Publicity run in the media at the decision of the media, not paid sponsors.

editorial print models Individuals who pose for the cover or the editorial pages of magazines and other print media.

evaluation Appraisal of the performance, people, places, and processes.

evaluation form Document used to summarize the evaluation process.

F

Fashion Calendar Calendar published weekly with the dates and relevant information regarding key national and international fashion events, serving as a guide for retailers, manufacturers, and the press.

fashion director Individual responsible for creating the fashion image for a particular retailer.

fashion dolls Historic miniature scale dolls wearing replicas of the latest clothing, also known as puppets, dummies, little ladies, or fashion babies.

fashion editor Individual at a newspaper, exclusively responsible for fashion.

fashion show director Individual charged with the responsibility of producing the show, planning all arrangements, delegating responsibilities, and accepting accountability for all details.

fashion show plan Schedule for a specific period of time, commonly six months or a year, of all the fashion shows that a firm intends to produce.

fashion show Presentation of apparel, accessories, and other products to enhance personal attractiveness on live models to an audience.

fashion trend show Show produced to introduce consumers to latest trends in silhouettes, fabrics, colors, and themes of new seasonal merchandise.

Fashion Week Designated time when many designer collections are brought together and shown as a series of fashion shows.

feature story Journalistic story in a media kit to provide insight into the event.

Federation Française du Prêt-á-porter Feminin Scheduling organization for the Paris ready-to-wear shows.

filler commentary Commentary planned for use at any time during the show to fill in unexpected pauses that may occur.

final lineup Complete listing of models and outfits in order of appearance, finalized after dress rehearsal.

finale Last impression of the show.

fit models Models of sample size who work in a manufacturer's design area. Sample garments are adjusted to a standard fit model's size.

fitting sheet Information sheet coordinated to the merchandise, including size, order number, and detailed description of the garment.

fittings Matching models to merchandise, planned and held when the tentative lineup is completed.

flats Temporary movable backdrops.

formal runway show Conventional presentation of fashion similar to a parade, featuring a series of models who walk or dance on a runway in a sequential manner.

full commentary Commentary written word for word on cards or in script form prior to the show.

full dress rehearsal Rehearsal with garment changes to check all aspects of the show, including timing, music, and other technical aspects.

full run Advertising that runs in all editions of a newspaper.

G

gratuities Cash tips given to service people, such as waiters or waitresses, or attendants in the coat check and rest rooms.

guaranteed audience Individuals who will attend the show regardless of the fashions displayed.

H

halftone Reproduced photographs or drawings using screens to convert the design into a series of dots, making shaded values in printing possible.

haute couture French high fashion industry featuring clothing produced from a client's made-to-order measurements.

headline Part of an advertisement or news article used to attract the attention of the reader and create interest.

headsheets Printed promotional card that includes the model's name, measurements, and agency contact information with various photographs. Also called a composite.

high board Where models, with the greatest level of experience and in the highest demand, are managed by their bookers.

historical fact sheet Page within a media kit to explain the historical nature of the show.

hosts People who greet audience members and show them where to sit.

I

ideal chart Plan listing all categories of merchandise that will be represented in the show.

impromptu commentary Commentary created spontaneously during the show using only brief cue cards for assistance.

individual model lineup sheet Form used in organizing the specific model's order of appearance, outfit, shoes, hosiery, accessories, props, and grouping.

informal fashion show Casual presentation of garments and accessories.

institutional promotion Promotion enhancing image.

in-store training fashion show Fashion show presented to train store personnel coinciding with fashion trend shows.

instructional video Video created for in-store training for store personnel.

J

junior Styles appropriate to the younger figure.

junior models Young models who are between the ages of 13 and 17.

K

knockoffs Copies of designer originals at lower prices.

L

layout Schematic plan or arrangement of the fashion show floor plan.

lead One or two sentences that summarize the news of a press release.

lease agreement Contract between leasing agencies and users drawn up prior to the show.

lighting Method and/or equipment used to provide illumination.

line drawing Illustration created by pen, pencil, brush, or crayon.

lineup Organized listing of models in the order they will appear and the outfit they will be wearing.

list of participants Page within a media kit to explain the participants.

live mixed music Use of a disk jockey and playback equipment to change music during various segments of the show.

live music Performance provided by musicians during the show.

local advertising Time bought on local television stations.

logo Copyright protected symbol or phrase used by an incorporated organization.

M

magazine tie-in show Cooperative fashion shows between major fashion publications and individual retailers.

male models Men who are hired to display clothing and accessories.

mannequin modeling Modeling in a store window or on a display platform by live models who strike similar poses to the stationary display props for which they have been named.

mannequin Live model used to present merchandise in fashion shows or a stationary doll or dummy used as a display fixture.

mannequins du monde High society women, millionaire wives, and the popular actresses from stage and screen became the fashion models in the 1930s.

mapped routes Paths planned for models to follow on the runway.

market calendar Published dates of trade shows known as market weeks.

Market Week Time designated for producers of a specific category of merchandise to open sales on the season's new styles.

mature models Women, such as Lauren Hutton and Christie Brinkley, who continued doing modeling jobs well into their 40s and 50s.

media coverage Number of exposures generated in the media about the show.

media kit Collection of materials delivered or mailed to the press in a folder with inside pockets. Contents include press releases, news stories, feature stories, fact sheets, photographs with captions, biographical or historical information about the event or people involved, and brochures or samples.

media list Locally or regionally generated list of media that might be used to publicize an event.

merchandise categories Divisions of merchandise, often corresponding with retail departments.

merchandise coordinator Individual in charge of the selection of merchandise for each scene and the entire show.

merchandise loan record Standardized form used by fashion show producers to record details of the merchandise borrowed from retailers.

merchandise pull Physically removing merchandise from the sales floor to an area reserved for fashion show merchandise storage.

merchandise selection Designation of apparel, shoes, and accessories for presentation in a fashion show to the target customer.

missy Conservative looks available at better, moderate, or budget price points.

missy models Models generally between the ages of 17 to 22 years of age, between 5′7″ and 5′ 10 1/2″, and wear the sample sizes 6 or 8.

model Individual employed to display clothing and accessories by wearing them.

model coordinator Individual responsible for selecting and training the models and coordinating activities that involve the models.

model group Two or more models who walk on the runway together.

model list Form that will include the model's name, telephone number, garment, and shoe sizes.

model order Rotation in which the models will appear throughout the show.

modeling agencies Companies that represent and act as scheduling agents for a variety of fashion models.

modeling schools Schools that train men, women, and children in modeling techniques.

moderator See commentator.

muse Designers may use their fit model, a friend, or a celebrity as an inspiration for their ideal customer.

music Vocal and instrumental sound environment.

music director Employee who will research and select appropriate music, obtain permissions to use copyrighted music, mix the music at the show, and prepare the sound system at the show site.

music mix The combination of different music styles to create a specified mood.

music play list Initial list of music selections, including the title and length of the song and recording artist.

music technician Expert in musical styles and sound system.

N

national promotion Primary and secondary promotion activities directed at the ultimate consumer.

network advertising Time bought on one of the three major networks.

news story Journalistic news story in a media kit to give basic information about the fashion show.

nonprofit organization An organization with 501 c3 status as designated by the Internal Revenue Service with published articles of incorporation, a board of directors, and all money earned by the organization is returned to the group.

O

online advertising Messages that appear on a Web site sponsored by a third party.

P

pace Timing of the show.

page of isolated facts Page in media kit about current and past fashion shows.

partial commentary Commentary written with only the major details about the outfit.

paste-up All elements of an advertisement placed in final arrangement, camera ready.

pauses Planned hesitations when models stop and pose on the runway.

personal selling Direct interaction between customer and seller with the purpose of making a sale.

petite models Models approximately 5′ 2″.

photographic models Individuals who pose for editorial and/or print media.

photography Reproduction of prints created by a camera.

pivots Turns executed by models on a runway.

pivot point Point on the middle of the runway where models turn.

pixel Smallest image-forming unit in video display.

planning All of the advance preparation to organize the show, including selecting leadership, delegating responsibilities, foreseeing problem that may occur, and continually reviewing the progress of the show.

plus size models Full-figure models.

point-of-purchase video Videos placed on the sales floor of a retail store.

portfolio Book of photographs that show a model in the most flattering way, showing the model's versatility.

preferred position Newspaper advertisement run at a specified page or position within the newspaper.

premier/premiere French term referring to the male or female head of the couture workroom.

press photograph Photographs prepared specifically for use in print media to accompany press releases or as part of a media kit.

press release Written article about a newsworthy event in a specified format, including all details about the event, sent to editors or news directors, for publication in the media.

press show Fashion show held specifically for the press to preview the fashions before public viewing.

prêt-á-porter Ready-to-wear fashion industry in France.

primary resources Manufacturers involved with the production of raw materials, including textile fibers, fabrics, trims, and notions.

production show Most dramatic or theatrical production type, may also be called a dramatized or spectacular show.

professionalism Acting in a manner accepted by the profession and/or occupation.

professional models Models trained in modeling techniques and hired through model agencies or modeling schools.

program editor Individual responsible for all activities related to creating a program.

program of events Page with a media kit that provides detailed information about the scheduled activities.

promotion Comprehensive term used to describe all of the communication activities initiated by the seller to inform, persuade, and remind the consumer about products, services, and/or ideas offered for sale.

promotional promotion Promotion for the specific purpose of selling products.

promotion coordinator Individual responsible for the creation and distribution of promotional materials required for the show.

props Items or symbols used in fashion shows to highlight the garments exhibited.

public address system Microphone, amplifiers, and speakers used to project voices.

public relations (PR) Interrelationship between service providers and the public, as it relates to the image of the organization through all levels of communication.

public service announcements (PSAs) Print or broadcast spots run free-of-charge to charitable organizations.

publicist Individuals hired to publicize a client or client's products in the media.

publicity Non-paid, un-sponsored information delivered at the discretion of the media initiated by the party seeking to tell others about the event.

R

rate card Published rates for the advertising units in print media.

ready-to-wear Mass-produced fashion.

rehearsal Practice performance, held in private, in preparation for a public performance.

responsibility sheet Form used in planning a show and delegating responsibilities to all participants.

retail promotion Store promotion directed at the consumer.

runway Extension of the walkway that generally projects into the audience.

runway models Men and women who find work at trade shows and major fashion centers.

run-of-paper position (R.O.P.) Newspaper advertisement run at any location in the newspaper.

run-through Rehearsal of the show sequence.

S

script commentary Commentary used in production shows, written out word or word for the commentator to read and speak like that of a broadcast.

secondary resources Clothing and accessory manufacturers.

show producer Individual hired to bring all of the fashion show elements together, including translating the designer's vision into a three-dimensional live show.

showroom models Men and women who work freelance or as a manufacturer's house model during market weeks.

slogan Catchy phrase that is appealing when spoken or viewed in print.

sound library Collection of records, cassettes, and/or CDs to be used by the public.

sound system Equipment needed to play music.

special events Activities sponsored by retailers to attract customers to their store while creating goodwill.

special events director Individual who works for a retailer, manufacturer, or designer to co-ordinate activities for special events.

special interest show Show presented to consumers that have special affinity with each other or a unique vocation.

specialty market shows Shows geared to a specific, narrowly defined group of consumers.

sponsorship Involves supporters who lend their name to an event and/or underwrite production costs of an event.

spot advertising Time bought on independently owned broadcast stations.

stage Raised area or platform that serves as a background area where the models enter and exit.

staging Process or manner of putting on a performance on stage.

stage manager Individual responsible for organizing the equipment and people providing services used behind the scenes.

stage strike Physically disassembling the set.

standard advertising unit (SAU) Space designated in print media by column inch.

starter Individual responsible for "cueing" the models to go on stage in the correct order at the right time.

stylist Individual hired to provide creative input to the designer and show producer and present the clothes immaculately.

subheadline Part of advertisement that further explains the headline.

survey Questionnaire distributed to ask people their opinions or reactions.

T

table seating Seating arrangements used at a show with some sort of meal service.

taped music Pre-recorded music from records, cassettes, and/or CDs copied to tape.

tea-room modeling Informal fashion show presented in a restaurant where models walk from table to table displaying garments.

tear sheet An advertisement torn directly from the newspaper to show proof of publication to the advertiser.

television commercial model Individuals who make the transition from modeling to acting in television advertisements.

tentative lineup Order of models and merchandise designed from the theme-grouped ideal chart and model order without input from fittings.

tertiary resources Retail organizations.

theater seating Chairs placed side by side next to stage and runway. This type of seating is best used for fashion shows without meal service.

theme Title of the show indicating the nature of the fashion show to the audience.

tone Manner of expression in speech or writing.

trade Any activity aimed at distribution of fashion and related products within the industry.

trade associations Groups of individuals and businesses acting as a professional, nonprofit collective in meeting common interests.

trade fair International trade shows.

trade promotion Activities designed to promote products from one business to another.

trade show Group of manufacturers presenting their lines to retailers and press one to four times each year.

trunk show Informal fashion show that features garments from one manufacturer or designer at a retail store.

U

ushers People who escort members of the audience to their seats and hand out programs.

V

venue The place where the fashion show is held.

video production Use of video technology to record fashion shows or special events.

visual merchandising Physical presentation of products in a nonpersonal approach, including window, interior, or remote displays.

W

white space Space between the copy and art of an advertisement.

Z

zoned edition Advertising run in selective editions.

INDEX